Rethinking Refugees

Rethinking Refugees
Beyond States of Emergency

Peter Nyers

Routledge
Taylor & Francis Group
New York   London

Published in 2006 by
Routledge
Taylor & Francis Group
270 Madison Avenue
New York, NY 10016

Published in Great Britain by
Routledge
Taylor & Francis Group
2 Park Square
Milton Park, Abingdon
Oxon OX14 4RN

Printed in the United States of America on acid-free paper
10 9 8 7 6 5 4 3 2 1

International Standard Book Number-10: 0-415-95231-X (Hardcover) 0-415-95232-8 (Softcover)
International Standard Book Number-13: 978-0-415-95231-6 (Hardcover) 978-0-415-95232-3 (Softcover)
Library of Congress Card Number 2005015139

Library of Congress Cataloging-in-Publication Data

Nyers, Peter.
   Rethinking refugees : beyond states of emergency / Peter Nyers.
      p. cm. -- (Global horizons series)
   Includes bibliographical references and index.
   ISBN 0-415-95231-X (hb : alk. paper) -- ISBN 0-415-95232-8 (pb : alk. paper)
   1. Refugees. 2. Humanitarian assistance--Political aspects. 3. Humanitarianism -- Political aspects.
4. Globalization. I. Title. II. Series: Global horizons.

HV640.N94 2005
325'.21--dc22
2005015139

Taylor & Francis Group
is the Academic Division of Informa plc.

Visit the Taylor & Francis Web site at
http://www.taylorandfrancis.com

and the Routledge Web site at
http://www.routledge-ny.com

Contents

Acknowledgments

This book could not have been written without the encouragement, support, and critical engagement of a great number of friends and colleagues. I am extremely grateful to all of them, and in particular to Sharry Aiken, Marshall Beier, Shannon Bell, Davina Bhandar, Lynette Boulet, David Campbell, Nergis Canefe, Ron Deibert, Mark Hiller, Jef Huysmans, Jennifer Hyndman, Engin Isin, Michelle Lowry, Mike Ma, Erin Manning, Jean McDonald, David Mutimer, Carlos Neves, Natasha Pravaz, Prem Kumar Rajaman, Alina Sajed, Sean Saraka, Christine Saulnier, Nicky Short, Claire Turenne Sjolander, Richard Stubbs, Chris Vance, Rob Walker, William Walters, Sandra Whitworth, and Cynthia Wright.

While writing this book, I had the good fortune of being surrounded by extremely supportive colleagues and staff at the Department of Political Science, Centre for International and Security Studies, Centre for Refugee Studies, and the Citizenship Studies Media Lab at York University; the Department of Political Science at the University of Toronto; and the Department of Political Science and the Institute on Globalization and the Human Condition at McMaster University. Thanks also to comrades in Red Hot, CUPE 3903, and STATUS for challenging me to rethink what it means to be political under current conditions. I am also grateful for the financial support provided by the Social Sciences and Humanities Research Council of Canada.

Parts of chapters 1 and 2 were published as "Emergency or Emerging Identities? Refugees and Transformation in World Order," *Millennium: Journal of International Studies* 28, 1 (1999). I acknowledge with thanks the permission.

Finally, I would like to thank Frank, Katalin, and Christina Nyers, and especially Oona Padgham and zoomates past and present for their unwavering love, support, and companionship during the writing of this book.

Introduction: Body Politics in Motion

> There is nothing more unsettling than the continual movement of something that seems fixed.

> —Gilles Deleuze

Refugees and States of Exception

Today's world, it is often remarked, is on the move like never before. Across the wide spectrum of human activities, there has been a vast expansion in the scope and a dramatic acceleration and intensification in the pace of socioeconomic and cultural relations.[1] That a single term—globalization—is usually attached to these dynamic processes should not efface the unevenness of their impact and effects. Globalization may have spurred some to proclaim the onset of an unprecedented condition of "time–space compression," however the question of how different people experience and are affected by this disruption to their received spatiotemporal orientations is still one that needs to be explored.[2] The enhanced mobility that is associated with globalization obviously means one thing for tourists and business class travelers and quite another for international domestic workers and "mail-order" brides. Doreen Massey comments on the "power geometry" of time–space compression, noting the unequal forms of power and privilege involved in one's relation to flows and movement: "Different social groups have distinct relationships to this anyway differentiated mobility: some people are more in charge of it than others; some initiate flows and movement, others don't; some are more on the receiving-end of it than others; some are effectively imprisoned by it."[3]

The politics of global movements involve many dimensions, as the flows of capital, labor, goods, services, information, and culture all have distinct, if interconnected, dynamics. The departure point for this study, however, is the movement of people and, in particular, the politics of people who are forced to leave their homes and flee as refugees. Refugees certainly constitute a class of moving people who occupy the lower rungs of Massey's power geometry. This book seeks to provide some answers to the ethical and political questions that arise whenever the complicated problem of refugees, their movements, and their political practices arise. I argue that to fully appreciate the politics of refugees, we must consider movement to be an ontological activity. It is through movement that bodies encounter and confront one another, thereby developing relationships that constitute the myriad ways of being and living in the world. How these encounters are structured and performed is of intense political significance. Will they be hospitable or hostile? engaging or effacing? equitable or hierarchical? To fully appreciate the politics of these encounters, I take the approach that the politics of moving bodies must be analyzed as being completely implicated in—indeed, immanent to—the movement of body politics. Put another way, it is not only the refugee's body that is moving but also the sovereign state—the body politic—that is in constant motion. The state is indistinguishable from the practices—historical and performed—that are constitutive of its self-identity. In this sense, I am not so concerned with the ontology of sovereignty or refugeeness so much as their ontogenesis, their historical constitution through ongoing political practice.[4]

Body—Politics—Motion. To establish a connection among these three terms is to invoke a very complicated politics. The aim of this study is to unpack, analyze, and assess the implications of this politics with reference to global refugee movements. What are the conditions under which it is possible to talk about corporeal political metaphors—such as the "body politic"—in a world where refugees and other forms of forcible displacement dominate the political landscape? As Lester Ruiz asks, how can we speak about "the political body, when, for the most part, they have been disembodied—banished from—not only by modern politics, but from both the *vita active* and the *vita contemplative*?"[5] Ruiz argues that the resolution to this dilemma lies in situating the bodies of "the dispersed, the displaced, and the dislocated"[6] in relation to contested accounts of political space, time, and practice. However, the "volatile bodies" that proliferate in the contemporary political landscape immediately complicate this project. These bodies, as Elizabeth Grosz has argued, are neither neutral nor passive but rather actively reconfigure, reinscribe, and resist as they move through, across, and between political spaces.[7] There is, in short, a diasporic quality to body politics today, with refugees playing a key role in pushing the boundaries of sovereign accounts of the political.

To insist on a diasporic framework when considering the body politic is no small request. Etymologies of the word state suggest that its origins lie with the Latin word *stave*, or "to stand." How can we speak about the grounded and territorial entity par excellence—that is, the state—as a body that is in constant motion? What would it mean to reformulate our political categories and practices with diaspora—or the refugee—as its starting point? These are difficult and provocative questions, not least because they directly subvert the received premises and tacit agreements on which modern conceptions of the political are based. This tradition asserts that sovereignty is the primary political category of the modern era. Sovereignty underpins and guarantees the basic discourse about the political. It provides a solution to the problem of political order, establishing the conditions for legitimate authority over time and within a particular space. What's more, as questions of order inevitably lead to questions of identity (i.e., the political body that is to be ordered), sovereignty also provides a powerful historical answer to the question of what kind of political subjectivities we possess (citizenship) and where political relations can be practiced (state). There is, therefore, an immanent connection between subjectivity and the social order that sovereignty makes possible.[8] Consequently, to suggest that the sovereign state is obsolete and redundant, as some of the literature on globalization does, is to say that the sovereign individual is also obsolete and dangerous.

The sovereign relation frames and fixes the political spatially. "Modern politics," Rob Walker argues, "is a spatial politics. Its crucial condition of possibility is the distinction between an inside and an outside, between the citizens, nations and communities within and the enemies, others and absences without."[9] According to this line of thinking, the modern state provides a spatial resolution to the problem of political order by insisting that all disputes within its bounded territory will be resolved by a legitimate sovereign power. The lack of such a common power to order and judge actions between states is interpreted as evidence of the anarchical nature of the international realm. From this perspective, the violence involved in securing the external borders of the state are justified as a necessary precondition for civil political relations to flourish within the political community. Thus, to the criticism that the state is, in the final instance, an administrator of violent and exclusionary powers, defenders of a state-centric conception of the political are able to respond by saying that this violence is indeed fundamental as it works to secure an ordered and safe inside from the dangerous and insecure forces from the outside. This not only allows for the safe performance of political relations but also provides the space for cultural, economic, and social pursuits to flourish. Sovereignty is, therefore, an intensely paradoxical concept: to have perfection, there must be violence; to have internal harmony, there must be external chaos.[10]

The sovereign state's claim to monopolize the legitimate use of violence within a given territory is also a claim to monopolize the entire conception of the political. In *On the Genealogy of Morals*, Nietzsche spoke of the coming of the state in the following terms: "They come like fate, with-out reason, consideration or pretext; they appear as lightning, too terrible, too sudden, too convincing, too 'different' even to be hated."[11] Following Nietzsche, the state is "too terrible … too convincing" to allow for any other alternative to its monopoly on political space, identity, and practice. It is sovereignty's dominant hold over the political imagination that is a central problematic of this book. While its account may be the prevailing one, it is in no way natural, normal, inevitable, or uncontested. To the contrary, it is the result—an effect, if you will—of a variety of performed historical practices. In the parlance of contemporary academic terminology, these practices are invoked whenever the state is referred to as a "social construction."[12] To say that the state is a social construction is an important development in political studies as it contributes to a more general renunciation of the trappings of reification in our political concepts. The state is neither given nor fixed, and it is certainly not a fully formed political agent. Rather, the state is a historical construct, created and sustained through continuous political activity. To underscore the significance of these constitutive practices, Warren Magnusson criticizes theories of the state that treat it as a static structure and instead encourages the idea that state is the product of a social movement: statism. It is only because the activities of statist movements have been so powerfully successful that the state has become normalized as the only authentic community that can serve as a site for political activity. To be sure, it is not that there are no other ways of being or acting politically but rather that the success of statism as a social movement has rendered these alternatives either unacceptable or unthinkable. As Magnusson states, "Such effacement of the past is not a sign of lack of movement, but rather of the overwhelming success of the statist movement. Like capitalism, the State just seems like a part of normal life, and people enact its routines— and hence re-create the State—day by day."[13]

The power of sovereignty, however, is not just rooted in inclusive and monopolistic practices. The capacity to decide what qualifies as a "normal" political identity, space, and practice also implies an obverse power—that is, the ability to decide what constitutes the exception. The concept of the "state of exception" is central to understanding how both sovereign power and refugee identity are constituted. The basic idea behind the state of exception is that the law can be legally suspended for the purpose of preserving the state and its system of law from some grave internal or external danger. In the earlier twentieth century, two very different thinkers recognized this element of sovereignty. Perhaps most famously, and notoriously, was Carl Schmitt, who declared that "Sovereign is he [sic] who decides on the exception."[14] Sovereignty is that "borderline concept" that marks the limit of the normal and the beginning of the exceptional. Walter Benjamin also referred to this dimension of the sovereign relation when he spoke of "law preserving violence." What concerned Benjamin was the relationship between this aspect of law and the challenges involved in founding a system of law in the first place, what he called "law making violence."[15] Every system of (state) law necessarily involves a dimension of violence in its founding. This violence, however, is not a discrete event, unique to the particular time and place of the act of founding. To the contrary, an element of this violence returns in the state of exception. Law and violence are indistinguishable during the state of exception. Consequently, the system of laws of any state always suffers from being founded by acts that are, from the perspective of law, criminal.[16] The persistent problem of sovereignty, therefore, is not just that its founding involves violence. Understood as a social construction, the founding of a sovereign political community (and its associated political subjectivity, citizenship) is not only locatable somewhere in a nation's past. Instead, the distinctiveness of every national culture has to be periodically refurbished, the population reassured, their affectations to the nation reaffirmed. In other words, every political community must, in short, refound itself.[17] With the sovereign political relation, however, the violence associated with founding returns in the form of the "state of exception."

The central argument of this study is that the subjectivity of the diasporic body—in this study, the refugee—is constituted by being exposed to the violent limit of the sovereign relation known as the "state of exception." From this perspective, the relationship between the refugee's identity and political subjectivity is not merely oppositional; the refugee is not simply excluded from the political realm. Rather, the refugee's relationship to the political can be described as a kind of "inclusive exclusion." Refugees are included in the discourse of "normality" and "order" only by virtue of their exclusion from the normal identities and ordered spaces of the sovereign state. As an object of classification, the refugee is trapped within the sovereign relation of the exception, a relation that Agamben argues is an "extreme form of relation by which something is included solely through its exclusion."[18] To banish is also to capture, according to the logic of the sovereign relation of power. Deleuze and Guattari also noted the powers of capture that distinguish the sovereign political relation. Sovereign power, they argued, is inseparable from "a process of capture of flows of all kinds, populations, commodities, or commerce, money or capital" and "never ceases to decompose, recompose, and transform movement."[19] This is a constitutive violence, Deleuze and Guattari stressed, as it is through its practices of capture that the state establishes the milieu of interiority—that is, domestic political space within which the various "spheres" of human activity (political, economic, social) take place. The power of capture, moreover, is also a negative power: it reacts to (and is dependent on) already existing primary flows of activity: "sovereignty only reigns over what it is capable of internalizing, of appropriating locally."[20] From this perspective, the state is but a secondary phenomenon; the sovereign relation is essentially an extractive power of appropriation.

The state logic that runs throughout the discourse of refugeeness can also be understood as a power of capture: subjects of the classification regime of "refugeeness" are caged within a depoliticized humanitarian space. There is, therefore, a fundamental tension between a sovereign power that tries to capture and overcode all that it encounters within its own logic of immanent relations of inclusion–exclusion and the remainder—the "political excess"[21] that evades or takes flight from such practices of capture. After all, the dynamics of presence–absence, inside–outside, included–excluded are never perfectly symmetrical or consistent. The contingencies of political life are far too messy and uncertain to allow for such an eventuality. This study seeks to demonstrate the variety of ways in which refugees are allocated characteristics—speechlessness, invisibility, passivity—that are the obverse of the sovereign identity of citizenship. It also seeks to demonstrate that the state of emergency that governs refugee identity is also an emerging complex of identity performances that are constantly recasting the meaning of refugeeness in ways contrary to the binary logic of sovereignty. In this way, the aims of this study seek to respond to the challenge that Agamben set for rethinking sovereign forms of political identity, community, and action: "If we want to be equal to the absolutely new tasks ahead, we will have to abandon decidedly, without reserve, the fundamental conceptions through which we have so far represented the subjects of the political (Man, the Citizen and its rights, but also the sovereign people, the worker, and so forth) and build our political philosophy anew starting from the one and only figure of the refugee."[22]

The Book in Brief

As the conditions and circumstances that give rise to refugee movements proliferate, a growing academic and policy literature has emerged to address its various political, social, and human dimensions. But what are the terms under which the refugee phenomenon has been framed? Why are refugees invariably framed as a "problem" in need of solution? What identities are constructed by the prevailing classification system of refugees and refugee movements? What political implications does this classification system have for how refugees can represent themselves as political actors? These are important questions, I argue, because despite the multiplicity of refugee experiences and reasons for flight, conventional analyses of the subject remain committed to a hierarchical mode of interpretation that works to efface this multiplicity. This is perhaps most evident by the striking absence of political "voice" or agency on the part of refugees in these studies. The prevailing attitude in conventional analyses of refugee movements is one that provides no place for refugees to articulate their experiences and struggles or to assert their (often collectively conceived) political agency. Refugees are silenced by the very discourses that attempt to provide solutions to their plight. This silence is not natural or inevitable but something that is produced by power relations that require explanation and critical analysis.

This book aims to problematize conventional perspectives on refugee flows that consider technical and operational "solutions" within a state-centric discourse to be sufficient for understanding this phenomenon. As such, it seeks to contribute to a growing critical literature that has broken free from the problem-solving approach and is exploring the complex challenges that refugees pose to the political.[23] Refugee identity is a limit-concept of modern accounts of the political and is constituted through an exceptional logic: whatever qualities are present for the citizen are notably absent for the refugee. The visibility, agency, and rational speech of the citizen is lacking in the prevailing representations of the refugee. Instead, qualities of invisibility, voicelessness, and victimage are allocated with the effect of effacing the political subjectivity of the refugee. I explore the politics of these representational practices with reference to the concept of "refugeeness."

Refugeeness is an admittedly ambiguous—some might say fuzzy—concept. It has been likened to a "generalized condition of homelessness."[24] Refugeeness is concerned with the various qualities and characteristics that are regularly associated with and assigned to refugee identity. Ambiguity, however, is an unavoidable, if unintended, consequence inherent to the practice of definition. The concept of refugeeness embraces this ambiguity by refusing to fix the meaning of "refugee" to any definitive definition. To do otherwise would be to enact closure on a concept that is constantly in motion. The concept's indistinct, ambiguous character has the advantage of making visible otherwise unnoticed political relationships. In particular, refugeeness touches on all the various "ensembles" of human life. As such, it is a concept with some force, as it breaks through the artifice of disciplinary divisions, emphasizing how the "realms" of culture, society, the economy, and the politics all coexist on an immanent field of interaction. This is important because how refugees are interpreted politically is not the exclusive domain of the legislative and judicial sectors. Legal definitions of refugees, while of immense significance, are not sufficient to understand the politics of refugees. The politics of being a refugee has as much to do with the cultural expectation of certain qualities and behaviors that are demonstrative of "authentic" refugeeness (e.g., silence, passivity, victimhood) as it does with legal definitions and regulations.

Refugeeness raises some fundamental questions about the location and nature of the body politic and political subjectivity. How does refugeeness figure into ongoing historical struggles over the meaning and location of the political? Here, it is important to note that refugeeness is not exclusively a condition that somehow exists outside the refugee, acting on his or her body. Refugeeness is, indeed, a social construction, but as such it is constituted not least by those who are experiencing forcible displacement of their political body. The concept and practices of refugeeness also include the possibility for emerging political practices, whereby refugees themselves recast the terms of their identity. The advantage of interpreting refugee situations in terms of refugeeness is that it highlights the very political process of becoming-refugee. This process is not a seamless, sudden, or otherwise dramatic shift from one static state to another (i.e., from citizen to refugee). Rather, it is a site of struggle, a continual process of identity construction, and one that highlights how the activity and practices of refugees are recasting the terms of ethical and political discourse.

In chapter 1, I examine the logic of sovereignty for how it works to tame the contingencies of refugeeness by subsuming both the phenomenon and the experience of refugeeness within a crisis vocabulary. A discourse of "the emergency" dominates the way that refugees and their movements are spoken of by governments, international humanitarian organizations, and academics. I show that one of the major effects of this framework is that it casts the whole phenomenon of the refugee in the form of a problem that is in need of practical, technical, and operational solutions. However, this same discourse plays an important role in structuring and ordering refugee identity in a way that imprints the qualities of speechlessness, invisibility, and emptiness onto the (nonpolitical) body of the refugee. These characteristics are neither natural nor inevitable. Rather, I read them as both supportive and subversive to the process of constituting the sovereign spaces and identities of the nation-state. To emphasize this doubleness of refugeeness, I analyze various photographic representations that have tried to convey the condition of refugeeness. By examining the images of refugees deployed by the United Nations High Commissioner for Refugees on its Web site and in its publications and the humanitarian photography of Sebastião Salgado, I argue that refugees are not just human subjects in a political crisis but also representative of a more generalized crisis in human political subjectivity.

The relationship that refugees have with the concept of the "human" is a close, yet problematic, one. On one hand, to speak of refugees is to enter into a plethora of discourses on the "human": their suffering is cause for humanitarian concern, raises important human rights issues, and is a barometer for human insecurity. To be sure, the 1951 UN Refugee Convention is generally lauded for replacing earlier regimes of classifying refugees according to their nationality or country of origin and, instead, defines refugees as human beings with certain inalienable rights. "Humanity" is the organizing principle here, not the nationality of the refugee applicant. The chorus of humanity, therefore, repeats throughout the saga of the refugee. And yet, despite the apparent universality of their condition, refugees are subjected to a wide variety of Othering strategies that, ironically, cast them as something less than human. The refugee is thus at once the purest expression of humanity and also its constitutive limit. What are the politics of being identified as "human," of belonging to the ever-elusive moral community of "humanity"? What is at stake in rethinking the relationship between the "political" and the "human"? In chapter 2, I address these questions by critically unpacking the assumptions informing the discourse, practices, and strategies of humanitarianism. Through a reading of key texts by Hannah Arendt, Michel Foucault, and Giorgio Agamben, I develop a biopolitical critique of humanitarianism and outline a critical framework for interpreting refugee situations and practices.

Chapter 3 is a study of the international legal definition of the refugee, namely, the clause in the UN Refugee Convention that awards refugee status to any person who flees their country of origin "owing to a well-founded fear of being persecuted for reasons of race, religion, nationality, membership of a particular social group or political opinion." The manner in which the definition establishes a relationship between reason ("well-founded") and passion ("fear") represents a key site where refugeeness is constituted in a way that is very supportive of sovereign accounts of the political. The Convention definition discursively produces the refugee as a human being identified by a close relationship with the human emotion of fear. The appeal of fear as the defining qualification for refugee status is that it is an emotion that is universally shared among all human beings. But human beings who are defined by their fear have a long history of being simultaneously defined as social outcasts, lacking full reasoning capacity, and incapable of presenting an autonomous, self-governing form of personal subjectivity. What emerges from this definition is a type of human that is not so much a universal as a restrictive category that can be employed to exclude, to produce difference, and to reinforce social and political hierarchies. Against this disabling view of fear, I offer examples of refugee poetry that constructively engage with the politics of fear in ways that both accept and defy sovereign accounts of the role of fear.

Human beings who have been defined as possessing fearful subjectivities often find themselves subjected to representational practices that define them as something less than human. In chapter 4, I analyze how this ontological reduction is enabled by hegemonic conceptions of refugeeness. The construction of the refugee as a figure who lacks the capacity for reasonable speech has historically been deployed to discursively establish an animal quality to refugeeness. My aim in this chapter is to examine how this animality poses a profound challenge to contemporary cultures of hospitality. Representing refugees as possessing a kind of animality suggests that Derrida's rereading of hospitality to include a hostile dimension—a kind of hostipitality—is an appropriate framework. "Hostipitality" allows for encounters with refugees without pretending that anxiety and conflict are absent but also without negatively characterizing refugees as bestial beings to be feared and controlled. I explore this problematic through the ambiguous Canadian response to two major refugee crises in the summer of 1999. While the humanitarian pride over the emergency evacuation of almost five thousand Kosovar refugees seems to stand in sharp contrast to the xenophobic hysteria over the appearance of almost six hundred Chinese "boat people" later that summer, I argue that the two cases share a number of disturbing commonalities. To demonstrate these similarities, the overlapping dynamics of animality, speechlessness, and detention are traced from the medieval institution of banishment all the way through to Microsoft's participation in cataloging the forcibly displaced.

Refugees are not supposed to be political agents—that is the prerogative of citizenship. And yet, refugees are everywhere demonstrating political agency. In chapter 5, I consider a limit category of refugees, the phenomenon of refugee warrior communities, to fully explore this paradox. Here, the refugee's relationship to the political is the clearest and most direct. As their name implies, refugee warrior communities are defined as autonomous political actors involved in armed struggle for clearly defined political purposes. As such, refugee warriors explode the civilian, humanitarian, and—above all—nonpolitical character of refugeeness. They operate at the limit of the humanitarian discourse on refugees, disrupting and unsettling the prevailing binaries of refugeeness (i.e., refugee–warrior, victim–agent, passive–active, speechless–vocal, humanitarian–political, etc.). The international response to the proliferation of refugee warrior communities has largely been aimed at reestablishing sovereign categories in situations made volatile by refugee warrior activity. However, the case of Afghan Muhajirin refugee warriors demonstrates how the meaning of refugeeness is being radically recast in ways that are counter to the prevailing expectations. I argue that the implications of this are far reaching and suggest that the concept of the refugee warrior community can be expanded to apply to refugees who strike out to reclaim their political identity, voice, and presence—and thus subverting traditional theories of the political based on the sovereign relation of the exception.

In sum, this study considers contemporary and historical narratives on refugees and their movements and assesses them for how they accommodate or resist, or both, sovereign resolutions to fundamental political relationships such as self and other, identity and difference, space and time, inside and outside. When the discourses and practices of humanitarianism take sovereign resolutions to these problematic relationships as obvious, normal, and inevitable, refugees invariably become transformed into "speechless emissaries."[25] My ultimate aim is to probe the conditions under which it is now possible to think about refugees, ethical responsibility, and political practice in ways other than sovereignty's strict logic of exclusion.

1

Emerging or Emergency Identities?

The tradition of the oppressed teaches us that the "state of emergency" in which we live is not the exception but the rule. We must attain to a conception of history that is in keeping with this insight. Then we shall clearly realize that it is our task to bring about a real state of emergency.

—Walter Benjamin

Introduction

Refugees and their movements regularly emerge as a "problem" to world order. To those whose principal concern is with the maintenance and security of this order, any situation that is constructed as a problem—or worse yet, a crisis or an emergency—is of obvious significance and warrants immediate action. The speeches of politicians, the scripts of news anchors, the field manuals of humanitarian aid workers, and the pages of academic policy journals all contain anxious expressions of concern over the global refugee crisis. "What is to be done?" is the collective chorus. While the urgency of finding an enduring solution to the global refugee crisis is one that is widely shared, the basis of this consensus goes well beyond feelings of moral obligation that come with the knowledge of human suffering. Indeed, at the same time that refugees are defined as "humanitarian emergency" and thus as an object of ethical concern, they are also defined as representing a crisis to world order and therefore as an immediate political concern.

Sadako Ogata, the former United Nations High Commissioner for Refugees (UNHCR), spoke to this point:

> The subject of refugees and displaced people is high on the list of international concerns today not only because of its humanitarian significance, but also because of its impact on peace, security and stability. The world cannot reach a new order without effectively addressing the problem of human displacement.[1]

The wording of the High Commissioner's statement is worth reflecting on, for it points to a fundamental ambiguity that characterizes conventional responses to the phenomenon of global refugee flows: what is the relationship between a commitment to the principles of humanitarian action on one hand and to the principles and norms that underline the "peace, security, and stability" of the international system of states on the other? While the first commitment appeals to a common human identity as the basis for humanitarian action, the second directs our concern toward maintaining a world order that insists on citizenship as the authentic political identity. How these competing commitments to humans and citizens are resolved reveals much about how contemporary visions of political identity and community are being (re)articulated today.

A useful way to begin a critical questioning of the politics of the refugee is to consider Walter Benjamin's views on states of emergency and counteremergency as represented in the epigram that opens this chapter. Refugees, as we shall see in this chapter, are cast as an abject population in a way that is systematically interrelated with the discourse of "the emergency." As a consequence, Benjamin's diagnosis of the "state of emergency" loses none of its relevance when it is applied to contemporary questions about humanitarianism, multilateral cooperation, and the global refugee crisis. Refugee identity is "not the exception but the rule" in the sense that the constitution of the normality requires the identification of difference, an Other through which coherence and unity of sovereign states and subjectivities are constituted and maintained.

Sovereign power is often thought about in terms of its inclusiveness. Indeed, the very language of liberal political theory encourages thinking about sovereignty in these terms: sovereign societies are brought together with the acceptance of a contract or a compact or through some vague general will. According to this view, a properly sovereign polity is one where the people (or their representatives) are empowered to determine the conditions that will structure and govern their own lives. In truth, however, this emphasis on inclusion obscures more than it illuminates, as modern forms of political sovereignty are as much based on the principles of exclusion as they are on inclusion, as much about dividing and differentiating practices as unifying and integrating the social order. One of the key performances of sovereign power, as Schmitt recognized, is to mark the limit of the normal and the beginning of the exceptional. "Sovereign is he [sic] who decides on the exception,"[2] said Schmitt, who went on to underscore how the sovereign relation makes possible the authoritative distinctions between friends and enemies, citizens and foreigners, insiders and outsiders. The dangers associated with such an account of the political are considerable, especially for an abject population such as refugees. With sovereignty, self–other encounters can readily be transformed into self–enemy confrontations. As a result, refugees can become stigmatized, made into a danger, and thus constructed as a threat to the nation-state and its citizen-subjects.

The refugee is a limit-concept that occupies the ambiguous divide between the binary citizenry–humanity. By "limit-concept" I mean a concept that expresses the limits of a certain logic of intelligibility—in this case, the political. By "political" I mean something much broader than just "politics." As Jenny Edkins points out, "The political has to do with the establishment of that very social order which sets out a particular, historically specific account of what counts as politics and defines other areas of social life as not politics."[3] As such, the refugee is constituted through a series of ontological omissions: whatever is present to the political subject (i.e., citizen) is absent to the refugee. The qualities of visibility, agency, and rational speech of the citizen-subject are conspicuously absent in conventional representations of refugees that cast them as invisible, speechless, and, above all, nonpolitical.

This chapter offers a critical assessment of the general discourse of "the emergency" within which refugees are subsumed. This discourse is thoroughly dominated by a problem-solving mentality that defines refugee movements as a technical problem in need of rapid solutions. This perspective not only is largely uncritical of prevailing and unequal global power relations but also discourages critical thinking about what constitutes a "normal" state of affairs. Situations deemed emergencies, however, are always interesting, for they bring to the forefront the unquestioned assumptions and tacit agreements that work to constitute a "normal" state of affairs. Consequently, to think of emergencies as Benjamin does—that is, as "not the exception but the rule"—means paying attention to those practices that work to reproduce and sustain prevailing conceptions of "normality" and "order." I argue that speaking about refugees as a technical problem in need of a solution has affected the way in which international efforts to resolve the refugee problem have been structured. To demonstrate this, I examine the history of the largely ad hoc, temporary, and crisis-orientated international refugee organizations of the twentieth century, arguing that their significance resides in how their insistence on the emergency terms of the refugee phenomenon imprinted the discourse of the emergency onto the very identity of refugees themselves. I consider in the remaining sections of this chapter the effects, as well as the constraints and possibilities, this emergency identity imposes on refugees.

Analyzing visual representations of refugees is an important part of understanding the politics of refugee identity and practice. To be sure, it is vital to include such representations if only for the simple reason that " photographs and other visual representations of refugees are far more common than is the reproduction in print of what particular refugees have said."[4] As a consequence, I consider in this chapter visual representations of refugeeness and assess how they affect the political subjectivity of people categorized as refugees. I contrast the visual images of refugeeness employed by the UNHCR with those presented by the noted humanitarian photographer Sebastião Salgado. Following this discussion, I offer some conclusions on what refugeeness can tell us about the contemporary status of sovereign accounts of the political.

A Crisis Vocabulary

The phenomenon of the refugee has a long history of being subsumed within discourses of crisis and danger. To be sure, words such as "problem", "crisis", "complex political emergency"—and let's not forget "border control" and "national security"—are commonly invoked whenever the subject of refugees and their movements arise. Refugee situations today are usually provoked by a complicated configuration of political, socioeconomic, and environmental forces that have conjoined to create a crisis situation. The suddenness and severity of post–cold war refugee flows has prompted a prominent UNHCR official to characterize these situations as "mega-crises" in a statement to the UN Security Council.[5] It is, therefore, not surprising to find that "humanitarian emergency" has come to be one of the most popular concepts in the refugee studies literature, dominating the vocabulary of the government officials, aid workers, refugee advocates, academics, and journalists. The concept attains a great deal of credibility for the way it connects the urgency of crisis situations with a heightened sense of moral obligation for individuals and groups caught in these violent and unstable situations. After all, the number of refugees and crisis situations worldwide does not seem to be diminishing. The 1.5 million refugees the UNHCR recognized in 1951 had increased to nearly 15.2 million by 2001, together with an additional 9.5 million "persons of concern" to the agency, including asylum seekers, returnees, and internally displaced persons (IDPs).[6] The financial costs of providing humanitarian assistance and protection to refugees have similarly increased: the UNHCR's original budget of US$300,000 has been dwarfed by recent budgets that have exceeded US$1 billion every year since 1992. Together, these growing numbers and institutional capacities are representative of a rapidly expanding global population of the displaced, the marginalized, the excluded.

The problem of refugees, however, does not lie with their numbers alone. It is a problem, first and foremost, of categorization, of making distinctions. All classifications have social conditions for their production and historical circumstances that make them credible.[7] However, the immediacy—indeed, the emergency—of refugee crises has left little time for critical self-reflection on the conditions and circumstances that make such a system of discrimination possible. On one level, this commitment to immediate action over critical reflection is not surprising. Researchers have often pointed out that the stakes involved in crisis situations are extremely high: "The rules which govern collective life no longer function; fear and hostility are intensified; the living conditions of the most vulnerable or exposed groups deteriorate; their very lives may be in danger."[8] Who would want to deny that refugee situations represent a real and urgent crisis to the affected individuals, families, and communities? Who would want to efface the emergency character of the refugee condition? It is not surprising that, put in these terms, critical questioning of the emergency discourse in which refugees find themselves is often dismissed as an unhelpful distraction. Daniel Warner spoke to this point when he recalled the reaction of a High Commissioner to an academic exegesis of refugee discourse: "That was all very well Professor, but what am I to do with the problem tomorrow morning?"[9]

One of the enduring consequences of being subsumed within a discourse of the emergency is that the refugee phenomenon is almost exclusively interpreted as a problem in need of a solution. How different actors articulate the nature of the problem does, of course, vary considerably. For instance, the UNHCR and other humanitarian actors seeking to provide protection and assistance to refugees interpret the problem of refugee flows in a very different way than, say, xenophobic, elements within (un)civil society and state institutions and legislatures. Despite their differences, these divergent perspectives nonetheless share some important commonalties. For instance, when faced with situations deemed emergencies, the desire to secure timely, policy-relevant analyses and recommendations is strong, irrespective of one's political views or moral position. Emergency situations, it is repeatedly stressed, require emergency responses: immediate, practical, and operational responses.

An example of this impulse to rapidly solve the problem of refugee crises can be culled from the ongoing policy-making debates held at the UNHCR. The "complex emergencies" that emerged from the violence and conflict in the Persian Gulf and the Horn of Africa in the early 1990s presented the UNHCR with such an "enormous and practical challenge" that the Executive Committee (EXCOM) of the organization commissioned "a detailed study of the organization's role and performance in [these] recent emergency operations."[10] The findings of the study approached the question of the UNHCR's relationship to humanitarian emergencies in an entirely practical and technical manner. Highlighted are operational issues such as logistics and the securing of lines of supply and communication. The question of agency coordination is similarly treated at length with recommendations for "closer integration of ... policymaking and operational functions" as well as for a lead agency to coordinate emergency response efforts to avoid "confusion," "inefficiency," and "duplication."[11] In general, the report is concerned with improving the efficiency and success rates of

UN emergency operations and so concludes that "greater emphasis must be placed on operational objectives, establishing a clear chain of command, decentralization and rapid decision making."[12]

The discourse on refugees and their movements is strongly allied to what Robert Cox identified as the "problem-solving" perspective. This approach is dominant not only among much of the academic scholarship on refugees but also within the policy-making circles of international humanitarian organizations dealing with refugees. It is an approach that is quite attractive to those responding to emergency situations, as its focus and emphasis is largely on practical and operational issues. It is also, however, an approach that is thoroughly implicated within a specific regime of power/knowledge that structures and orders the discourse on refugees and their movements. As Cox argued, the problem-solving approach "takes the world as it finds it, with the prevailing social and power relationships and the institutions into which they are organized, as the given framework for action" and in general works to "make these relationships and institutions work smoothly by dealing effectively with particular sources of trouble."[13] Thus, typical problem-solving questions with respect to refugee flows include the following: What causes the "complex emergencies" that produce so many refugee movements? What are the political implications or effects of these movements? How can we remedy these situations? Indeed, how can we control and solve the problem of the refugee?

Who is this "we" that will solve the problem of refugees? This is a crucial question because, as the scare quotes highlight, the capacity to speak authoritatively about populations, problems, and solutions always involves a power relation. However, the political character of knowledge claims is one that is rarely given much reflection in the problem-solving literature. In fact, the major concern with this perspective is precisely the unwillingness of its practitioners to be self-reflexive on their origins, contexts, and purposes. The crisis vocabulary reinforces this intransigence, as the strict temporal limitations imposed by "emergency" situations leave little time for critical self-reflection. The effect of this inattention, however, is that the problem-solving perspective tends to concentrate on realizing practical ways in which order and normalcy can be reinstated. Critical questioning of both the unequal power relations and the desirability of this order are deemphasized, marginalized, or ignored. As Sandra Whitworth notes, "When questions are posed in strictly technical terms, not only are a whole series of political questions silenced, but a whole series of interested actors are excluded from the discussion. Technical questions are answered by technical experts."[14]

Thus, the question of what a "crisis" or an "emergency" means in the context of refugee movements is one that needs to be explored. The first step in doing this is recognizing that the meaning of a crisis is never a simple or self-evident fact. The positivist assumption that the world is an open book that, once read, will offer up its enduring truths should be viewed with great suspicion in this context. There is no universal interpretative key—no Rosetta stone, as it were—to make the world completely transparent to our inquiries. "The world is not an accomplice to our cognition," said Foucault in an often-quoted passage. "There is no pre-discursive providence that makes the world well-disposed towards us."[15] Rather, the world is discursive; it is a text that is constantly being written and rewritten with no other authors except us. Therefore, for a critical perspective on refugees to proceed, some questioning of the discourse that structures the characteristics and polices the boundaries of intelligibility is in order.

Like any other discourse, a discourse of "the emergency" operates according to what Foucault called a "system of exclusion." Here, discourse is understood as a (coercive) practice through which the objects and practices that constitute the world are categorized and evaluated, regulated and controlled. In this way discourses work to enable some questions, while disabling others; they attempt to control which objects, propositions, and forms of analysis are "normal" and thus acceptable as a measure of "truthfulness" and those that are not.[16] Within every discourse, moreover, classification plays a crucial regulatory role. Classification—the process of assigning characteristics or an identity to an entity—gives order to the world by marking off limits, assigning positions, and policing boundaries. Distinct classifications, however, would not be possible without a process of differentiation. In the case of events classified as emergencies, this form of differentiation is profoundly influenced by a dichotomous logic. To speak of emergencies is to at once enter into a dualistic dance with all that which is taken to constitute a normal and ordered state of affairs. This oppositional relationship between order and crisis, the normal and the exceptional is not a symmetrical one, and it is not natural, equal, or innocent. Instead, as Zygmunt Bauman has noted, the very existence of dichotomies "testifies to the presence of differentiating power."[17] This power lies in the capacity of dichotomous categorizations to produce difference, to keep things apart and maintain separateness. According to this logic, an event is considered a "crisis" only to the extent that it differs in some fundamental way from an "ordered" state of affairs.[18]

Such logic can be seen to work even in some of the most thoughtful reflections on refugee emergencies. For instance, the authors of a recent article on humanitarian emergencies argued against making unwarranted generalizations about crises, insisting instead that these events must be appreciated in their specific locality and historical context. At the same time, however, the authors were quick to declare (within their opening paragraph, in fact) their consensus on what are shared and common characteristics of "all" crises:

- a crisis is temporary;
- it is unstable;
- it can rarely be resolved without the help of an intermediary;

- its outcome is uncertain;
- its resolution will mark a change, in that the outcome cannot be simply a return to the preexisting situation.[19]

The emergency, from this point of view, is precisely that which is aberrant, unusual, not normal. A crisis and an ordered existence constitute separate and distinct worlds; their relationship is one of strict difference. The UNHCR, for one, underscored this sentiment with respect to its capacity to develop protection and assistance during humanitarian emergencies: "Emergency operations cannot be managed as if they were regular programmes running at an accelerated pace."[20] Crisis situations, in other words, are not a sped-up version of the Same but something that is decidedly different, Other.

If the emergency is excluded from the accepted boundaries of order, it is also included at the same time within this realm by virtue of its exclusion.[21] Policing discursive practices to ensure this exclusion is, moreover, essential for incorporating, regulating, and constructing the identity of the inside. To be sure, part of the power of normality is precisely its capacity to portray itself in a positive normative light—that is, as permanent (vs. temporary), stable (vs. unstable), autonomous (vs. help of an intermediary), rational (vs. uncertain), secure (vs. change). The certainty, trust, and order of normal existence are made possible by the identification of a realm of uncertainty, fear, and chaos. The implication here is that a crisis cannot be recognized as a self-evident objective fact that somehow presents itself naturally to an external observer, as the problem-solving approach assumes. Rather, the crisis is revealed as a hotly contested social construction, involving a variety of competing political, cultural, and identity practices. As Jutta Weldes has stated, "As these divergent narratives indicate, there are no objective crises out there waiting to be discovered or observed by state officials or analysts. Instead, events are differently constructed as crises, or not constructed as crises at all, in different cultural contexts and in relation to the discursively constituted identities of states."[22]

Refugees: Aberration and Accident

What, then, is the normal state of affairs with respect to refugees? A 1939 review of international cooperation on the "refugee question" offers a conventional answer that is still relevant today. The author, an international lawyer, commented on how the refugee condition should be understood as a temporary condition: "The status of the refugee is not, of course, a permanent one. The aim is that he [sic] should rid himself of that status as soon as possible."[23] The lawyer probably felt justified in so easily incorporating the phrase "of course" into his discussion because (as noted previously) a crisis mentality can prejudice one toward a shortened temporal horizon. His casual acceptance, however, can also be interpreted as a claim about what is the "proper" and "enduring" form of political identity and community—that is, the citizen and the sovereign nation-state. In his review of modern theories of the state, Andrew Vincent highlighted the idea that the state brings presence to the political: it represents a "continuous public power" that provides "order and continuity" to the polity.[24] Crisis situations, however, are negatively defined by their capacity for absence—that is, for how they negate order and bring about disorder, chaos, and contingency. Refugees—displaced as they are from the "authentic" political identities and communities of citizenship and nation-states, respectively—are therefore seen as no more than a temporary aberration to the norm, as hiccups that momentarily disturb what Liisa Malkki called the "national order of things."[25]

Refugees are represented as a mishap, an accident that scars the moral and political landscapes of the international order. But if they are an accident, they are so in the sense that Paul Virilio has argued:

> Accidents have always fascinated me. It is the intellectual scapegoat of the technological; accident is diagnostic of technology. To invent the train is to invent derailment; to invent the ship is to invent the shipwreck. The ship that sinks says much more to me about technology than the ship that floats.[26]

Refugees, from this perspective, can be said to constitute an "accident" of the modern territorial nation-state.[27] The ontogenetic practices of modern statism work to secure the "normality" of citizenship and the state, yet do so by producing the "accident" of the refugee. To invent the citizen is to invent its opposite, the refugee. How the category of the refugee has been invented and naturalized as a crisis situation facing the modern states system is therefore of considerable significance.

This view of the refugee as an aberration, an accident if you will, is one that has been prevalent throughout the modern history of international cooperation on refugee issues. As such, it is important not to overstate the novelty of today's refugee crises. The current numbers are considerable and the diversity of refugee situations is great, to be sure. However, the alignment of refugees with notions of crisis and emergency predates contemporary post–cold war problems of forced displacement. The suddenness of mass refugee flows, the complex and varied conditions and circumstances causing flight, and (especially) the vast numbers seeking protection and asylum are all contributing reasons for refugees having been historically classified in crisis terms. Consequently, despite all the evidence that refugees are a "diffuse and enduring"[28] phenomenon of modern political life, the international organizations charged with protecting refugees have consistently been conceived in terms of crisis or emergency management.

While select groups of migrating people have been called "refugees" for almost as long as the Westphalian system of states—the term was first applied to the French Huguenots who fled to England after the Edict of

Nantes was revoked in 1685—the refugee phenomenon became a "problem" for the international system of states only beginning in the twentieth century.[29] Prior to this time the international migration of people was left largely unregulated. Passports were commonly employed more to control internal migrations within, for example, the Russian and Ottoman empires than to regulate interstate travel, where they became a common requirement only in the 1910s.[30] While it is still a matter of debate whether the number of individuals forced to migrate as refugees is unprecedented, it is widely accepted that the scope of protection offered to refugees by the international community is without precedent.[31]

The conventional wisdom regarding the origins of the refugee problem is well expressed in the historian Michael Marrus's history of twentieth-century refugee movements. Marrus prefers the term exile to refugee when characterizing individuals who fled their home countries because of political persecution before the twentieth century. Marrus argues that during the nineteenth century, for instance, European political exiles were generally "individuals who had chosen their political path, rather than large masses of people torn loose from their society and driven to seek refuge."[32] Moreover, while political exiles were certainly exposed to hardship and suffering, a degree of prior affluence was usually a necessary precondition for procuring the means to flee abroad in the first place. The class privilege that characterized the political economy of exile of the nineteenth century was such that "the world of political exiles was that of the relatively well-to-do or, at least, of the once well-to-do."[33] Radical political activists from the lower classes faced much bleaker fates. For them, "the consequences of defeat were more likely to be incarceration, transportation to penal colonies (such as Australia for the Irish and Algeria for the French), and even massacre, as occurred in Paris in June 1848 and again in the spring of 1871."[34]

Refugees, by this logic, became a problem when they ceased to be individual cases and appeared, instead, as a mass phenomenon.[35] As a result, conventional narratives on the rise of the modern regime of international refugee protection place its roots in the extraordinary and violent events that transformed early-twentieth-century Europe. The First World War, the Russian Revolution, and the collapse of the Ottoman and Austro-Hungarian empires had caused an unprecedented mass displacement of peoples in Europe—twenty million by most estimates. These refugees, moreover, were denied the protection that the comparatively cosmopolitan life of exile had previously offered some. As Hannah Arendt grimly observed, the violent transformations of the early twentieth century brought about

> migrations of groups who, unlike their happier predecessors in the religious wars, were welcomed nowhere and could be assimilated nowhere. Once they had left their homeland they remained homeless, once they had left their state they became stateless; once they had been deprived of their human rights they were rightless, the scum of the earth.[36]

The scope of the refugee problem, it was felt, was such that no state acting by itself could hope to address it effectively. Refugee flows, such as those fleeing the civil war and famine in Russia, were too intense, their movements too uncertain, their numbers too overwhelming. International voluntary relief organizations such as the International Committee of the Red Cross (ICRC), Near East Relief, the Save the Children Fund, the International Union for Helping the Children, and others were similarly overwhelmed. The recognition that some form of international cooperation was required to adequately meet the refugee problem was thus the conclusion of an international meeting of humanitarian aid organizations, convened by the ICRC, in February 1921. This appeal for a multilateral solution to the crisis posed by ever-increasing and diverse refugee flows led to a decision by the League of Nations to appoint its first High Commissioner for Refugees, the Norwegian explorer Fridtjof Nansen.

If modern international refugee protection was born from a perception of crisis, the organizations created to implement a protective mandate were similarly touched by what seems to be a congenital "crisis mentality." From the outset, the League of Nations was dominated by a mode of thought that conceived refugees and their movements as discreet and episodic crisis situations. As such, the League placed great constraints on the spatial and temporal orientations of the international organizations it created to deal with refugee flows. The League faced considerable pressure from governments dealing with large refugee movements for its "refugee work [to] be liquidated with the utmost rapidity," and so it consistently conceived the refugee problem as a temporary one.[37] Consequently, the international organizations the League established to deal with refugees were all conceived as short-term, ad hoc operations with limited mandates. The precisely worded designations of the League's refugee offices betray their ad hoc, geographically specific character: for example, "High Commissioner on behalf of the League in connection with the problems of Russian Refugees in Europe" (1921) and, later, the "High Commissioner for Refugees coming out of Germany" (1933).[38] These geographical and national limitations were matched by strict financial constraints. League funds were to be spent only on administrative matters and were not to be used for funding direct relief operations for the displaced. The funding of these operations came not from states but from philanthropic sources that were funneled through private voluntary organizations (e.g., ICRC). The result, as one commentator observed, was that for "most of the interwar period, the international refugee regime ran on extremely limited ad hoc budgets put together without benefit of long-range planning."[39]

In the refugee studies literature, the ad hoc character of these early attempts at international cooperation on the refugee question is usually presented as evidence of an imperfect and incomplete refugee regime still in the process of development. To be sure, the refugee regime is generally considered to have gone through two major stages of development. The first stage consists of those international organizations that predated the UNHCR. Here, the League of Nations High Commissioner for Refugees (1921), the Nansen International Office for Refugees (1930), the Intergovernmental Committee on Refugees (1938), the United Nations Relief and Rehabilitation Administration (1943), and the International Refugee Organization (1947) are all seen as representing progressive steps in the evolution of an effective regime of refugee protection. Nevzat Soguk suggests that the conventional refugee studies literature interprets the significance of these early, tenuous, and nonsystematic attempts at international protection as lying not so much in their successes or effectiveness (which anyway were always limited) but rather in their promulgation of the idea of international protection for refugees. This idea, the story goes, was only fully realized in 1951 with the adoption of the Convention Relating to Status of Refugees and the establishment of the UNHCR.[40]

While it is surely correct to make a distinction between the more extensive activities and permanent offices of the UNHCR and the limited capacities of its predecessors, the evolutionary explanation is less than satisfying. In the first place, it is important to consider the strikingly similar way in which each international refugee organization—the UNHCR included—was initially conceived. Like its predecessors, the UNHCR, too, was initially considered to be only a temporary organization. The UNHCR was established to deal specifically with refugee flows caused by the Second World War, as well as with émigrés from the communist regimes of Central and Eastern Europe. The number of displaced people in Europe at this time was considerable. A 1945 U.S. State Department report estimated the number of uprooted people as being anywhere between twenty to thirty million.[41] The refugee problem, however, was once again framed as episodic, as a periodic crisis that required an immediate problem-solving response. As such, the UNHCR was given a limited mandate and a projected life span of only three years. The High Commissioner, with his staff of twenty-three, was allocated a small administrative budget of only $300,000 and was prohibited from raising revenue directly or even spending any funds directly on refugees.[42] As originally conceived, the organization would not be involved in the direct delivery of emergency aid to refugees but rather would facilitate "the coordination of the efforts of private organizations concerned with the welfare of refugees."[43]

The most significant line of continuity between the various international institutions, however, is their shared view of what constitutes a refugee. Here, the juridical definition of the refugee is less important than the pervasively shared cultural conception of what the experience of displacement—or "refugeeness"—involves. As Randy Lippert argues, the creation of the category of "refugee" was formed alongside international attempts to cooperate on the refugee crisis:

> Contemporaneous with and inseparable from the emergence of the international refugee programs and organizations ... was the

rise of the refugee as both an object of the aspirations of various Western authorities and as a new kind of person.[44]

The shared view that refugees constitute something different, unusual, and strange and hence require a unique identity can be traced all the way back to the early attempts to constitute an international refugee regime made by the League of Nations. Soguk argued that the LNHCR represents a significant development in dealing with refugee events and that it was during its tenure that the ontology of the refugee was fully determined and thoroughly formalized, thus enabling the subsequent regime activities.[45] The real significance of the ad hoc, temporary, and crisis-oriented international refugee organizations resides in how they established certain expectations for refugee identity. Their insistence on speaking about the refugee phenomenon in crisis terms ended up creating an emergency out of the people who found themselves labeled as refugees. The effects, as well as the constraints and possibilities, this emergency categorization creates for individuals and groups finding themselves labeled as refugees are, therefore, ones that need to be explored.

Visualizing Refugeeness

Attempts to explain the meaning and character of refugeeness often begin by asking the question, "Who is a refugee?" The 1951 UN Convention Relating to the Status of Refugees is the model that most national governments have employed to answer this question. The Convention defines a refugee as any individual who "owing to a well-founded fear of being persecuted for reasons of race, religion, nationality, membership of a particular group or political opinion" has crossed an international border to seek protection. Despite the widespread adoption of this definition, the question of who qualifies for refugee status remains a contested issue and one that is deeply implicated in political and ideological calculations. During the cold war, for example, the criteria for designating people as refugees was often overdetermined by ideological considerations, as Western governments regularly offered asylum to people from the Soviet bloc on the assumption that collectivized, command economies were unnatural (and thus political) arrangements imposed by totalitarian regimes. At the same time, the flip side of this assumption was that market economies were somehow natural and nonpolitical, and so the asylum claims from people originating from third world countries could be rejected on account that they were merely "economic migrants."[46]

The UNHCR, by contrast, insists that it is motivated by an altogether different, humanitarian set of concerns. Indeed, Article II of the organization's founding statute insists on the organization's nonpolitical character and its "humanitarian and social" disposition. To help cultivate this disposition in others, the organization employs a variety of tactics to communicate not so much who a refugee is (this is a political decision) as to relay what it is like to be a refugee. By far the most effective way the UNHCR and other humanitarian organizations have pursued this tactic is through visual images. The nightly televised newscasts are all too regularly filled with images of the violence and horror, the desperation and fear facing refugees in the various hot spots of the world. Indeed, governments regularly justify their "humanitarian interventions" in places like Kosovo by appealing to collectively consumed images of human suffering. The visual images of refugees presented in these different contexts are therefore of considerable significance. They play an important role in articulating and placing into general circulation a certain image of refugees that dominates what Malkki has referred to as the "transnational social imagination of refugeeness."[47]

An exemplary illustration of such representational practices can be found in the UNHCR's Web site of refugee images.[48] The Web site sees itself as providing a visual supplement to the rather abstract legal definitions that are typically employed to explain the condition of the refugee. As such, the Web site's purpose is summed up by its title—What is it like to be a Refugee? The ensuing photographs attempt to answer this question. On one screen we see a Rwandan family who fled as refugees with two hundred and fifty thousand others all on the same day in April 1994. On another, we encounter a photograph of an elderly Bosnian woman who has become "internally displaced" within her own community. These photographs—and others representing the struggles of Tajik, Somali, Vietnamese, and other refugees—reflect how the recent proliferation in refugee numbers has been matched by an unprecedented polymorphism and complexity in the causes, underlying dynamics, and effects of global refugee flows. Refugees are products of an extraordinarily large and varied global phenomenon of coerced displacement. Consequently, viewing the visual archive can leave one with the sense that no simple or singular answer to the question of refugee identity (or refugeeness) is possible. Refugeeness involves not a single identity position but a multiplicity of them, as can be witnessed in the recent proliferation of categories to describe the extraordinarily large and varied global phenomenon of coerced displacement: Charter refugee, political refugee, environmental refugee, nonstatus refugee, internally displaced person, asylum seeker, émigré, oustee, deportee, relocee, involuntary displaced person, involuntarily resettled person, forced migrant, involuntary migrant, and so on. Faced with such an explosion of categories for human displacement, current conditions strongly suggest that the answer to the Web site's initial question must necessarily be plural, ambiguous, and historical.

The diversity in the lived experiences of the refugees represented in the UNHCR's visual catalog is testament to the sheer scope and complexity of contemporary refugee is. At the same time, however, the organization insists that behind these experiences born out of particular contexts and circumstances lies a common underlying identity that is universally shared among all refugees. This universalist, humanitarian perspective is well represented in the title page photograph. At first, the photograph seems to be a rather enigmatic choice for a title page representation. No actual person—refugee or otherwise—can be found anywhere in the picture. Portrayed rather is a single long-sleeved shirt suspended in front of a makeshift shelter. The shirt hangs in a way that produces the illusion that a human body—the body of the refugee—is occupying it. We expect to *see* the refugee, but that individual is missing, absent, invisible. What is clear, however, is the underlying humanitarian message: the emptiness of the shirt signifies the emptiness that all refugees feel when they are forced to sever their ties with their home. To the question "What is it like to be a refugee?" the answer must therefore be understood in terms of a profound sense of lack. The condition of the refugee is an exceptional one in that all that fills so-called normal existence is absent. Like the empty shirt, the life of the refugee is typically seen as suffering from emptiness.[49]

The humanitarian photographic representations that are deployed to establish identity and presence to refugees ironically do so by highlighting the theme of absence and lack. This is especially the case when the question of upholding the human and political rights of refugees is raised. Take, for instance, the 1998 UNHCR report, *The State of the World's Refugees: A Humanitarian Agenda*.[50] This publication features a photograph of refugees at the beginning of each chapter; each photograph complements and further conveys the chapter's central theme. The chapter titled "Defending Refugee Rights" is accompanied by a highly enigmatic photograph of a Sri Lankan refugee child in Tiruchi, India. The child is standing beside several large trunks, holding, no doubt, the only possessions the child's family could transport during the flight from their homes. What is most striking about the photograph is that its subject—the refugee child, standing behind a backlit curtain—can be seen only as a shadow. Absent is any indication of even the most basic physical features; not even the child's gender can be discerned. Just as the opening photograph of the UNHCR's Web site is notable for how it links refugeeness with invisibility, acorporeality, and emptiness, the image of the refugee child is striking for how it effaces all traces of presence on behalf of a refugee when it comes to discussing his or her political and social rights.

What is the significance of this? Why would a photograph chosen to illuminate the challenges of defending refugee rights present an anonymous, two-dimensional outline of a child's human form? While it is true that humanitarian representations of refugee life can often capture much of the material and psychological difficulties that result from the experience of being forcibly displaced from one's home, they are still far from being unproblematic. The photojournalist who assumes that he or she can somehow be an objective witness to refugees caught in or taking flight from humanitarian emergencies often ends up taking a superior and distanced subject position. David Levi Strauss has explored the dangers associated with such a stance:

> Photographs taken from this position may elicit pity, sorrow, or guilt in their viewers, but they will never provide information for change. They only work to reinforce the construction of the center and the periphery: North and South, rich and poor, superior and inferior. It cannot be otherwise.[51]

Representations, therefore, cannot merely expect to convey one thing as another without political effect. This is especially true given how the discourse on the subject of the refugee works to codify displaced people with empty, invisible, and voiceless identities. Consequently, one explanation of the photograph of the refugee child is that "the visual prominence of women and children as embodiments of refugeeness has to do not just with the fact that most refugees are women and children, but with the institutional, international expectation of certain kinds of helplessness as a refugee characteristic."[52] This expectation leads to a very strange discourse of human displacement. As Nevzat Soguk has argued, it is a discourse that provides "no place for the displaced human, a discourse on the question of the refugee that affords no place for the refugee and the refugee's voice."[53]

Humanitarian representations of refugees act as a powerful intervening force in world politics. Malkki notes how photojournalists, the mass media, and the publications of humanitarian and international organizations systematically deploy representations that transform refugees into what she calls "speechless emissaries." Humanitarian representational practices often aim to disrupt the common distinction between refugee and nonrefugee by promoting a vision of a shared and common humanity. However, the humanitarian representations of refugees often end up portraying a rather undifferentiated "raw" or "bare" vision of humanity that works to mask the individuality of refugees as well as the historical and political circumstances that forced them into this identity. Malkki argues that "in their overpowering philanthropic universalism, in their insistence on the secondariness and unknowability of details of specific histories and specific cultural or political contexts, such forms of representation deny the very particulars that make people something other than anonymous bodies, merely human beings."[54]

The central difficulty with portraying refugees as "merely human beings" is that all notions of political agency are, in a word, emptied from refugee subjectivity. What is most at stake politically with the refugee phenomenon is that refugees are silent—or rather, silenced—because they do not possess the "proper" political subjectivity (i.e., state citizenship) through which they can be heard. Refugees are negatively defined as registering a twofold lack with respect to the privileged resolutions to questions of political identity (citizenship) and community (nation-state). Whereas citizens are firmly and securely rooted in the territorial space of the state, refugees suffer from displacement: they are uprooted, dislocated, and unwilling exiles from the community of citizens. Refugees signify an emptiness, an incompleteness vis-à-vis the meaningful positive presence to political subjectivity that state citizenship provides. Without citizenship, refugees are denied not only political rights but also something more fundamental—the capacity to speak politically and the expectation that they will be heard. Denied the political identity of citizenship, refugees are shut out from what Balibar describes as "cultural initiative or effective presence in the public space (the capacity of be 'listened to' there)."[55] Consequently, refugees, as Hannah Arendt recognized, represent a problem not of geographical space but of political space.[56] Refugees are people deprived of their human rights first and foremost because they are denied access to a political space that allows for a meaningful political presence: "They are deprived, not of the right to freedom, but of the right to action; not of the right to think whatever they please, but of the right to opinion."[57]

The refugee is an aberration only when people accept as a matter of common sense that citizenship is the only authentic political identity of modern political life. Refugees are voiceless not in any essentialist way but only through the congenital disorder that comes with being classified as the absence of the sovereign voice capable of intervening in the public sphere. But this space of politics, it must be recalled, is not just *there* in some timeless fashion. Rather, political space is created and sustained by ongoing human activity—much of it bloody, unfair, and prejudiced. Thus, to assume that the concepts of citizenship and sovereign state are somehow unproblematic, foundational principles of modern political life is to engage in an act of reification which obfuscates the historical practices of identity and community formation and contestation.[58] As an historical construct, the modern state has sought to either incorporate or decree all alternatives to it as unacceptable. "The State is sovereignty," Deleuze and Guattari say, "but sovereignty only reigns over what it is capable of internalizing, of appropriating locally."[59] What it cannot internalize, naturalize, or co-opt, it excludes, displaces, and alienates. This effacement of the variety of historical struggles over what it might mean to be political does not alter the fact that other ways of being or acting politically have and continue to exist. Rather, the conceptual governance that is one of statism's effects works to mask the significance of social, cultural, economic, and political practices that do not necessarily abide by the logic and codes of the sovereign territorial state. Sovereignty, from this perspective, is not so much a juridic principle to be invoked as an effect of various discursive and material practices.[60] As such, state sovereignty should not be assumed so much as explained. Cynthia Weber explains,

> It is not possible to talk about the state as an ontological being—as a political identity—without engaging in the political practice of constituting the state. Put differently, to speak of the sovereign state at all requires one to engage in the political practice of stabilizing this concept's meaning.[61]

The state, in short, is not a static and reified thing. Rather, it involves dynamic and historical practices that are constantly performed.

The representational practices of the UNHCR reinforce an image of refugeeness that negatively establishes the refugee as the inverted mirror image of the citizen. These practices are not only consistent with but also reproduce sovereign accounts of the location and nature of "authentic" political identities and spaces. However, not all representations of refugees align themselves so neatly to this sovereign logic. Next, I consider the case of renowned humanitarian photographer Sebastião Salgado and assess his recasting of refugeeness for how it resists and, as we shall see, subscribes to the logic of state sovereignty.

Taking Exodus?

Salgado made a name for himself by taking a snapshot for *Newsweek* of John Hinckley's bullet going into the sovereign body of Ronald Reagan; he has made a lifetime pursuit out of documenting the lives of people—refugees, involuntary migrants, the internally displaced, and so on—violently expelled from the sovereign body politic. His photographs of the Brazilian landless movement gained him notoriety, while his portrayal of the struggles of industrial workers at the close of the twentieth century secured his position as a photographer of the underclass, the marginalized, and the dispossessed.[62] Recognition for Salgado's talent in this regard has been widespread. He is the recipient of major photographic prizes in Germany, Spain, Holland, Czechoslovakia, Sweden, and the United States as well as the recipient of the French government's W. Eugene Smith Award for Humanitarian Photography. Salgado's work has been widely and popularly exposed in the top news magazines (*Time, Newsweek*, etc.), and he has regularly been given feature spreads in widely distributed popular magazines such as *Rolling Stone* and *Match*. All in all, Salgado's images have an important currency in the global "mediascapes" that play such an important part in developing and structuring a standardized moral imaginary of refugeeness.[63]

"Humanity is on the move; urgently, chaotically." These words—the curator's—are the first to greet viewers of Salgado's major photographic exhibit at the Museum of European Photography in Paris in the summer of 2000. Titled *Migrations: Humanity in Transition*, this project has been hailed as an epic documentation of the phenomenon of mass migration.[64] Salgado is renowned for eschewing the photo-documentarian's claim to "objectivity" and instead engages with his subjects in an attempt to capture the meaning—and underlying structures—of coerced human displacement in all its diverse forms and contexts. The scope of Salgado's study is extremely broad; the photographs were taken over a period of seven years and cover thirty-five countries. Many of them were taken at the request of humanitarian relief organizations, such as Médecins sans Frontières (Doctors without Borders). As such, all the recent and current hot spots of human population flows are featured: the U.S.–Mexican border, the former Soviet Union, the Strait of Gibraltar, Bosnia, Kosovo, Mozambique, Rwanda, Afghanistan, and many others. Walking through the exhibit rooms one encounters again and again faces filled with fear, pain, and desperation. Salgado's photographs are often said to convey suffering in such a way that the courage and dignity of the individuals photographed are preserved. To be sure, Salgado has made his career in sociodocumentary photography by taking such an involved, empathetic view. Strauss has argued that it is the ability to convey an "extraordinary balance of alterity and likeness, of metaphoric and documentary function [that] is part of the Salgado signature."[65] Eduardo Galeano has made a similar point and has distanced Salgado from the one-dimensional representations of refugeeness found in the UNHCR examples discussed previously. He remarked, "Salgado photographs people. Casual photographers photograph phantoms."[66] It is not surprising, therefore, that Salgado has been designated as the "family photographer" of the Third World.[67]

The curator's notes at the Paris exhibit inform us that the photographs in the exhibit strive to "capture tragic, dramatic, heroic moments in individual lives." The viewing public is warned that while individually the photographs offer no absolute answers, collectively they do pose a fundamental question: "As we enter the future, are we to "leave behind" a good part of humanity?" To my eye, one of the most extraordinary features of the exhibit is how it encourages the viewer to leave behind the familiar categories that are employed to conceptualize global movements of human beings. Viewed as a collection, Salgado's photographs challenge us to deconstruct the common distinction made between refugees and other migrants, especially so-called economic migrants. While Salgado is very successful in accomplishing this, his photographs are nonetheless caught in a paradoxical relationship with the logic of the sovereign political relation. Like the refugees he documents, Salgado's attempt to escape is never an unqualified success. As we shall see, the sovereignty effect is still discernible within his representations of refugeeness.

Let us begin by considering Salgado's attempt to subvert conventional classification schemes on human migration. As noted previously, his exhibit catalogs all the hot spots of recent humanitarian emergencies. However, he also photographed the factories, markets, and slums of Bombay, Cairo, Manila, Shanghai, and Jakarta. The lives of economic migrants—some legal, some not—are considered alongside those of refugees. Legal classifications seem less important for Salgado than capturing the dynamics of global patterns of estrangement that comes with unregulated (yet highly policed) movement of all kinds. While some photojournalists are drawn to humanitarian emergencies to capitalize on the drama and tragedy of these situations, Strauss has applauded Salgado for his demonstrated

> understanding of the geopolitical and economic background of the situations he documents (he was a development economist before becoming a photographer in 1973) [which] gives his images proac-

tive urgency and address. Pathos is not his aim. Single images may appear nostalgic, but seen en suite and in relation to one another, as Salgado intends, they reveal a conflicted and often concealed history.[68]

Refugee and migrant are thus considered together—"in relation to one another"—in this exhibition. They are portrayed together not to highlight their categorical differences but to better describe the way they are both important members of a growing yet extremely diverse population of what Jan Jindy Pettman calls the "international political economy of bodies."[69]

We should take inspiration from Salgado's attempt to disrupt conventional ways of thinking, seeing, and talking about refugees. We should also, however, show great caution as well. For despite their best efforts at subverting the refugee–migrant binary, Salgado's photographs still express values that are derived from the logic and assumptions of state sovereignty. This subsumption within a statist discourse of inside–outside is most clearly expressed when the tropes of "hope" and "fear" are used to distinguish and separate migrant from refugee. As the curator put it,

> Most migrants leave their homes filled with hope; refugees usually do so out of fear; both are driven by the survival instinct. Caught in maelstroms of poverty and violence beyond their comprehension, their only escape is to move on.[70]

The impact of this distinction can be measured throughout the exhibition. When portrayed as individuals or small groups, the photographs of refugees tend to highlight expressions of fear, anguish, helplessness, and urgency. Portrayed as a mass, the photographs overwhelmingly portray sprawling camps, long columns of people in flight, masses of slaughtered bodies, long lines for humanitarian aid, and so on. Many of the photographs—especially those documenting the genocide in Rwanda—are extremely difficult to view, let alone forget. Therefore, it is almost a relief when the exhibit moves away from the zone of crisis and fear that characterizes the refugee component of this exhibit. Upstairs in the Museum—note the spatial segregation—the photographs consider the lives of migrants. Make no mistake: the transition to consider the poverty-stricken lives of migrants evokes its own malaise. However, there is an interesting and significant difference. Unlike the images of the refugees, the photographs of migrants in this exhibition are shown as active participants in a social, cultural, and economic lifeworld. They trade, they work, they build homes, they worship. They play guitar and sing and dance. The exuberance and multiplicity of life—of living—that is represented in these photographs is simply remarkable.

The enthusiastic participation in "normal" life, however, is almost entirely absent in the photographs of the refugees. This absence, I fear, is consistent with the way the sovereign political relation structures the relationship between hope and fear. Migrants are not just hopeful subjects but also individuals who have a greater access to the space of hope. This space assumes the secure space of sovereignty as a condition of its possibility. Sovereignty, Rob Walker argued, allows not only for the space of politics to exist but also for the pursuit and articulation of specific notions of truth, beauty, and goodness. Inside, there is the possibility—the hope—of attaining the "good life." Outside, all bets are off as individuals must struggle with the uncertainty, contingency, and fear of being outside the "protection" of a state.[71] Thus, while migrants travel between spaces of hope, refugees are condemned to the zone of fear that exists in between states. Here, there is no hope. Rather, the refugee's condition portrayed in Salgado's photographs is not too dissimilar to one UNHCR characterization:

> In some ways, becoming a refugee makes life desperately simple, and empty. No home, no work, no decisions to make today. And none to make tomorrow. Or the next day. Refugees are the victims of persecution and violence. Most hope that, one day, they may be able to rebuild their lives in a sympathetic environment. To exist again in more than name.[72]

Unlike the lives of migrants, the condition of refugee has no normality; it is a life in a state of emergency and is stripped bare of all cultural and political qualities.

The logic of state sovereignty is reinforced in Salgado's exhibition, as the only time refugees are seen "to exist again in more than name" is when the possibility of returning "home" emerges. The cultural and community activity regularly displayed in the photos of the migrants is visible only among refugees in these cases. The possibility of leaving their condition of exile and making a move to return home creates a huge transformation in Salgado's representation of refugeeness. His photos of soon-to-be-repatriated refugees from Mozambique are exemplary in this regard. Here, refugees are shown not as afraid or helpless but as actively engaged people. This is demonstrated in a photograph of members of a refugee family who demonstrate their determination to "go home"—and new signs of a purposive agency—by burning down the house that served as their home during exile. Refugees, moreover, are portrayed not as dirty and disheveled but as displaying qualities of elegance and beauty. While Salgado seems to have a particular fondness for a group of women combing and styling each other's hair, the frames in this portion of the exhibit overflow with images of people of all ages dressed up and looking their best. The faces of these refugees show not only joy and happiness but also spiritual contemplation as religious activity among refugees is documented here for the first and only time in the exhibit. Indeed, the photographs of the refugees returning to Mozambique are unfortunately unique in this exhibit. While it is visibly apparent that the prospect of returning home is of immense significance to this community, what is not so clear is why cultural activities are absent in all the other representations of refugees. One is struck with the impression that during their exile, refugees never worship, trade, build, sing, or dance.

It is as if only in the context of welcoming the return of statist identities that such activity can be seen.[73]

These criticisms are not meant to undermine Salgado's credibility or confer upon him unwarranted intentions. Rather, my comments are intended to demonstrate just how persistent and pervasive the sovereign conception of social and political life is. Like the refugees and migrants it documents, Salgado's exhibit was soon set into motion to travel a global network of movement and cross-cultural encounters—in this case, a rather privileged movement and set of encounters through the global exhibition network of elite museums and exhibition halls in various world cities (New York, Rio, Rome, Berlin, etc.). I should note, however, that *Migrations: Humanity in Transition* is only the traveling name of Salgado's exhibit. The Parisian exhibit went under the much simpler, older, and infinitely more evocative title of *Exodes*.[74] While Salgado's exhibit is powerful and note-worthy in many respects, it also needs to explicate itself—take exodus, if you will—from the conventional forms of categorizing refugees and their movements.

Conclusion

All solutions are deeply implicated in the conditions that make the problem possible in the first place. The great limitation of the conventional litera-ture on the global refugee crisis is that the sovereign identities of state and citizen unproblematically serve as the starting point of analysis. If refugees constitute a crisis it is because they are not citizens, they are not sedentary, they do not presently possess a home in the form of a sovereign territorial state. Refugees and their movements are thus categorized as an "absence made possible by the insistence of the presence of sovereignty."[75] The refu-gee and the citizen thus share an immanent relationship, with each clearly making the other possible. The solutions that rectify this crisis, moreover, come in an entirely state-centric language as well. In general, humanitarian solutions to the phenomenon of the refugee enact a spatial reversal of the binary citizen–refugee to transform the refugee's lack into a positive pres-ence. These solutions take the form of restoring statist identities and com-munities to refugees. Traditionally, the UNHCR has pursued a dual strategy of securing asylum for refugees (i.e., settlement and integration into anoth-er state) or facilitating the voluntary repatriation of refugees (i.e., return-ing to country of origin). Of course, the most extreme solution within this state-centric logic is to create a new state for the refugees, as was the case for Jewish refugees (Israel) and is still one of the major goals of the ongoing struggle of Palestinian refugees.

The modern account of the location and character of the political con-tinues to be powerfully compelling. Even actions residing on the limit of modern politics—such as humanitarian representations and multilateral interventions on behalf of refugees—tend to be, in the end, overdetermined by the statist prerogative to claim the authentic subjects and spaces of politics as its own. The humanitarian ethic in these cases is subsumed within the political logic of state sovereignty, a logic that already posits a resolution between the moral obligations we feel toward the one and the many, the universal and the particular, humanity and citizen-subjects.[76] The point to be emphasized here is that conventional humanitarian responses to refugee crises focus on returning to refugees statist identities so as to restore the conditions under which they may once again enjoy a properly human life as citizens.

Taking our cue from Salgado, perhaps it is time again to take the concept of exodus seriously and learn of ways to include it within our critical armory. The concept has its original and most famous roots as a term to describe the biblical flight of the Jews—that is, their escape from the Pharaoh's army and their slave existence in ancient Egypt. More recently, the Italian political theorist Paolo Virno has campaigned for the reintroduction of the concept exodus into our political vocabulary.[77] Inspired as much by the "refusal to work"[78] movement of radical Italian workers in the 1960s and 1970s as by the line of flight taken by the ancient Jews, Virno conceived of exodus as a form of political action based on the strategy of refusal, of defection, of flight. Exodus is not a dialectical politics of direct opposition and confrontation but a politics of "engaged withdrawal" and "subtraction."[79] Rather than seizing power and holding political and public space, the political theory of exodus begins by refusing to acknowledge as legitimate the received accounts of what and where "power" and "the political" is and can be. "The state will crumble," according to this view, "not by a massive blow to its head, but through a mass withdrawal from its base, evacuating its means of support."[80]

When faced with the statist overdetermining discourse that engulfs refugees and their movements, we should choose defection and exodus—as quickly as possible! The concept of exodus is a useful political metaphor not least because it reminds us of how much activity is required to maintain and reproduce the political space of the sovereign state. To take exodus is to go beyond declaring that some government or regime lacks legitimacy; rather, it calls into question the whole conceptual system of governance that serves to underpin the idea of the state and the citizen as the only authentic political space and identity. To choose this line of flight, we should stress, is "not a negative gesture, exempt from action and responsibility. On the contrary, because defection modifies the conditions within which conflict takes place, rather than submit to them, it demands a particularly high level of initiative—it demands an affirmative 'doing.' "[81]

In this way, as Homi Bhabha has pointed out, the "state of emergency is also always a state of emergence."[82] There is always some "political excess" that allows us to consider how a phenomena such as refugees can figure into the process of transforming world order by virtue of how they "contest borders, put states into question (without rendering them irrelevant), rearticulate spaces, and reform identities."[83] Emergency discourses cannot completely control or disarm political phenomena that challenge, exceed, or simply sidestep the limits of modern accounts of political space and identity. Refugee situations should therefore be understood as complex, multidimensional sites of identity practices. Refugee identity is not merely the negative, empty, temporary, and helpless counterpart to the positive, present, permanent, and authoritative citizen. What we need are perspectives that are open to the possibility of political and ethical engagements that do not reproduce the sovereign codes that doom refugees to the status of "speechless emissaries."

2

On Humanitarian Violence

The ontological category of "the human" and "human nature" has been inextricably associated with the violence of Western history. If the human is itself revealed as a conflictual concept it can no longer be presented as an undisturbed ethical end.

—Robert Young, *White Mythologies*

Introduction: Humanitarian Violence

Humanitarian violence? At first glance, the concept seems to be an oxymoron, an almost insulting contradiction in terms. While "humanitarianism" and "violence" have certainly been employed together in recent scholarly and popular discourse, their conjunction is usually made on the understanding that they constitute an opposition. The two are presented as separate and distinct forms of activity, occupying opposing poles in the chain of causality of contemporary instances of conflict and violence. According to this view, the excesses of state, ethnic, and nationalist violence have created the untold human suffering that has motivated various global and local actors to humanitarian action. The causal relationship here is clear: if violence is the problem, then humanitarian action is presented as the moral remedy.

The disjuncture between humanitarianism and violence is consistent with the separation commonly invoked between ethical and political forms of activity. The received tradition of Western political thought (or at least its Realist variants) teaches us not only to separate the political from the ethical but also to impose a normative framework on this supposedly fundamental distinction. When Augustine distinguished the City of God from the City of Man, it was understood that it was the former realm—that of eternity, heaven, and life beyond the contingencies and indeterminacy of the temporal world—to which we were to hold our primary allegiance. Compared to these lofty heights, politics was an activity that was considered as somehow fallen, inferior, and amoral.

This separation continues to have a considerable—if contested—currency in the discursive economy of humanitarianism. The much-heralded concept of "humanitarian space," for one, depends on the explication of "humanitarian" actors from the field of the political. As the former United Nations High Commissioner for Refugees (UNHCR) Sadako Ogata repeatedly underscored during her tenure, the creation of humanitarian space must be "premised on the principles of impartiality and neutrality" and be "independent from political goals and considerations."[1] The former president of the International Committee of the Red Cross (ICRC) put the issue even more bluntly in an address to the UN General Assembly: "humanitarian endeavour and political action must go their separate ways if the neutrality and impartiality of humanitarian work is not be jeopardized."[2] According to the conventional wisdom, therefore, humanitarian action is the opposite of political activity. The two constitute a hierarchical binary, the normative character of which has one element carrying positive connotations ("humanitarianism is compassionate, principled, impartial") while the other is seen in negative terms ("politics is cynical, amoral, self-interested").[3]

To speak of "refugees" and "world politics" together is to enter into a discourse where international ethics, humanitarian principles, and morally derived arguments for international action have some claim to prominence. The end of the cold war brought many changes to world politics, and the increasing relevance of international humanitarian action must certainly be considered as one of the most significant developments. This development is reflected in the scholarly literature on world politics, where there has been a resurgence in interest in ethical questions, or what has been called "new normative approaches" to international theory.[4] To be able to highlight moral and ethical issues when assessing global politics is a noteworthy development. Until quite recently, to speak of "ethics" and "international politics" as anything other than two separate and distinct fields of inquiry (and practice) would have been interpreted as proof of a profound, perhaps even dangerous, naïveté to the "realities" of world politics. Questions of ethical responsibility in the international realm were seen as altogether incommensurable with the doctrine of political realism that dominated discussions of world politics during the cold war. At the time, any perspective that did not interpret world politics as the pursuit of power politics by amoral, self-interested, and utility-seeking sovereign states acting in a dangerous and anarchic realm was effectively marginalized or ignored.[5]

On one level, the resurgence of interest in humanitarian ethics can be interpreted as reflective of a general shift toward a more reflexive and critical approach to understanding world politics.[6] There are good reasons, however, for taking pause before celebrating the onset of an alleged ethically situated approach to understanding world politics. In the first place, the emergence of "new normative approaches" still largely relies on specifically liberal, rights-based ethical theories drawn from the dominant traditions of Western moral and political theory.[7] This point becomes especially important when we are confronted with what seems to be a plethora of available ethical approaches to international relations. This apparent wide range of choices actually serves to obfuscate the fact that they are derived from a single—if differentiated—Western tradition.[8] The easy (and often openly chauvinistic) manner in which non-Western ethical traditions are excluded from serious consideration is certainly cause for alarm, not celebration. Rob Walker has pointed out the dangers involved in such myopic moralism, noting that "one person's normative project may well be another person's reification of contingent dominations or expression of chauvinistic arrogance on a global scale."[9]

A second set of concerns arises from how the so-called new normative approaches uncritically accept some very old categorical distinctions between life inside and outside sovereign states. There is a whole literature on humanitarian ethics that readily accepts (and forcefully advocates for) the continued division of the world according to what Michael Shapiro called "sovereignty's moral cartography."[10] The logic of sovereignty establishes a moral hierarchy that directs people to place their primary moral obligations with their fellow citizens and not with humanity at large. Robert Jackson summed up this view when he argued, "Humanitarian concerns and human rights still take a back seat to the rights and legitimate interests of sovereign states and—by extension—of the citizens of those states."[11] The acceptance of sovereignty as the ordering principle of global politics creates considerable difficulties when the ethical categories of state-centric moral philosophies are applied to the global stage that humanitarianism demands. The major concern here is that such applications tend to forget the conditions under which these moral philosophies owe their existence. In particular, they obscure the considerable violence that is expended to sustain and reproduce the sovereign political space that allows for the development and performance of ethical principles.

My aim in this chapter is to critically unpack the assumptions of sovereignty's moral imaginary. I do so by focusing on how humanitarianism has been constituted as an engaged—yet somehow neutral and impartial—ethical practice. Humanitarianism's core principles (humanity, impartiality, neutrality) are defined in a way that requires a strict line to be drawn between the ethical and the political. While there has been recognition in recent years that humanitarianism has been thoroughly politicized, my position is that humanitarianism has always been an inherently political concept. As such, it maintains an often hidden—yet increasingly all too apparent—relationship with coercion, violence, and the political. Far from being isolated and disconnected, these realms share a connected—indeed, immanent—relationship.

I begin with a critical assessment and unpacking of the concept of humanitarianism and emphasize its constitutive relationship with the "political." I go on to investigate some specific articulations of this relationship in order to highlight the violence that is the constitutive limit of these relations. A critical analysis of Mervyn Frost's writings highlights how the contemporary range of ethical possibilities is inextricably connected to ongoing violent performances that serve as an important condition of possibility for sovereign political spaces and identities. I also critically assess claims that humanitarianism is part of a movement to construct a world community based on the common identity of "humanity" and argue that the category of "humanity" (which provides the universal orientation of humanitarianism) must be situated in relation to the political discourses about state sovereignty. In doing so, I argue for the practices and strategies of humanitarianism to be understood in a biopolitical framework. I discuss the recent writings of Giorgio Agamben to demonstrate how the "bare life" that humanitarianism sets up as the recipient of its magnanimous assistance not only is thoroughly implicated in political relations but also serves as the condition of possibility for sovereign power to exist in the first place.

The Politics of Humanitarianism

Despite its popularity and widespread use, a great deal of confusion surrounds the nature and meaning of the term humanitarianism. While in its broadest sense, humanitarianism is "concerned with promoting human welfare," the term is prone to a more narrow usage to describe "emergency action, taken by recognized, independent organizations, in foreign parts, in the context of war."[12] Caught between these two axes of social transformation and emergency management, a number of commentators have pointed out the ambiguous character of the concept of humanitarianism. UNHCR staff have expressed their dissatisfaction with the confusion that results when the differences between humanitarian action, assistance, and protection are left unexplained. Similar complaints have been registered as to the unclear differences between humanitarian and human rights organizations.[13] Still others have argued that not enough thought goes into distinguishing humanitarian principles from the principles of humanitarian action.[14] The ambiguity of the concept is further evidenced by the slippery deployment of humanitarianism to justify a range of contradictory activities. For instance, international voluntary agencies providing emergency food and medical aid are designated as being humanitarian actors; yet, state military action—often of a most grizzly nature—also has been justified as being of a humanitarian character, as was seen in the 1999 NATO bombing of Kosovo and Serbia. Indeed, the sheer diversity of nouns attached to the adjective humanitarian—for example, humanitarian aid, assistance, and protection have been joined by humanitarian bombing, war, and deterrence—are such that the current list of so-called humanitarian actions cannot help but read like a catalog of contradictions.

To understand the role humanitarianism plays in world politics today requires some critical reflection on the concept as well as recognition of its historical emergence. After all, the notion that we have obligations to humanity is hardly a new one. Such moral impulses have motivated the activities of a wide range of religious, workers' and merchants' movements throughout history. In its modern guise, however, the ICRC has profoundly influenced the development of humanitarianism. The ICRC's pivotal role in putting humanitarian considerations onto the global agenda is evidenced by the widespread acceptance of the organization's definition of humanitarianism. The meaning of humanitarianism has seen its fair share of debate within the Red Cross movement, and the core principles of humanitarianism have been altered and modified several times over the course of the twentieth century. However, throughout all these debates three core principles—humanity, impartiality, neutrality—have stood constant as constituting the "essence" of humanitarianism since the first Geneva Convention of 1864. It is worth reflecting on these principles as the ICRC definition of humanitarianism has been accepted by a great number of global actors, including most international aid organizations as well as the UN system. Indeed, the United Nations interprets the humanitarian mandate of its various "nonpolitical" agencies in a way that draws obvious inspiration from the humanitarian principles of the ICRC. For example, in a General Assembly resolution from 1991, the UN body declared, "Humanitarian assistance must be provided in accordance with the principles of humanity, neutrality, and impartiality."[15]

Putting aside the concept of "humanity" for the moment, let us consider the principles of impartiality and neutrality. According to the ICRC, the principle of impartiality means that the Red Cross "makes no discrimination as to nationality, race, religious beliefs, class or political opinions. It endeavors to relieve the suffering of individuals, being guided solely by their needs, and to give priority to the most urgent cases of distress." The ICRC further defined the principle of neutrality as follows: "In order to continue to enjoy the confidence of all, the Red Cross may not take sides in hostilities or engage at any time in controversies of a political, racial, religious or ideological nature."[16] In each case, the principles gain their force from a prior distinction made between humanitarianism and politics. The ICRC, however, has from its outset been criticized for holding on to a conception of humanitarianism that cannot help but be implicated in a field of political relations. For example, the organization does not oppose war directly; it aims only to provide structure and order to combat so that human suffering can be minimized. The practice of providing impartial assistance to the wounded on the battlefield often has been criticized for sanctioning the very notion of combat and of merely "humanizing slaughter."[17]

How do the principles of neutrality and impartiality influence how international protection is provided to refugees? In the first place, these principles work to establish the refugee phenomenon as a nonpolitical occurrence. It is well known, for example, that the "humanitarian and social" disposition of the UNHCR (as stipulated in Article II of its founding Statute) is articulated only *after* the agency's work is defined as "nonpolitical." This distinction between humanitarianism and politics, however, predates the emergence of the UNHCR. To be sure, the history of the international organizations that were created to manage and control the refugee "problem" is one marked by a recurring tension between the "political" and the "humanitarian."[18] For example, each of the High Commissioners for Refugees during the interwar period sought to carefully draw a line between what they perceived as their humanitarian actions and any sort of activity or position that could be construed as "political." The first High Commissioner for Refugees, Fridtjof Nansen, exemplified this nonpolitical stance of early coordinated humanitarian actions on behalf of refugees in his letter to the Turkish government dated November 9, 1922: "I cannot in any way denounce the proceeding of the Turkish authorities, whatever my personal opinion may be. I am obliged to confine myself to appealing on strictly humanitarian grounds for assistance for the [Greek and Armenian] refugees."[19]

The capacity for humanitarian actors to maintain their neutrality and impartiality has been put to severe tests in the post–cold war era. Determining what impartiality and neutrality mean in "complex humanitarian emergencies" has come to dominate much of the discussion among academic policy makers and aid workers in the field. The tendency toward critical self-reflection on these concepts is not surprising given the waning optimism for effective and meaningful humanitarian action that is free from political forces or effects. The optimism for effective and meaningful humanitarian action that gripped the international NGO community at the beginning of the 1990s had largely dissipated after the humanitarian disasters of Somalia, Bosnia, and Rwanda as well as the increased use of humanitarian discourse by states as a cover for actions based more on national security interests than moral altruism. The malleable character of humanitarian discourse has prompted some defenders of humanitarianism to respond with attempts to fortify the concept against political incursions. Nicholas Leader, for example, has made the case for distinguishing "humanitarian principles" from "principles of humanitarian action." Whereas the former refers to a moral principle that tries to lessen the "destructive impact" of war (e.g., distinction between combatants and noncombatants), the latter refers to principles such as impartiality and neutrality that are intended to guide humanitarian actions (and separate them from political action). Leader complains that while humanitarian principles are well developed within international humanitarian law, the principles of humanitarian action suffer from a less than solid legal status. What is more, even when principles such as impartiality and neutrality are mentioned, they are usually not defined. As a result, the concepts possess a looseness, a fuzziness to them that Leader considers to be "problematic."[20]

For many defenders of humanitarianism, the concepts of impartiality and neutrality become truly problematic when they are subject to forces that result in their "politicization." To be sure, a common response to the sobering experiences of Somalia, Bosnia, Rwanda, Kosovo, Afghanistan, and elsewhere has been to lament the various ways in which humanitarian action has become implicated in political fields of action. There is an emerging and expanding literature that assesses how the politicization of humanitarianism (intended or unintended) is undermining the ability of humanitarian actors to maintain their neutrality and impartiality in conflict or crisis situations.[21] Adam Roberts, for example, has demonstrated how in the contexts of warring violence or political crisis the cherished principles of neutrality and impartiality often simply become a matter of perspective. Humanitarian organizations invariably have to cooperate to some degree with governments, yet their mere association with these authorities can damage the perception of neutrality. What is more, in cases where humanitarian emergencies occur within the context of a so-called policy vacuum (as, say, in the case of Bosnia) humanitarian aid workers are often left with no other choice but to fill this vacuum and become political actors and make their own policies in the field.[22]

The politicization of the neutrality and impartiality principles offers some important insights into the paradoxes and limits of contemporary humanitarian action. At the same time, however, the challenges facing humanitarian actors today is a much more complicated set of affairs than the politicization criticism allows. This is because the politicization criticism usually retains a commitment to the idea that a "pure" or "unspoiled" nonpolitical humanitarianism is somehow possible. This can be seen in the "Providence Principles" that Larry Minear and Thomas Weiss developed as part of the Humanitarianism and War project:

1. Relieving Life-Threatening Suffering
2. Proportionality of Need
3. Non-Partisanship
4. Independence
5. Accountability
6. Appropriateness
7. Contextualization
8. Subsidiary of Sovereignty[23]

Despite the solemn and highly paradoxical genuflection to sovereignty, humanitarian ethical action is presented here as a matter of applying an external set of normative principles to a volatile and complex political situation. According to this view, the main challenge facing humanitarian action today is to somehow preserve the integrity of basic humanitarian principles while recognizing the political context in which moral actions must take place. As Leader has put it, humanitarian actors need to figure out "how to sup with the Devil without getting eaten."[24] This perspective retains a commitment to a pure, nonpolitical conception of humanitarianism that has not been spoiled by a negative interaction with political forces. As well, not only is the distinction between the ethical and the political realms of human life reaffirmed but a normative framework is imposed so that the former realm is granted positive attributes and the latter is cast negatively as the domain of cynical, self-interested, "devilish" behavior. Humanitarian action and political action are cast as two distinct and separate modes of acting and being-in-the-world. From this perspective, it is the encroachment of politics into the ethical sphere that poses the greatest threat to humanitarian action. As we shall see next, it is by emphasizing global obligations to humanity that humanitarianism is salvaged from the effects of politicization. Humanity, however, is a concept that is immanent to, and not separate from, the sovereign political relation. As a result, the problem of humanitarianism's relationship to the political is not as easily deflected as some of its defenders might hope.

Humanity and the Logic of Sovereignty

One of the great hopes of humanitarianism has been its potential to challenge and transcend the sovereign codes that regulate patterns of inclusion and exclusion and relations between self and other. Refugees, in this view, are part of a wider community that is beyond the moral confines of state sovereignty. Sovereignty, after all, is based on the principle of exclusion; its power comes from its capacity to authoritatively distinguish friends from enemies, citizens from foreigners, insiders from outsiders. But whereas the principle of state sovereignty insists on the citizen as the authentic political subject, humanitarian principles attempt to transcend this particularism by positing a universal—that is, the whole of humanity—as an ordering principle. In a manner similar to the proponents of international human rights, cosmopolitan citizenship, global civil society, or various other promoters of a "post-Westphalian" or "postsovereign" world order, the goal of humanitarianism is to avoid the degree of violence associated with carving out the world's territories and moral sympathies along strict sovereign lines.

The willingness to think of humanitarianism in a way that will effect a "widening of the moral boundaries of political communities"[25] is certainly a laudable endeavor. However, the easy division between humanity on one hand and citizenship on the other is a bit misleading. What this opposition misses is how the logic of humanity is already accounted for by the logic of state sovereignty. Indeed, sovereignty, I want to suggest, provides the very conditions of possibility for what is commonly understood as human identity. Thus, the principle of humanity—which provides both the justification and orientation of humanitarian action—must be reconceived as an inherently political concept. Far from relating to one another as distinct and segmented logics, humanitarianism and politics share an immanent connection. What connects them is precisely that principle that informs and orders modern claims to political identity and community—that is, the principle of state sovereignty.

The moral conflict between civic and humanitarian virtues, between claims to citizenship and claims to humanity, is one that has puzzled social and political theorists for some time. Does one place an obligation toward humanity and strive for ethical universality, or does one privilege the duties we have toward fellow citizens in a political association and therefore settle for ethical particularity? The modern resolution to this dilemma, as Andrew Linklater has argued, was predicated on the early modern trade-off between "men" and "citizens."[26] The terms of this trade-off, classically represented in the work of Thomas Hobbes, stipulate that priority is given to the moral claims of citizenship in the particular political association of the state. Hobbes resolved the conflict between the universal and the particular by positing a theory of state sovereignty that allows for one international system with many particular states. Walker explains the logic of this citizen–human resolution:

> As a response to questions about whether "we" are citizens, humans, or somehow both, the principle of state sovereignty affirms that we have our primary and often overriding political identity as participants in a particular community, but asserts that we retain a connection with "humanity" through our participation in a broader global—international—system. As citizens, we may aspire to universal values, but only on the tacit assumption that the world "out there," that supposedly global or states system, is in fact a world of particular states—of dangers, or of other communities, each aspiring to some notion of goodness, truth, and beauty.[27]

Emphasizing the obligations we have to humans as primary—as humanitarianism claims to do—has the potential of provoking a whole-scale reconceptualization of what it means to be an ethical and political subject or community. Linklater, for example, has contributed to this project by constructing a countersovereign discourse to affirm a universal vision of rights and duties based on the figure of the human. For Linklater, the structural inequities that are reproduced because of sovereignty's hold on the moral imagination makes it urgent that we rethink where we choose to direct our ethical energy and political loyalty. Shall we continue to subscribe to identities and moral obligations of statism? Or will we be seduced by the so-called primordial call of the substate affiliations of tribes, clans, and other ethnic groupings? Linklater rejects both of these options and instead has called for a "transformation" of our political categories to realize a truly universal ethical and political community.[28]

The choice between citizenship and humanity is not a simple or straightforward one. It is not simply a matter of contrasting a statist power politics with a more rational, cooperative, and global humanitarian civil society. In his many writings, Rob Walker has been critical of presenting the issue here as one of a dualistic choice of humanity or citizen, the universal or the particular, the one or the many. He argues that this apparent choice between citizenship, on one hand, and humanity, on the other, is a false one in that they are the effect of a prior resolution made by state sovereignty.

> Sovereignty and subjectivity express the possibility of resolving the relationship between universality and diversity in a particular place. They do so ... by resolving all relations of unity and diversity, space and time, and self and other in a space/body that is in principle capable of attaining universality in its particularity while taking its proper place as one particular space/body among other particular space/bodies.[29]

"In this way," Walker continues, "state sovereignty and subjectivity express a series of relationships."[30] The limit of Linklater's analysis is that he does not appreciate enough the relational character of claims to universality and diversity. What is involved here is not a simple matter of choosing or emphasizing one logic over the other but an appreciation about how claims to humanity are always already implicated in the logic that informs our categories of where or what the political can be. Consequently, there is always the danger of universal impulses like the humanitarian one expressing their worldliness within the very terms and categories set up by the theory of state sovereignty.

A humanitarian ethics that forgets the constitutive spatial and identational practices that serves as its condition of possibility can risk reproducing violent political relations that it claims to be resisting, not perpetuating. The dangers involved with this peculiar form of amnesia can be clearly demonstrated by a critical reading of Mervyn Frost's Ethics in *International Relations: A Constitutive Theory.* Frost's book is in part a reaction to the emergence of a global (if unevenly distributed) humanitarian and human rights culture. He considers his project as one of developing an ethical theory that can resolve the relationship between the universal and the particular. In doing so, he seeks to provide a moral justification for both the international system of sovereign states as well as provide recognition of fundamental human rights. This would allow him to solve some "pressing normative issues" that are without clear precedent or without an established set of rules to structure one's ethical response. Included among his "hard cases" is the politics of global refugee flows. On this issue, Frost asks,

> How should refugees from one state be treated by other states? Who is responsible for them? Should they be allowed to choose a

new home state or are they obligated eventually to return to their state of origin?[31]

Frost proceeds by identifying two norms that are essential to his ethical theory: the preservation of the states system and the principle of state sovereignty. Frost's understanding of global ethics is thus unabashedly state-centric: all normative concerns in international relations are predicated on what is good for states. This is an important point, and it is worth critically analyzing for how it eventually points to the violent relationships that underpin ethical relations that assume a world where political sovereignty reigns.

Frost considers the existing justifications for the state system—order-based theories, utilitarian theories, and rights-based theories—to be insufficient to the task of reconciling norms that are centered on the preservation of state sovereignty with norms seeking to preserve the rights of autonomous individuals.[32] He attempts to bridge these two ethical concerns with a "constitutive theory of individuality" that draws heavily on arguments from Hegel's *Philosophy of Right*.[33] However, while Frost goes into some detail to demonstrate that individuals simultaneously constitute themselves as moral and ethical subjects by virtue of their participation in institutions such as the family, civil society, and the state, he stops short of describing the violent performances Hegel considered integral to the constitution of ethical subjects. Here, Frost's reading of Hegel is consistent with most political theorists in that he emphasizes those constitutive practices that are internal to the state.[34] What is missing, however—and this is curious for a theorist of *international* ethics—is recognition of the significance Hegel placed on those constitutive practices that are external to the state. In particular, Frost's analysis excludes from consideration the important role *war* plays in Hegel's theory of actualizing ethical life for both the individual and the state. This omission is significant for it effaces an important process by which the coherence and unity of the state is created and sustained. Moreover, since Hegel believed that such coherence is achieved through the dynamics of negation, warring violence can be understood as one of the ultimate acts of negation—that is, the violent effacement of an Other's subjectivity to bolster and maintain the identity of the Self.[35]

For Hegel, war is an important, even "necessary"[36] practice in the quest to actualize the ethical community of the state. Hegel criticized the Kantian notion of "perpetual peace" on the basis that individuals in a peaceful civil society tend to assume that this form of human association is the final and most desirable form of political community. Civil society, however, is only one "moment" (albeit an important and necessary moment) in the development of social relations. A condition of civil peace, in Hegel's estimation, leads people to become entirely individualistic; that is to say, they tend to understand political community and social organization only as a means of maximizing their own private ends. Consequently, the centrifugal forces of civil society are always at risk of going too far, of exceeding the state's capacity to contain individualistic interests and desires within an organic whole. For Hegel, civic life threatens the ethical unity of the state; individuals in civil society thus need to be shaken out of their complacency and compelled to recognize that political community involves much more than just their own narrowly defined interests.[37] Hegel considered war a positive means by which the divergent and particular interests of civil society can be made to coalesce into a unified whole. In a state of war, individuals cease to consider only themselves and instead become aware of their membership in the larger community of the state.[38] Consequently, for Hegel, war should be seen not as a negative or contingent feature of the modern state but rather as an important and positive means by which the competing forces of civil society can be contained and thus reestablish the ethical unity of the state.

Theories of international ethics, including those of a humanitarian disposition, that assume the logic of sovereignty need to be more self-reflective of the violent performances that come along with this political relation. Frost's attempt to sidestep such a criticism by claiming that his is a "secular interpretation" of Hegel that "does not require us that we understand or accept Hegel's metaphysical system" comes across as rather unconvincing.[39] There is much more at issue here than whether one accepts or rejects Hegelian metaphysics. What is at stake is as much political as it is metaphysical. For instance, even if Frost can wriggle out of the particularities of Hegel's conception of the state, the relationship between the state and violence is not so easily sidestepped, as numerous studies of the bloody practices of state-building attest.[40] In the end, the issue comes down to being self-reflective about the violent underpinnings that serve as the silent assumption of sovereign political communities. Indeed, what is most illuminating about Hegel's writings on the relationship between ethics, war, and the state is his willingness to recognize and confront the violent practices that help constitute the space within which the performance of ethical relations is possible. A humanitarianism that declares itself as "impartial and neutral" without first considering its condition of possibility is bound to create confusion, engender contradictions, and work to recast violent relations in unexpected contexts.

Humanitarianism and the Politicization of Life

The moral geography that governs representations of refugees stands in contrast to the one that governs the citizen. According to the prevailing representations, citizens belong to a secure political community of conationals, whereas refugees have been forcibly displaced into the elusive moral community of humanity. To be sure, most discussions about the subjectivity of refugees commonly associate this identity with that of humanity. For example, international NGOs providing relief and assistance to refugees do so as a result of a humanitarian impulse or from a concern about human rights. Concerns over the human security of refugees and other forcibly displaced people have led to global conversations about the justification for military intervention into failed states. The refugee has even been included in discussions about cosmopolitan political projects, with Pierre Hassner arguing that by virtue of their membership in the family of humanity, refugees should qualify as "a special case for cosmopolitan citizenship."[41]

When humanitarian justifications for international action are invoked, what motivates this sentiment is ultimately a belief in the sacredness of life, of human life. This principle is important for justifying the allegedly nonpolitical character of humanitarian actions: political, economic, and other self-interested motivations are not primarily at issue here. Rather, there is only a concern with helping people, securing them a chance to live, to survive, to escape—whatever it takes to protect their human existence. Life is sacred, and so we should resist the artifice of political boundaries to help those caught in emergency situations that threaten their dignity as human beings. The moral appeal of humanity thus gains its force from the universal character of a shared "human existence." Consequently, to consider the phenomenon of the refugee is to consider an inescapable question: What is the politics of being human?

As we saw earlier, the human is by no means an innocent, neutral, or impartial category. Humanity, as Thomas Keenan argues, implies all sorts of borders: "it is riddled with differences, internal and external, and the simple proclamation of a new borderless condition, in the name of humanity, hides more than it reveals."[42] Hannah Arendt has perhaps most famously described the deep dilemmas facing refugees in their struggles with being recognized as human. In her essay "The Decline of the Nation-State and the End of the Rights of Man"—aptly titled for how it holds the political community and human rights in a symbiotic relationship—she revealed that

> the conception of human rights, based upon the assumed existence of a human being as such, broke down at the very moment when those who professed to believe in it were for the first time confronted with people who had indeed lost all other qualities and specific relationships—except that they were still human. The world found nothing sacred in the abstract nakedness of being human.[43]

Arendt gave a clear articulation of the paradox of modern claims to human rights: to possess rights one has is to be other than human; one has to become the human's other; one has to become a citizen.[44] The question of what is the politics of being human cannot, therefore, be resolved within an allegedly neutral space of humanitarianism. Rather, the issue must be addressed on the terrain of the political. This is because what is ultimately at stake with being human is who can be considered a political subject in the first place.

In his *Politics,* Aristotle famously pronounced "man" to be a political animal. For Aristotle, human life is uniquely qualified to be a political form-of-life. More accurately, it was the human lives of free adult Athenian men that Aristotle considered fit for this kind of existence. This qualification is significant not only for how it reveals Aristotle's sexism and classism but also for how it demonstrates the divided character of human life. Agamben describes this division as a difference between qualified and unqualified life:

> The ancient Greeks did not have only one term to express what we mean by the word life. They used two semantically and morpho-logically distinct terms: *zoé*, which expressed the simple fact of living common to all living beings (animals, humans, or gods), and *bios*, which signified the form or manner of living peculiar to a single individual or group.[45]

Aristotle, therefore, declared that "man" is an animal (*zoé*), but one that is distinguished by "his" capacity for political existence (*bios*). The key indicator of this qualified form-of-life is the unique human capacity for speech (*logos*), which can be distinguished from the mere possession of a voice (*phônê*). All animals possess the latter as the means through which they indicate feelings of pleasure or pain. For Aristotle, humans (again, only some humans) are distinguished by their ability to express what is useful and harmful, just and unjust, good and evil, and so on. Whereas animals cry out their pleasures and pains, humans can discursively articulate grievances, making them uniquely qualified for a political existence. According to dominant accounts in the received traditions of political theory, this politically qualified life finds its peculiar existence within the state (*polis*) and expresses its identity in the figure of the citizen.

The equivalence made here between speaking beings, human beings, and political beings has always been problematic in that its logic is easily manipulated to exclude entire categories of people—for example, women, children, workers, non-Europeans, and so on—into a marginalized non-political life. Jacques Rancière explains, "If there is someone you do not wish to recognize as a political being, you begin by not seeing them as the bearers of politicalness, by not understanding what they say, by not hearing that it is an utterance coming out of their mouths."[46] For the ancient Greeks, the unqualified form-of-life—the "bare" or "naked" life of nonpolitical humans—was excluded from the public realm through its inclusion in the domestic sphere. Feminist theorists have aptly demonstrated how the creation of the "domestic" sphere has been a historically powerful strategy for effacing political subjectivity, serving as the "home" of the citizen's others (women and children, workers and slaves). Rancière argues that because this space is kept separate from the audible and visible public sphere, "only groans or cries expressing suffering, hunger, or anger could emerge, but not actual speeches demonstrating a shared aisthesis."[47]

The analytical frameworks that are commonly employed to make sense of the refugee movements work to reinforce the speechlessness of the refugee's form-of-life. Here, so-called objective factors such as war and civil conflict, the degree to which a society is democratic, the "push–pull" of the global economy, and demographic inequities are usually considered to be the most important factors in understanding the dynamics of forced migration. When human movements and migrations are understood as largely structural processes, the voices of individuals and collective groups often get marginalized and ignored. In the case of refugees—that is, those individuals whose global movements can be explained by their "well-founded fear of persecution"—it is invariably an agent of a sovereign state, and not the asylum seeker, who gets to determine whether the refugee's fear of persecution is "well-founded." An other holds the capacity to reason, the human's Other: the citizen. All the refugee is left with is an agency effacing fear.[48]

The close connections between human life and political life constitute a very complex problem for humanitarianism. These connections cut to the core of sovereign conceptions of the political. Foucault argued that in the modern era, the relationship between life and power claims a prominent role in questions about the political. The capacity to manage, manipulate, and control living matter is a defining feature of modern forms of political power. The conjunction of life and power under the term "biopower" serves to highlight those forces that "brought life and its mechanisms into the realm of explicit calculations and made knowledge-power an agent of transformation of human life."[49] Biopower, therefore, refers to those "numerous and diverse techniques for achieving the subjugation of bodies and the control of populations."[50] Agamben applies the concept of biopower to demonstrate how refugees are caught up in the "mechanisms and calculations" of sovereign power. He departs from Foucault by suggesting that the inclusion of human life within the political realm is not exclusively a modern phenomenon but one that can be traced back to the Ancient Greek distinction between different forms-of-life. Aristotle declared that "man" was an animal (*zoé*) but one distinguished by his capacity for political existence (*bios*). Those who are not capable of living the politically qualified form-of-life as citizens are represented in terms of a "bare" or "naked" form of unqualified existence. A politically qualified life, moreover, was to find its peculiar existence within the state (*polis*); an unqualified bare life was, by contrast, excluded from this realm and instead confined to the domestic sphere (*oikos*).[51] This classical distinction, however, became superseded in the modern era once bare human life was made immanent to the ontogenetic practices of constituting the sovereign subjects and spaces of modern conceptions of the political. Agamben therefore extends Foucault's original thesis—that biopolitics involves the administration of life—to consider how bare life coincides with the political. As Agamben states, "The entry of *zoé* into the sphere of the polis—the politicisation of bare life as such—constitutes the decisive event in modernity and signals a radical transformation of the political-philosophical categories of classical thought."[52]

Agamben's approach to biopolitics has important implications for contemporary forms of humanitarianism. The common belief that humanitarian action is motivated by a desire to protect humanity and provide relief to life-threatening suffering takes on new—political—meaning in this context. What is noteworthy about Agamben's analysis is that he situates the whole question of human life in relation to—indeed, as part of the process of—constituting the sovereign spaces and identities of politics. The normative distinction between "human life" and "political life" is thus a misplaced one in that they are both conceived on a mutual and immanent plane of coexistence. Agamben is not so much concerned about what sovereignty is (a question of Being) as figuring out how sovereign power operates—how it works (a question of becoming). To make sense of this, he draws on Schmitt's idea that the structure of sovereignty is based on the notion of the exception.[53] Sovereign power, according to this view, derives its force from its capacity to suspend normal rules and laws; for example, by decreeing a state of emergency. The legalities behind suspending the system of law are accomplished from a position outside the law. As Michael Shapiro notes, "The law is effectively outside itself inasmuch as sovereignty, as the power to make exceptions, operates outside the law in the process of suspending it."[54] The paradox of sovereignty is that it is at the same time inside and outside the juridical order.

How does human life—and, in particular, the human subject of the refugee—figure into these sovereign performances? How does the "bare life" of (some) human beings become "included in the mechanisms and calculations of State power"?[55] For Agamben, bare life holds a special relationship to the sovereign capacity to decide on the exception, as it enters the sphere of the political through what he calls an "inclusive exclusion." Bare life, in other words, is included in the political sphere by virtue of its exclusion. Agamben argues that the problematic of sovereign power and its relationship to bare life finds its expression in the figure of *homo sacer.* An obscure category of ancient Roman law, the *homo sacer,* Agamben explains, was a form of bare life that suffered from a paradoxical condition of being included in the law by virtue of its exclusion. The terms of this "inclusive exclusion" are hardly favorable for the degraded bodies condemned to this identity. The *homo sacer* could be killed but not sacrificed; their life was considered sacred, yet they could be killed without the criminal act of homicide having been committed. The individual conferred an identity of *homo sacer* is, therefore, subjected to a double exclusion: he or she is outside both human law (he or she can be killed without any crime being committed) and divine law (his or her life is unworthy of sacrifice). Agamben is quick to point out, however, that this tag team of exclusion is also simultaneously a double inclusion. At the same time that *homo sacer* is excluded he or she is also included. The condition of a *homo sacer* is one of an individual whose "entire existence [has been] reduced to a bare life stripped of every right by virtue of the fact that anyone can kill him without committing homicide; he can save himself only in perpetual flight or a foreign land. And yet he is in a continuous relationship with the power that banished him precisely [because] he is at every instant exposed to an unconditioned threat of death."[56]

The challenges facing humanitarianism today are not dissimilar to Agamben's project—that is, they both seek to unravel the relationship between politics and the bare life of the human that is considered to be sacred. His thesis is that the paradoxical figure of *homo sacer*—the life that is sacred, yet can be killed—in fact structures and orders the logic of sovereignty. It is precisely a human being's life—and not some social contract or an individual's free will—that functions as the foundation for the state's legitimacy and sovereign power. "From the point of view of sovereignty," Agamben argues, "only bare life is authentically political" as it is "the always present and always operative presupposition of sovereignty."[57] Humanity— far from being a neutral concept—is seen to be inextricably and inescapably connected to our modern understanding of the location and character of the political.

From this perspective, the principal reason refugees constitute a "problem" or "emergency" to the international system of states lies in "the very ambiguity of the fundamental notions regulating the inscription of ... life ... in the juridical order of the Nation-State."[58] "Humanity" is already present within the concept of citizenship; it appears as the "hidden difference" between birth and nation, bare human life and the political. Agamben's point is that refugees make what is hidden (i.e., bare life) come to light, thus "unhinging" the state–nation–territory trinity that conventional theories of the state take for granted. Refugees pose a challenge to sovereign power precisely because "by breaking the continuity between man and citizen, nativity and nationality, they put the originary fiction of modern sovereignty in crisis."[59] As the modern political imagination remains fixated on the citizen as the authentic political identity and ethical subject, it is not surprising that refugees (as the absence of that identity and subjectivity) are stripped of all political agency and deemed temporary, "emergency" situations.

In this way, a humanitarianism that insists that it be separated from politics, but that nonetheless focuses on the sacred or bare human life of individuals to justify itself, can have the effect of working in perfect symmetry with sovereign state power. This is because sovereignty, based on the relation of the exception, is a violent relation in the sense that it is a practice that works to keep things apart, create boundaries, and maintain separateness. And because the concept of "humanity as bare human life" relies on the sovereign exception for its condition of possibility, then we must look at humanitarianism not as a neutral, impartial, and nonpolitical concept but as one that is implicated in a fundamentally political—and, when pushed to the limit—violent relationship.

Conclusion

To consider questions of ethics and morality when determining what to do about the pressing and harrowing complex emergencies that distinguish the post–cold war era is certainly a move in the right direction. However, humanitarian action must also reflect on the conditions and circumstances that allow its cherished principles to have rhetorical force. My goal in this chapter has been to provide a critical reflection on these conditions and circumstances. The concept of "humanitarian violence" highlights the intimate, interconnected, and immanent character of the relationship between coercion and altruism, violence and morality, the political and the ethical. The view advanced here is that a humanitarianism that assumes itself to possess an autonomous existence, separated from the vicissitudes of political life, is—and always has been—an impossibility. Instead, humanitarianism is an inherently political concept, and one that is always already implicated in a relation of violence. This relationship is rarely considered because humanitarians are resistant to a critical reflection on their statist conditions of possibility. Indeed, the idea that humanitarianism's current popularity is leading the way to some form of global civil society, or a universal world polity based on an expanded dialogic community, tends to underestimate the way that the theory of state sovereignty produces this option in the first place. The question is not "Should I be universal or particular in my ethical obligations and political commitments?" but rather "What relation of universality and particularity allows me to express my humanitarian vision?" This latter version is helpful, I think, because it more accurately points out both the possibilities and the constraints of current global ethical practice. In the case of refugee flows, for example, it is a perspective that allows one to appreciate how the prevailing humanitarian "solutions" to the refugee's plight focus on returning to refugees statist identities so as to restore the conditions under which they may once again enjoy a properly "human" life as citizens. Humanitarian organizations face a grave danger of maintaining "a secret solidarity with the very powers they ought to fight."[60] As Jenny Edkins argued, "The relationship between humanitarianism and either violent militarism or politics is not an oxymoron. Humanitarianism is essential to both: it is deeply implicated in the production of a sovereign power that claims monopoly of the legitimate use of force."[61]

3

Fearful Subjects: Reason and Fear in the UN Refugee Definition

Fear is the direct perception of the contemporary condition of possibility of being-human.

—Brian Massumi

Introduction: The UNHCR at 50

The international human rights and humanitarian communities celebrated a number of significant anniversaries in the years immediately leading up to the new millennium. The fiftieth anniversary of the Universal Declaration of Human Rights was celebrated in 1998. The following year marked one hundred years of the Law of The Hague as well as the fiftieth anniversary of the Geneva Conventions. In the year 2000, it was the United Nations High Commissioner for Refugees' (UNHCR) turn, and the fiftieth anniversary festivities of this organization arrived with a great deal of fanfare. The agency established a handsomely endowed organization, the UNHCR-50 Foundation, to organize and promote anniversary celebrations around the world. The Foundation's public relations campaign has been truly global in its scope. The Foundation distributed eleven print advertisements and a sixty-second television spot to magazines, newspapers, and television stations around the world. Calendars, posters, board games, commemorative stamps all were commissioned, printed, and distributed with the aim of raising public awareness of refugee issues and the continued relevance of the UNHCR in managing the refugee problem today. Similarly, the UNHCR-50

43

Foundation played a pivotal role in establishing the first World Refugee Day on June 20, 2001. Finally, international conferences and special issues of academic journals were sponsored and funded by the Foundation, as were theatre productions, film and music festivals, and sporting events in places as diverse as Ecuador, England, and Ethiopia.

The public relations campaign aside, the fiftieth anniversary of the UNHCR also sparked off a great deal of reflection and debate on the accomplishments and shortcomings of the UN agency. How well has the agency served the cause of protecting refugees? Is the mandate of the UNHCR still relevant given the increasingly complex and controversial character of global refugee flows? Does the 1951 Convention Relating to the Status of Refugees and its 1967 Protocol continue to serve as the most appropriate definitions for refugees?[1] The agency has responded to these questions by taking a proactive stance: the UNHCR entered the new millennium by launching an ambitious two-year program of "Global Consultations," the purpose of which was to solicit ideas on how to revitalize and improve the international refugee protection regime.[2] The UNHCR's position within this debate followed a twofold strategy: (1) a demonstrated openness to new ideas, and (2) a firm commitment to existing frameworks and instruments. On one hand, the agency recognized the great challenges it faces in the increasingly complex world of contemporary political and humanitarian emergencies. Then UN High Commissioner for Refugees Ruud Lubbers readily conceded that the dynamics of contemporary population flows involve an "entanglement of migration and asylum" that create huge challenges to the "social stability, security, and the environment" of many countries.[3] Similarly, the globalization of migration, the emergence of vast populations of internally displaced people, and the problem of responding to violence both within and around refugee camps, among many more issues, have made UNHCR officials very open to novel and innovative approaches to providing humanitarian assistance and protection to refugees.

At the same time, however, the UNHCR is steadfast in its commitment to the principles set out in the 1951 Convention. Whatever shifts in refugee management that must be taken to respond to the changing conditions of forced migration, the UNHCR argues that these efforts must work within the paradigm established by the 1951 Convention. The High Commissioner was adamant on this point in his statements to a February 2001 meeting of European Union ministers:

> The Global Consultations—first and foremost—will promote the full and effective implementation of the Refugee Convention. The Convention has proven its resilience by providing protection from persecution and violence to millions of refugees over five decades. It is the hub upon which the international protection regime turns, and we would tamper with it at our peril.[4]

For the High Commissioner, protecting refugees who have fled their countries of origin is the "core concern" of his agency.[5] Indeed, the great advantage of the Convention and its Protocol, the High Commissioner argued, is its capacity to provide a clear framework for determining who qualifies as an "authentic" refugee.

> The Convention and its Protocol give coherence to the protection system because they are clear on basic principles, focused on rights and grounded in universal values. These instruments allow us to start from a basic consensus regarding the most fundamental issues. Who is a refugee? Who does not deserve protection? And when—exceptionally—do a state's security or public order interests overcome the fundamental obligation not to return a refugee to danger.[6]

The High Commissioner's position seems to have been taken seriously. Many of the 141 states party to the 1951 Convention or its 1967 Protocol, or both, took the occasion of the UNHCR's anniversary to reaffirm their commitment to these instruments for dealing with the phenomenon of forced migration today. For example, the May 2000 Inter-Parliamentary Union meeting in Amman saw 648 parliamentarians from 124 states reassert their commitment to upholding the principles of the Convention. Similar affirmations of support came from the October 1999 European Union leaders meeting in Tampere, Finland, as well as from the 56 members of EXCOM.[7]

The significance of the 1951 Convention definition of the refugee lies in its powerful influence in setting the standards for determining who qualifies as a refugee and, thus, for the protection that comes with legal refugee status. However, as previous chapters have indicated, being an authentic refugee involves much more than securing the appropriate legal status. It also involves an expectation of displaying the appropriate qualities associated with "refugeeness" (e.g., speechlessness, placelessness, invisibility, victim status). The Convention defines a refugee as someone who flees across an international border because of a "well-founded fear of being persecuted" for his or her political, social, or religious beliefs and activities. In this chapter, I argue that the Convention definition effectively splits the refugee in two: the human capacity to reason ("well-founded") is held in tension with the emotion ("fear") that motivates an individual's flight. This split in the refugee's subjectivity is representative of the paradox of humanity we saw in the previous chapter. Whereas the concept of "humanity" is often considered to embody universal qualities, it nonetheless operates as a restrictive category. Paradoxically, this exclusivity emerges when the Convention attempts to assert a universality to the refugee condition on the basis of the human emotion of fear. But human beings who are defined by their fear are often simultaneously subjected to social practices that also define them as social outcasts, lacking full reasoning capacity, and incapable of presenting an autonomous, self-governing form of personal subjectivity.[8] As Kay Anderson explains,

> Human beings "in the raw"—supposedly motivated in their conduct by naked impulse rather than rational deliberation—have included those variously savage peoples, the mentally disordered, some women, and the so-called dangerous classes who in different ways have been deemed either beyond, or potentially improved by, the cultivation of self-government.[9]

In this chapter, I argue that the fearful human assumed by the Convention definition is not a universal category but an exclusive category that can be employed to exclude, to produce difference, and to reinforce social and political hierarchies. In fact, when read in relation to the project of constituting sovereign power, fear is something much more than a mere subjective experience. Fear is instead a crucial part of the process by which modern political subjectivities are formed. It is, as Brian Massumi suggests, "part of what constitutes the collective ground of possible experience."[10]

Mick Dillion argues that refugee identity is best understood as a "figure of the 'inter'—or the in-betweenness—of the human way of being, as a figure of the 'inter' of international relations and as a figure of the political abjection that is integral to the political subjectification of political modernity."[11] Refugees occupy this ambiguous "inter" zone whereby they are paradoxically included within the realm of humanity by virtue of their exclusion from it. Despite conceptual and institutional frameworks that define refugees as a social and humanitarian (and decidedly nonpolitical) problem, the constitution of a fearful refugee identity is crucial to the process of creating and stabilizing sovereign political identities and spaces. I advance this argument in this chapter by examining how fear came to constitute the core of the 1951 UN Convention Relating to the Status of Refugees. Next, I introduce and assess the concept of fear for its place in modern theories of the political. This section focuses on a reading of the role fear plays in Thomas Hobbes's *Leviathan*. In particular, I read the temporal and spatial orientations of fear in relation to Hobbes's project of establishing an ontology of sovereignty to act as the precondition of modern politics.[12] The fearful subject is placed both outside and prior to the political and subjected to all forms of "Othering" strategies. In the following section I explore the consequences of these strategies in relation to the Refugee Convention. An examination of a UNHCR handbook that explains how the refugee's fear should be assessed demonstrates how this determination works within the ontology of sovereignty and reproduces sovereign identities and spaces as the only authentic expression of the political. Finally, I conclude this chapter by considering some of the countervailing efforts by refugees to politically question their fearful subjectivities. I assess the cultural practices of refugees and refugee communities and, in particular, refugee poetry for how they contribute to current reassessments of refugeeness at the beginning of the twenty-first century.

Reason, Fear, and the UN Refugee Convention

According to the UN Refugee Convention, a refugee is someone whose well-founded fear of being persecuted has caused him or her to take flight from his or her country of origin and seek asylum abroad. In international law, Article 1 A(2) of the 1951 United Nations Convention Relating to the Status of Refugees establishes a "refugee" as a person who,

> owing to a well-founded fear of being persecuted for reasons of race, religion, nationality, membership of a particular social group or political opinion, is outside the country of his nationality and is unable or, owing to such fear, is unwilling to avail himself of the protection of that country; or who, not having a nationality but being outside the country of his former habitual residence as a result of such events, is unable or, owing to such fear, is unwilling to return to it.[13]

A well-founded fear of being persecuted. The interrelationships of these terms constitute a very complicated politics. The first thing to note about this definition is how it established the ability to reason ("well-founded") and the experience emotion ("fear") as the basis for the definition of the refugee. The relationship between these two elements is key to understanding how the refugee does and does not figure into sovereign accounts of the political. The Convention definition establishes the expectation that to be a refugee and to possess a fearful subjectivity are one and the same thing. This alleged symmetry, we shall see, has enormous implications for refugees, especially in terms of how they are or are not recognized as active, visible, and vocal subjects.

While the various implications of this argument are worked out in future sections, in this part of the chapter I explain why the reason–fear nexus within the UN refugee definition must be taken as the subject of serious political analysis. Such a justification is necessary because in the vast majority of studies on the UN refugee definition (both conventional and critical), it is the term "persecution" that has attracted the greatest degree of attention. For the purposes of determining refugee status, persecution is usually understood as "a deliberate act of the government against individuals."[14] However, exactly what qualifies as persecution is a hotly contested topic among policy makers, refugee scholars, refugee advocates, and, of course, refugee claimants. While the UN Convention claims to be based on grand universal principles, its criteria for persecution have been widely criticized for its limitations and parochialisms.

The Convention definition lists "reasons of race, religion, nationality, membership of a particular social group or political opinion" as acceptable criteria for the existence of persecution. It also insists that the refugee claimant be outside his or her country of origin and that he or she no longer trust or expect protection from this state. These criteria have been subjected to a number of critiques, as they a priori exclude "victims of general insecurity and oppression or systemic economic deprivation, and people who have not crossed national frontiers to seek refuge."[15] However, some of the most incisive and trenchant criticisms of the Convention definition's criteria for persecution have come from feminist refugee scholars, activists, and claimants. Their criticisms have focused on the gendered implications of international refugee law. This system of law is identified as being rooted in the liberal political tradition of rights-based individualism and so reproduces core liberal distinctions, such as the public–private divide.[16] Jacqueline Bhabha argues that the Convention's preoccupation with persecution occurring within the typically male-dominated "public" sphere has the effect of de-emphasizing the significance, and even disregarding the legitimacy, of persecution arising from activities that are classified as "private." Bhabha explains,

> Refugee law has evolved through an examination of male asylum applicants and their activities: men have been considered the agents of political action and therefore the legitimate beneficiaries of protection for resulting persecution. The fears of female relatives of activists have been considered "personal" rather than "political," thereby excluding them from protection as refugees.[17]

Because it is usually women who are fleeing oppressive "private" activities (e.g., restrictions on sexual conduct, personal relationships, dress codes, etc.), the liberal values inherent within the Convention definition of the refugee contribute to a gender-blindness that has created serious obstacles and difficulties for female asylum applicants.[18]

This focus on the way in which the UN refugee definition structures and limits what qualifies as persecution is obviously an important and pressing political issue. The argument presented in this chapter is in no way meant to sideline these concerns. However, the point that I argue is that the interacting dynamic of reason also works to structure what qualifies as persecution and, by extension, what constitutes refugeeness. Moreover, the reason–fear element of the UN refugee definition has its own history and was not included by accident. Let us now look at how this twin dynamic was included within this definition.

The UN Convention definition of the refugee represents a significant break from earlier attempts to classify refugees. Previously, during the interwar period, refugees were defined primarily in accordance to their nationality or country of origin (be it Russian, Armenian, German, etc.). In addition to being outside their country of origin, people were recognized as refugees because of their prior membership in groups of persons who had been denied formal *de jure* protection from their country of origin. This is evident in the very names of the international organizations created to deal with interwar refugee movements. For example, in 1933 the League of Nations created the Office of the High Commissioner for Refugees from Germany. Throughout the interwar period, therefore, the criteria for being considered a refugee followed a strict state-centric logic, one that consistently asserted the importance of possessing certain ethnic or territorial origins on behalf of claimants.

The 1951 Convention, by contrast, is much more general in scope, defining the refugee in a manner keeping with the ethos of the Western liberal universalism of the immediate postwar era. The refugee was defined no longer by the country from which he or she fled but as a human being with certain inalienable rights. "Humanity" is the organizing principle here, not the nationality or citizenship status of the refugee applicant. In the words of the Universal Declaration of Human Rights (1948), the role of the international community was now to recognize and promote "the inherent dignity" and "the equal and inalienable rights of all members of the human family."[19] Included among these universal rights is the "right to seek and enjoy in other countries asylum from persecution."[20] In terms of international refugee law, the way in which refugees were included within "the human family" was to promote a common emotion (fear) as constituting an essential feature of modern-day refugeeness.

The idea that fear should lie at the core of refugeeness was first articulated in the Constitution of the International Refugee Organization (IRO). The IRO was a temporary and ad hoc agency created to manage massive refugee flows. Its mandate was to administer the millions of refugees moving through Europe in the immediate postwar context. The agency defined a refugee as any person who gave "valid reasons" for not returning to their home state, including "persecution, or fear, based on reasonable grounds of persecution."[21] This definition is important because it served as the immediate terms of reference to the members of the UN's Ad Hoc Committee on Refugees and Stateless Persons. Indeed, each of the three initial draft definitions submitted to the committee by the American, French, and British delegations, respectively, invoked "fear" as the central motivating element to being a refugee.[22]

What, then, is the effect of prioritizing the experience of fear in the UN refugee definition? As we saw earlier with respect to Salgado's humanitarian photography, the tropes of fear and hope play a powerful role in distinguishing refugees from other classifications of migrants and, thus, in establishing their authenticity (or lack thereof). It has already been noted that the refugee subjectivity promoted in the Convention is nothing less than a classic example of Western liberal individualism. Here, it is important to note that the text of the Convention was drafted in the early years of the cold war, when East–West ideological tensions were running high. Western states were eager to bring attention to the massive population movements in Central and Eastern Europe in an effort to stigmatize both the Soviet Union and its communist ideology. During the debates that took place during the drafting of the Refugee Convention, the UN delegates of Western states consistently advocated for a refugee definition that would prioritize international protection efforts for people whose flight could be construed as being motivated by pro-Western values. The result of this debate, of course, is a Convention that promotes respect for liberal civil and political rights and makes no mention at all of socioeconomic rights. Instead, the classic liberal separation of the "political" from the "economic" is invoked, whereby people displaced by market forces are excluded from qualifying for refugee status.

According to this view, the term "economic refugee" is a misnomer, a category error, because the liberal worldview considers market activity to be natural and nonpolitical. From this perspective, the only noun that the adjective economic can legitimately qualify is migrant. Conversely, liberal economic thought declared the collectivized command economies of the communist nations as unnatural—indeed, as political—arrangements imposed by totalitarian regimes.[23] This assumption created an ideological loophole through which migrants from the Soviet bloc could claim refugee status. The Hungarian refugees of 1956, for example, were granted prima facie group eligibility as refugees in a way reminiscent of the earlier classifications of refugees in the interwar period. Even when so-called economic migrants are motivated by fear—fear of hunger, of poverty, of homelessness, and so on—this fear is emptied of any political quality and is recast as "despair." Indeed, because only economic migrants exist within the liberal lexicon, these people are seen as entering global migration networks inspired by the hope for a better, more economically successful life. From the liberal perspective, the economic migrant may feel despair about leaving her home country, but fear of state persecution cannot be said to be the central motivation for his or her movement.

If the category of the "economic migrant" is caught within a dualism of hope–despair, the Convention establishes a binary of courage–fear for refugee applicants. To be sure, the UN Convention encourages the idea that refugee status is a kind of reward for heroism and bravery. As we saw in the feminist critiques discussed previously, the social construction of refugeeness involves a profound gender dynamic. Bhabha argues that the Convention definition not only reflects the liberal political values of "non-discrimination, individual autonomy and rationality" but it also sets up the figure of the refugee as "someone heroically seeking to assert his (typically male) individuality against an oppressive state."[24] The Convention's focus on the fear of state persecution evokes visions of autonomous, articulate citizens who voice their opinions and beliefs in the public sphere. Refugees, from this perspective, are courageous citizens who, because of their words, actions, or thoughts, are forced out of their political identities (citizen) and communities (state). The refugee's Fear is thus a product of a prior Bravery or Courage. The social construction of refugees as heroic "freedom fighters" oppressed by their (typically communist) states is classically represented during the 1956 Hungarian refugee crisis. Gil Loescher explains, "UNHCR appeals to governments for the resettlement of Hungarians generated numerous offers from governments all over the world. A tremendous groundswell of sympathy and support for the Hungarians arose. Spurred by extensive television coverage of students hurling paving stones and Molotov cocktails at Soviet tanks, the Western public viewed the Hungarians as heroes who deserved their help."[25]

The 1951 UN Refugee Convention expresses some profound paradoxes about the relationship between "humanity" and the "political." On one hand, the Convention breaks from earlier refugee definitions by refusing to limit refugee identity to groups of people coming from some specified state. Instead, the Convention promotes an open-ended definition, one that is potentially open to all of humanity. It does so, moreover, by positing an emotional experience (fear) as the core essence of refugeeness. On the other hand, this claim to universality has been challenged from the outset as merely the reflection of the global reach of Western cultural and political values. The UN Convention may not specify which states refugees must come from, but until 1967 it did posit a "European" arena as the privileged limit of state obligations to refugees. Similar liberal borders separating the "economic" and "political" and the "public" from the "private" have worked to exclude the unique problems of people forced to flee for economic or gender persecution. The effect of this is to introduce a hierarchy to the reasonable grounds on which the fear of persecution can be based. In the next section I further explore this political quality by focusing on the political dimensions of the core quality of the Convention refugee: fear.

Fear and Sovereign Power

Fear is an enigmatic concept, one that expresses some of the deepest contradictions and paradoxes of modern political life. On one hand, the meaning of fear is all too apparent and obvious. Fear, we know, is an intense emotional reaction to a real or perceived danger; it is something that causes us either to fight or to take flight. And yet, to pin down the meaning of fear is a decidedly slippery task. "Fear, like pain, is overwhelmingly present to the person experiencing it, but it may be barely perceptible to anyone else and almost defies objectification."[26] When fear is present, its effects may be too intense to consider it with any degree of detachment. Conversely, when the emotion is absent, its meaning remains elusive. It is not surprising, therefore, that Aristotle once referred to fear as "a kind of depression or bewilderment."[27] Or that Edmund Burke was compelled to write, "No passion so effectually robs the mind of all its powers of acting and reasoning as fear."[28] These views are still commonly held today. Fear, it is often said, involves a kind of forgetting of oneself, a loss of self that can lead to feelings of intense alienation and anxiety. Instead of providing a solid foundation on which personal subjectivity is founded and cultivated, fear is a radically decentring and deauthentifying experience.

There is, as Michael Taussig has argued, a relentless doubleness to fear: it is at once obvious and elusive, both the rule and the exception. This poses the problem of how to escape the effects of fear. To paraphrase Taussig, "How does one sidestep fear's side stepping?"[29] What are the grounds for discussing a concept that seemingly escapes all attempts at grounding? William Burroughs offered some sage advice: "Never fight fear head-on," he said. "That rot about pulling yourself together, and the harder you pull the worse it gets. Let it in and look at it. You will see it by what it does."[30] Following Burroughs, I undertake a conceptual unpacking of fear to provide some clarity on the politics of fearful practices. In doing so, I ask a variety of critical questions, including the following: What does fear do? What are its effects? What spaces and identities does fear constitute? These questions are answered in relation to modern theories of the political that presuppose an ontology of sovereignty and, in particular, the writings of the early modern political theorist of sovereignty, Thomas Hobbes. Hobbes remains a relevant thinker in this context because he fully explored the paradox of fear—that is, it at once poses a problem and provides a solution to the modern project of constituting political spaces and subjectivities.

Etymologies of fear suggest that the word once referred to the experience of being in transit. Consequently, the close connection between fear and the movement of the refugee is apparent even at the level of language. The history of the concept of fear is replete with associations with movement and, in particular, the experience of moving between spaces of safety and protection. Thomas Dumm outlined the etymological connections between fear, movement, and danger:

> Fear is a word rooted in the experience of being in transit. It shares a common root with the word *fare*, and in Teutonic languages it shares a root with danger, the word *fahren* expressing their common meaning as early as the ninth century. The word *far*, distant, is also associated with these words. *Fare* originally meant travel, and then came to mean the price of travel. The price of travel is removing oneself from protection … and can be thought of as fear, fear of calamity, of sudden disaster.[31]

Fear is, therefore, much more than a subjective response to danger. It is symptomatic of the condition of being outside the zone of safety, external to the bordered, territorial community that provides the individual with protection. As Dumm explains, to experience fear is to experience that "moment of vertigo that accompanies the movement from a place of protection to a place of exposure, experiencing the vertigo of uncertainty, not knowing, and admitting that one does not know, what threats to well-being lay in wait."[32]

According to the received tradition of political and international theory, it is the modern sovereign state that serves as the site of safety and protection. Along with the power and authority that comes from its claim to a monopoly on the legitimate use of violence, the state has also taken responsibility for providing security to the citizen-subjects within its territory. The state thus can make a legitimate claim to provide an enduring solution to the problem of fear. To unpack the politics of fear, therefore, one must read the concept in relation to the practices of sovereignty. The etymologies suggest that fear moves, but this movement is structured by the political space–time of sovereignty: fear is at once spatially outside and temporally before the political. Fear is something that becomes present only in the absence of laws and political institutions. The practices of sovereignty are designed to keep danger—and hence, fear—at bay.

Because the modern territorial state claims a monopoly over the space of politics, the space of fear is logically external to the state. State-centric thinking declares that this "outside" of the state is the international realm, an anarchical space where uncertainty and insecurity reign. Theorists of international relations have long considered fear to be a fundamental political category. The canon of political realism is replete with references to fear. In *The Peloponnesian Wars*, Thucydides had the Athenian ambassadors in Sparta remark to the Lacedaemonians that Athens had secured its international success "chiefly for fear, next for honour, and lastly for profit."[33] Machiavelli, too, recognized the centrality of fear to the practice of politics and counseled incipient princes to cultivate an atmosphere of fear over love in their polities, if they are somehow incapable or otherwise prevented from ensuring a good balance of the two.[34] The subject of fear similarly appears at pivotal points throughout Thomas Hobbes's writings. For example, he established a logical connection between Fear and Liberty immediately prior to his famous discussion of how Liberty and Necessity are consistent.[35]

Hobbes understood that fear was a formidable force, difficult to manage, and yet crucial for his project of creating the conditions under which sovereign political spaces and subjectivities could emerge. For Hobbes, fear was an emotion more fundamental than courage and was key in tempering the political effects of hope.[36] It is, however, his description of the nasty, brutal, in short, fearful condition found in the state of nature that is most regularly invoked by international theorists as the defining essence of the international realm. To be sure, Hobbes's relevance to international theory is typically framed in terms of how relations between states are analogous to relations between individuals in the state of nature. Hedley Bull, for instance, maintained that students of world politics are "entitled to infer that all of what Hobbes says about the life of individual men [sic] in the state of nature may be read as a description of the condition of states in relations to one another."[37] A state of war, "where every man is Enemy to every man," is the defining condition of Hobbes's state of nature. It is the fear of violent death, along with a rational capacity to recognize laws of nature that direct humans toward peace, that compels individuals to agree to (partially) renounce their natural right of self-preservation to a common power: the modern sovereign state. The sovereign state provides a spatial resolution to the problem of political order by insisting that all disputes within its bounded territory will be resolved by a legitimate sovereign power. It is the lack of such a common power to order and judge actions between states that is presented as evidence of the anarchical nature of the international realm, full of conflict, uncertainty, and war. As international relations scholars have interpreted this logic, within states civil politics can occur; outside states only fearful relations exist.[38]

If the space of fear is external to political space, then the temporality of fear appears to occupy an altogether different time zone than the modern state. The time of fear and the time of politics are out of sync, and this temporal disjuncture is often attributed to the prepolitical quality of fear. Even at the level of language it is apparent that fear and the state are opposing concepts. Fear is an emotion, and the temporal quality of the Latin root for the word emotion ("to move") stands in stark contrast to the spatial character of the Latin root for state ("to stand"). The temporal quality of fear is invoked whenever it is presented as a primal emotion or elementary passion, an involuntary response to danger that is somehow "hardwired" into the human psyche. The temporality of fear suggests that it lies somewhere before culture, before civility, and certainly before politics. Fear emotes a barbarism of distant past, when reason was undeveloped, passions were dominant, and life was more "primitive."[39]

In Hobbes's time, this distant past was interpreted as the seemingly observable present among the indigenous people of the Americas. Hobbes's description of the state of nature is therefore of further relevance here for developing an understanding of the temporal quality of fear. While it could be said that Hobbes's understanding of the state of nature is nothing more than an exceptional application of the deductive logic of Galileo's "resolutive-composite" method, Hobbes entertained the possibility that empirical cases of the state of nature might actually exist. The natural, fearful condition of humans is not merely the abstract creation of a political philosopher but, Hobbes suggests, an observable condition in the newly discovered people of America:

> It may preadventure be thought, there was never such a time, nor condition of warre as this; and I believe it was never generally so, over all the world; but there are many places, where they live so now. For the savage people in many places of America, except the government of small Families, the concord whereof dependeth on naturall lust, have no government at all; and live at this day in that brutish manner, as I said before.[40]

The logic of Hobbes's political anthropology in this passage insists that a society without a government, without a state, is not really a society at all.

Hobbes's textual strategy here is one of "othering," negatively identifying difference to reaffirm one's own claim to normality. David Campbell comments, "Hobbes's text is replete with examples of others from whom the self of rational, disciplined 'man' must be distinguished."[41] Here, Hobbes's reference to the "savage people" is presented as an empirical validation of the state of nature argument. Hobbes, of course, made no attempt to seriously understand or respect the social, economic, kinship, and political practices of these "savage people." Their difference is not understood and respected *as difference* but interpreted according to a logic of identity that negatively understands these societies in terms of a fundamental and pervasive lack—that is, the lack of a state to serve as the most rational, authentic, and "civilized" form of human community.[42]

These textual strategies of otherness are important because they establish the conditions whereby normative distinctions between fear and security, inside and outside, refugee and citizen can be made. Hobbes's text is full of these othering strategies. He wrote for effect, and he hoped that people will be suitably frightened by the state of nature so that they accept the constraints placed on them by the state.[43] Thomas Dumm has noted the intimate connection between the experience of fear and the production of political subjects, arguing that fear is "a feeling that makes vivid the experience of facing the priority of law in its various manifestations, such as the moments of the constitution of personhood."[44] William Connolly has given a similar emphasis in his reading of Hobbes, noting that "every element in the Hobbesian order functions in its way to pull the self together."[45] From this perspective, the state of nature argument appears as a form of "shock therapy" designed to compel subjects to recognize what their lives would be like if there were no sovereign power to protect them. Fear, in this sense, is an entirely "useful passion" for how it subdues unruly subjects and persuades them to accept the state and its regulations as a necessary part of securing their continued existence. As Connelly states,

> The fear of death pulls the self together. It induces subjects to accept civil society and it becomes an instrumentality of sovereign control in a civil society already installed. So, while Hobbes seeks to dampen the unruly and lustful passions, he seeks to elicit and accentuate this one. It is a useful passion, useful to an ordering of the self and to peace and quiet in the social order.[46]

The sovereign order, in other words, arises from the terrifying unanimity of a populace that comes face-to-face with their fear. Fear, recalling Burroughs, does indeed work: it works to stabilize anxious subjectivities, discipline disordered identities, and give the citizen-subject political coherence.

We can see how important fear is to Hobbes's project of constituting modern political space and identity by the distinctions he made between different types of fear. Not all fears are useful, and Hobbes considered some to be downright dangerous to his political project. For example, Hobbes had little positive to say of the concept "Panique Terror." In *Leviathan* he defined this passion as "Feare, without the apprehension of why, or what."[47] People caught up by this type of fear are unable to ground their fear in any determinable reason or cause. Often they cannot even identify the object of their fear. This was disturbing to Hobbes—whose nominalism insisted that "truth consisteth in the right ordering of names"[48]—as he had already defined fear as an object of sense that arouses a sense of aversion within the subject.[49] The problem of Panique Terror is that it is fear based on the absence of a sensible object. The individual does not know exactly what it is he or she fears; he or she supposes, like everyone else, that others know what is the object to be feared. Hobbes negatively associated this type of fear with a sort of mob mentality, driven and intensified by rumor and found only among "a throng, or multitude of people."[50] To anyone concerned with the maintenance of public order, this type of fear has its obvious problems. But for Hobbes, the difficulties with Panique Terror go much deeper than sporadic disturbances of civil peace. More important to Hobbes was the danger Panique Terror represents to the ongoing production of sovereign power. Sovereign power relies on the individual's capacity to recognize the proper hierarchy of fear, based on the sensible character of each fearful object. As William Sokoloff states, "Panique Terror disrupts the potentially stabilizing force of fear because it has a mediated relation, or possibly no relation to the realm of sensibility."[51]

For Hobbes, any reasonable person would identify sovereign power as an important object to fear. Indeed, Hobbes's entire theory of the political depends on sovereign power inspiring the second greatest fear, overawing all others except the fear of the state of nature. Consequently, Hobbes only validated fearful experiences that have a rational component to them, in that they allow for the apprehension of future harm or insecurity. Useful fears work in tangent with reason. Hence, Hobbes dismissed the utility of Panique Terror, employing a textual strategy of otherness, to reaffirm the idea that legitimate passions are those that work to legitimate and, indeed, produce and sustain sovereign power. An important connection between the production of knowledge and the legitimation of political authority needs to be underscored in this context. As Karena Shaw comments, for Hobbes, the relation between the two is an especially intimate one:

> It is the ontology of sovereignty that guarantees and authorizes knowledge claims. In the absence of sovereignty, words have no meaning; covenants without swords are mere words. Because the ontology of sovereignty gives words their authority (a political authority can only be considered sovereign if it can guarantee the meaning of its words), this ontology necessarily provides the basis for authority and legitimacy throughout society.[52]

Fear flourishes under conditions of ambiguity: "Denunciations, gossip, innuendos, and rumors of death lists create a climate of suspicion. No one can be sure who is who."[53] Hobbes's theory of sovereignty is precisely about creating the conditions where everyone "can be sure who is who." The constitution of sovereign spaces and subjectivities is the modern response to the terrifying uncertainty of living in fear. As such, the sovereign relation is infused with ontological status out of a fearful desire that Richard Bernstein has called the Cartesian Anxiety—that is, a desire "for some fixed point, some stable rock upon which we can secure our lives against the vicissitudes that constantly threaten us."[54] Sovereignty is thus spatialized through its encounters with the dangerous temporality of fear. This is reflected in Realist theories of international relations, which read Hobbes's state of nature argument in a fairly linear fashion. The shift from a state of nature to a state of laws is interpreted as a progressive move from one distinct state to another. As we have seen, however, this dualistic movement involves a host of other distinctions and produces a disturbingly familiar hierarchical pattern of identity and difference: when we move from a state of fear to a state of laws, we are told that we are also making the shift from war to peace, primitive to modern, human being to citizen-subject. This, of course, creates a host of problems for individuals and groups who are defined by a close relationship to fear. In the next section, I explore this dynamic with reference to the UN Refugee Convention.

A Handbook of Reasonable Fear

The 1951 UN Convention definition of the refugee does much more than just promote a particular cold war ideology. Not only is the impact of the Convention limited to how it individualizes the whole phenomenon of refugees and their movements through its appeal to Western liberal political values;[55] but at a more fundamental level, the Convention works to reproduce the entire architecture of sovereignty on which the Western concept of the political is based. The UN Convention, for all its enthusiasm for a refugee definition that universally applies to all human beings (by virtue of a common fearing), actively assumes a world where meaningful and authentic political identities (i.e., citizenship) are the monopoly of particular sovereign states. This can be seen in the Convention's insistence that refugee status be applied only to people who have been forced to flee across an international border. Fear, we have already established, is located externally to the modern sovereign state. The refugee—motivated by his or her fear—similarly occupies this zone outside the state, the "inter" of the international realm.[56] The problem with this, as many critics have noted, is twofold. First, it evades the internal or intrastate conflicts that have produced vast populations of internally displaced people. Contemporary patterns of coerced displacement—including the movement of internally displaced people, environmental refugees, involuntary resettled people, and so on—do not necessarily involve the type of interstate movement that the Convention definition demands. Second, Western states, in particular, reject the idea that people fleeing from civil war or generalized persecution should be eligible for legal refugee status. The impetus for international flight should not come from some general "society of fear" but instead be firmly fixed on the fear that an individual feels when persecution from one's state becomes a real or likely occurrence. Here, the Hobbesian claim that fear must at all times be focused on the state is firmly reinforced.

The idea that a refugee is someone who has a "well-founded fear of being persecuted" is one that is widely incorporated into the refugee law of nation-states. The 1951 Convention or the 1967 Protocol, or both, has been ratified by 145 countries, many of which incorporate its language into their national legislations. Despite this near unanimity as to what defines the central element of the refugee's condition, it is nonetheless the prerogative of sovereign states to develop the specific judicial and administrative mechanisms to determine an applicant's claim to refugee status. Indeed, states have developed an extensive volume of policy and case law to determine whether a reasonable risk of persecution exists. The language through which a "reasonable likelihood of risk" is expressed varies from one country to the next. In Spain and Portugal, for example, there must be a reasonable likelihood of persecution; in Germany, a "considerable likelihood"; in Switzerland, a "strong probability." French case law concludes that "it must be taken as certain or sufficiently probable that the person would be subject to persecution." In Canada, the degree of "reasonable chance" is located in "the field between upper and lower limits; it is less than a 50% chance (i.e., a probability) but more than a minimal or mere possibility."[57] In the United States, the Cardoza-Fonseca case of the U.S. Supreme Court (1987) found that "one can certainly have a well-founded fear of an event happening when there is less than a 50% chance of the occurrence taking place." What's more, on several occasions U.S. case law has indicated that a risk of around 10 percent can be sufficient.[58] The point to be emphasized about these variations is that the ability to judge one's capacity to reason is firmly held by officials of a sovereign state and not the refugee claimant. The refugee's fearful subjectivity is always suspect for how it might inhibit his or her rational capacity. The refugee claimant, however, is not so much denied his or her rationality as has demands placed on him or her to demonstrate a certain percentage, or ratio of likelihood. In other words, the claimant must be sufficiently rational to calculate the probability of persecution.

The UNHCR's position on the relationship between reason and the refugee's fear is discussed at length in its *Handbook on Procedures and Criteria for Determining Refugee Status under the 1951 Convention and the 1967 Protocol Relating to the Status of Refugees*. This publication is widely recognized as being the authoritative interpretation of the UN Convention and its Protocol. In it, the phrase "well-founded fear of being persecuted" is clearly identified as comprising the key element of the 1951 Convention and 1967 Protocol definition of a refugee.[59] The official interpretation of this phrase splits it in two, highlighting the so-called subjective and objective elements. The first element—the subjective—is recognized as fear. The Handbook defines fear as "a state of mind and a subjective condition."[60] Here, the liberal individualism of the Convention definition shines through as the Handbook posits a fundamental difference as being the defining element of the human condition. As individuals, people possess a notoriously wide variety of temperaments and dispositions, and so the "psychological reactions of different individuals may not be the same in identical conditions."[61]

The UNHCR defines fear as subjective, and so determining the level of fear requires an evaluation of a refugee applicant's personal statements regarding his or her plight. According to the Handbook, however, the subjective quality of an individual's fear necessitates an objective evaluation:

> To the element of fear ... is added the qualification "well-founded." This implies that it is not only the frame of mind of the person concerned that determines his refugee status, but that this frame of mind must be supported by an objective situation.[62]

The subjective quality to fear is, therefore, used to justify the intervention of "competent authorities"—that is, the immigration officials of individual states. Their task is to "objectively" evaluate the applicant's statements to determine whether the experience of fear is "well-founded."[63] The Handbook states, "It will be necessary to take into account the personal and family background of the applicant, his membership of a particular racial, religious, national, social or political group, his own interpretation of his situation, and his personal experience—in other words, everything that may serve to indicate that the predominant motive for his application is fear."[64]

The Handbook recommends a variety of strategies for determining who is an "authentic" refugee: "A typical test of the well-foundedness of fear will arise when an applicant is in possession of a valid national passport."[65] The Handbook recommends that, in general, the refugee should not possess a passport. If the refugee truly possesses a "well-founded fear of persecution," he or she will behave like someone who has lost the protection offered by his or her home country and will, therefore, either not possess a passport or readily surrender it to officials representing the state to which he or she is applying for asylum. The Handbook admits that the possession of a passport cannot automatically be interpreted as an indication of an absence of fear. After all, a state may in fact want this person to leave the country, and so the simple possession of this document does not mean that the state is not persecuting the refugee applicant. Nevertheless, the Handbook goes on to stress that if

> an applicant, without good reason, insists on retaining a valid passport of a country of whose protection he is allegedly unwilling to avail himself, this may cast doubt on the validity of his claim to have "well-founded fear." Once recognized, a refugee should not normally retain his national passport.[66]

The analysis here appears dated (the Handbook was written in 1988), as the refugee and immigration laws of many, and, in particular, Western, states have created very strict legal (and physical) barriers to refugees who lack official papers or identity documents.[67] Nevertheless, the Handbook's analysis of passports is significant for the links it establishes between refugees, fear, and political identity. A form of what Daniel Warner has called the "liberal mathematics"[68] of refugee determination is employed to establish a series of equivalencies that result in either an authentic refugee or a nonauthentic refugee.

1. Nonauthentic Refugee Equation: Passport = state identity = state protection = no fear = citizen = no international protection/asylum.
2. Authentic Refugee Equation: No Passport = no state identity = no state protection = fear = refugee = international protection/asylum.

These equations represent a clear example of the connection between the production of knowledge and the legitimation of political authority that was identified in the previous section. Fear and Reason appear as a Janusfaced figure in the UN Convention definition of the refugee. "Fear must be reasonable," insists the Handbook, echoing Thomas Hobbes. Without reason as its guide, fear is a destabilizing force, the obverse of the state order. State refugee law on "well-founded fear" attempts, among other things, to disarm and sanitize fear, bringing order to disorder. The applicant's fear may make the refugee's speech less than trustworthy.[69] The claim to "objectivity" on behalf of state refugee adjudicators is therefore made in part to impose some coherence to the explanation offered by refugees. The Handbook argues that state officials should make special arrangements to deal with refugee applicants who are seemingly overwhelmed by their fear:

> The nature and degree of the applicant's "fear" must also be taken into consideration, since some degree of mental disturbance is frequently found in persons who have been exposed to severe persecution. Where there are indications that the fear expressed by the applicant may not be based on actual experience or may be an exaggerated fear, it may be necessary, in arriving at a decision, to lay greater emphasis on the objective circumstances, rather than the statements made by the applicant.[70]

The experience of fear, in other words, can have a silencing effect, making once eloquent political dissidents mute: "while a refugee may have very definite opinions for which he has had to suffer, he may not, for psychological reasons, be able to describe his experiences in political terms."[71] In this sense, refugees are not only individuals without authentic political identities but also subjects who are made incapable—because of their fear—of uttering political speech.

Cultures in Contention

Global politics has been transformed in many ways since 1951, when the UN Convention Relating to the Status of Refugees was established. Much has changed even since 1988, when the UNHCR Handbook was written. Refugees and their movements no longer fall into the simple ideological choices of the cold war (if they ever did). Refugee flows in the post–cold war era, it is often said, are much more complex and confusing; they blur and call into question distinctions that were once considered common sense (e.g., refugee–migrant, public–private, inside–outside). Still, the UNHCR is committed to preserving the 1951 Convention as the center of the international refugee protection system, but it also has recognized the need to take a more flexible approach and be receptive to forced migrants who do not meet the strict qualifications of the Convention. The rationale for providing humanitarian aid and protection to the people caught in these "refugee-like" situations is that all people who have been coerced to leave their homes and take flight (regardless of whether they have crossed an international border) suffer from a form of "human insecurity."[72] As the UNHCR explains in its 1998 *State of the World's Refugees* report, "Refugee movements and other forms of forced displacement provide a useful (if imprecise) barometer of human security and insecurity. As a rule, people do not abandon their homes and flee from their own country or community unless they are confronted with serious threats to their life and liberty. Flight is the ultimate survival strategy, the one employed when all other coping mechanisms have been exhausted."[73]

According to the UNHCR, a clear indicator of human insecurity is the fear that motivates people to take flight. Therefore, what connects Convention refugees to other forcibly displaced people is that they all experience the insecurity of fear and thus they are all "human" in the bare sense assumed by the 1951 UN Convention. The Convention encourages a vision of refugeeness that identifies refugees for their base drives, their proximity to the "state of nature," and their lack of political voice. Refugees are human beings "in the raw," so to speak, because they are motivated by a feeling—the subjective emotion of fear—rather than by rational deliberation. By defining refugees in terms of a naked fearful impulse to take flight from persecution, nation-states, the UNHCR, and other humanitarian organizations risk reproducing the extremely "thin" conception of humanity envisioned in Hobbes's state of nature argument. In Hobbes's fearful state of nature, the focus is on bare human survival. The constant fear that defines this condition does not allow its occupants to act politically, develop knowledge, or otherwise pursue a cultured form of existence. All that remains is a form of "bare life" that Agamben spoke of: a life included in the sovereign political community (state) only by virtue of her exclusion from it and its authoritative, articulate identity (citizen). In a similar way, the humanitarian organizations responding to today's complex political and humanitarian emergencies are working under conditions where the supply of the basic necessities of life (food, shelter, protection) is often highlighted above all other considerations.

We have already seen in previous chapters how this focus on the technical and logistical problems of refugee management has the effect of de-politicizing refugees and refugee situations. Here, I want to emphasize how refugees, already adept at escaping oppressive situations, evade the conceptual trappings that attempt to impose speechless, invisible, and nonpolitical identities on them. I highlight this with reference to the refugee's relationship to culture. The fearing subjects of the Hobbesian state of nature do not possess the individual or collective security to pursue cultural activities. Similarly, the fearing refugees of the UN Convention are typically seen as emaciated figures requiring the basic fundamentals to sustain life, and not something as elusive as "culture." Yet refugees all over the world continually emphasize that the provision of, say, pen and paper and a postal system is as fundamental a "human right" as is the provision of food and shelter.[74] That this demand for a life that is not merely a "bare life" comes from refugees is significant for it underscores a basic reality that often goes unnoticed: in the shift from citizen-subject to refugee-human, refugees do not lose their capacity to sing, to recite poetry, to dance. In fact, as we shall see next, they continue to engage in these cultural performances in spite of their fear and even in environments (such as refugee camps) that do not appear at all hospitable to the arts.[75]

International humanitarian organizations have begun to realize that important policy lessons can be learned from the cultural dynamic of refugee life. For instance, the United Nations Development Programme has funded a Theatre for Development project in the Zambezia province of Mozambique, which has had considerable success in using theatre to promote reconciliation in postconflict communities.[76] Similarly, the Norwegian Refugee Council has promoted a project that uses music, art, theatre, and sport to encourage the social and educational rehabilitation of internally displaced children in Azerbaijan.[77] In general, humanitarian organizations have found that encouraging the expression of cultural identity can have a positive effect on the mental, physical, and social health of refugees and refugee communities. As David Parkin noted, "When people flee from the threat of death and total dispossession, the things and stories they carry with them may be all that remains of their distinctive personhood to provide for future continuity."[78]

The significance of culture among refugees is not limited to how international humanitarian agencies use these practices to fulfill their mandates and promote the smooth functioning of their operations. The impact culture has among refugees and their communities exceeds the problem-solving perspective of these agencies; there exists a polyphone of refugee cultural practices than cannot be contained by the technical view. These practices are, instead, better assessed for how they work as a transformative force, unsettling the prevailing conception of the "proper" (i.e., negative)

relationship between refugee identity and the political. There is a growing recognition of how cultural practices act as an intervening force within
world politics. For example, in his introduction to a special issue of the
journal *Alternatives* titled "Poetic World Politics," Roland Bleiker promoted
the value of poetry to the project of understanding the processes of change
and transformation in world politics:

> Poetry is ideally suited for rethinking world politics because it re-
> volves around a recognition that (aesthetic) form and (political)
> substance cannot be separated. The manner in which a text is writ-
> ten, a speech is uttered, a thought is thought, is integral to its con-
> tent. There is no neutral way of representing the world, a form that
> is somehow detached from the linguistic and social practices in
> which the speaker or writer is embedded.[79]

In the same issue, Costas Constantinou also underscored the productive
connection between language and politics, noting, "Words are not just narrative material, but can themselves have stories to tell."[80] The word "human"
certainly has a story to tell, the fearful dimension of which we recounted
in this chapter. We saw how the UN Convention grounds its definition of
the refugee on the basis of a common human emotion, that of fear. But the
story of the refugee's fear cannot be wholly contained by the logic of sovereignty. While fear has a close relationship with motion, it nonetheless har-
bors distaste for linear motion. Fear flows, transverses, sidesteps. Similarly,
there is a polyphony of refugee cultural practices that recast the meaning
and effects of fear in a way that evades the sovereign codes of the state.

Mohamed Ali Aissaoui is a refugee claimant living in Leeds, England.
He has fled for reasons of political persecution from his home country of
Tunisia. His poem "I Am a Refugee And" evokes a conception of refugeeness that is at once inside and outside of the conventional expectations of
this identity.

I am a refugee and
I am a prisoner in your country,
I am a student,
I am political,
I am opposed to any military dictatorship,
I am the grandfather of two girls,
I am the father of four children—one girl and three boys,
I am a Muslim,
I am a good practitioner,
I am very happy with my teacher,
I am friendly, honest and serious.[81]

Aissaoui's poem is remarkable for how it asserts a refugee subjectivity that
speaks only in the confident voice of the first-person tense. "I Am a Refugee

And" captures the multidimensional character of refugeeness, demonstrating that not all characteristics coincide with the humanitarian and nonpolitical expectations found in the UNHCR's definition. This definition, we have seen, casts the refugee as nonpolitical, as a bare life, as speechless, as temporary, as criminal, as a victim. The refugeeness found in the Convention definition establishes the refugee as someone whose fear has overwhelmed the capacity for reason effectively. But Aissaoui did not mention "fear" in his inventory of refugeeness. Rather, he identified a variety of characteristics that run counter to the conventional expectations of refugees. He is indeed a refugee (as the title establishes), but he is also a student and a religious person. He is not simply an individual but also a member of an extended family—a family, it should be noted, that is not the bare life of the "family of humanity." Similarly, he has a developed human personality (he is "friendly, honest, serious") and is not just a one-dimensional bare life. Finally, in a gesture that purges the sovereign relation out of refugeeness, he declared that not only does he possess political opinions ("I am opposed to any military dictatorship") but also he is, in fact, political.

Agustin Nsanzineza Gus is another refugee-poet living in England. One of his poems, "The Sweetness of Being a Refugee," engages in the story of the human, attempting to open up a space for an alternative conception of humanity than that imposed on him by the UN Convention.[82] I discuss the poem in detail later, but we should immediately note that from the very first line ("I'd like to be a refugee") Gus's poem makes a strong case for the allure, the "sweetness" of refugee identity. As he is already a refugee, Gus uses the rhetorical technique of irony to great effect. Irony allows him at once to highlight the paradoxes of refugeeness as well as to offer some alternative answers to what it means to be "human" to those provided by the fearful ontology of sovereignty. Given the problematic quality of the UN Convention, an ironic approach seems appropriate enough. This rhetorical technique employs techniques of overstatement and understatement: the former, to make seemingly ordinary forms of classification outrageous; the latter, to say very little while implying that there is much more to be said. "Irony," Donna Haraway has argued, "is about contradictions that do not resolve into large wholes, even dialectically, about the tension of holding incompatible things together because both or all are necessary and true."[83] Irony recognizes that representation always involves an engagement with the political. There is always a gap between a representation and that which is represented, and ironic writing recognizes and plays with this ambiguity.[84]

In a similar fashion, Gus sets up a stark ironic contrast between the different, paradoxical elements of refugee identity. At first, the desirability of the refugee is promoted in insistent, repetitive assertions:

> I would be the king of the world
> I would go wherever I want to

> I would fearlessly knock at every door
> I would be assisted by whosoever
> I would be cared for by everybody
> I would inspire compassion in people's hearts

In this world, refugees possess an elevated status; they move freely and would not be at all fearful for they would be secure in the knowledge that they are welcome wherever they go. In a manner similar to Aissaoui's poem, the purposeful agency of the refugee is evident in the repetition of the pronoun I. Soon, however, the refugee encounters the practices of sovereignty and the state's monopoly on politically active subjectivities (citizenship). The otherness of the refugee is established through a logocentric exercise that portrays the refugee as everything the citizen is not. From the perspective of citizenship, the refugee does not qualify for a subjectivity that can speak in the first person (the Is above). Instead, the refugee's fear unplugs the rational capacity of this "human," reducing her to an abject and objectified condition (the As below).

> ... a refugee is a citizenshipless citizen
> A heartless human being
> A consciousless conscience
> An unbearable burden
> A society dirt and toy
> A spier and a spoiler
> And what not ...

Kathy Ferguson, reflecting on the political implications of irony, concluded that irony is "subversive to unity, but crucial for solidarity across differences."[85] Gus's poem promotes a new solidarity between humans, one that does not rely on the exclusionary logic of the sovereignty relation.

> We all belong to the family of Humans
> Did I say humans?
> No, sorry
> The world of potential refugees
> Or better than that
> The world of refugees to be

From this fragment we can see that the distinction between "refugees" and "humanity" is, in fact, a misnomer. The relationship between the two is rather one of indistinction: humanity is in a continual process of becoming-refugee. To assert that all humans are "potential refugees" or "refugees to be" is, of course, no small claim, as it challenges some of the central assumptions of modern political and international theory. The received wisdom of this tradition is that obligations to fellow citizens within the bounded community of the sovereign state take precedence over obligations to the rest of humanity. Gus's poem, by contrast, suggests that the modern resolution to global–local moral obligations be revised: it is humanity and not citizens that must take precedence in questions of moral obligation and responsibility. This "humanity," moreover, is not the negative reverse image of the citizen-subject (voiceless, agentless, defined by a "naked" fear) that is found in the UN Convention. On the contrary, it forgoes the usual distinctions between different states of being (citizen vs. humanity), promoting an alteration (as opposed to an alternation) of states of being. The refugee-becoming of humanity disrupts the categories of sovereign power, thereby creating a space in which refugees can begin to speak, to engage in a dialogue, about their condition, their hopes for return and for justice, and their fears.[86]

Conclusion

The fiftieth anniversary of the UNHCR prompted a call to rethink the way in which refugees are conceptualized by states and international humanitarian agencies. The UNHCR insists that any modifications to the existing protection regime must nonetheless accept the centrality of the UN Convention. This insistence, however, will likely limit the range of possible alternatives to dealing with contemporary patterns of forced migration. The Refugee Convention is allied to a mode of political thinking that already defines the possible array of alternatives. In the case of the refugee's fearing humanity, we have seen how that alternative is not much of an alternative, because it promotes a vision of humanity that is based on the nonchoice of the "state of fear" vs. "state of law" binary. The ontology of sovereignty encourages the individual to see this binary as a transition between two opposed states of being (i.e., from a fearing human condition to a secure citizen state). The "alternative" expressed by the Convention merely flips the already existing hierarchy of citizen–human; it is an alternative that relies on a spatial crossover, or a reversal of one side of the binary in favor of the other. As such, the system of dualistic and exclusionary codes—a system that sovereignty both fosters and relies on—remains intact. A serious tautological dilemma arises when one confronts the fact that the alternative of humanity has been anticipated by a mode of political thinking that has already set the terms for how to conceive "alternatives" in this first place.[87]

One of the consequences of this line of argument is that the inclusion of fear as a fundamental attribute of refugeeness has implications that go well beyond the terms of the Convention definition. Here, the focus within the refugee advocate community to "broaden" the criteria of persecution must be viewed with caution. This is not to say, of course, that the terms of the definition should not be expanded. Quite the contrary. Amending the refugee definition to include, for instance, a well-founded fear of being persecuted for allegedly "private" activities of women and sexual minorities is an important political project. So too are the calls to amend the definition to include a well-founded fear of war, "generalized persecution," or (more radically) poverty. But expanding the list of potential reasons for the fear of persecution or suffering, or both, is not sufficient to the task of recasting refugeeness. Rather, the constitution of the refugee's subjectivity in terms of fear is a large part of the problem and so adding these other categories to the legitimate causes of fear will not solve it.

4

Human Hospitality/Animal Animosity: Canadian Responses to Refugee Crises at the Millennium

Wolf-men, bear-men, wildcat-men, men of every animality, secret brotherhoods, animate the battlefields. War contained zoological sequences before it became bacteriological. It is in war, famine, and epidemic that werewolves and vampires proliferate. Any animal can be swept up in these packs and the corresponding becomings; cats have been seen on the battlefield, and even in armies. That is why the distinction we must make is less between kinds of animals than between the different states according to which they are integrated into family institutions, State apparatuses, war machines, etc.

—Gilles Deleuze and Félix Guattari

Introduction: Refugee Policy for the Dogs?

To be a refugee means that one must become a dog, at least according to one prominent Canadian newspaper columnist. In an article titled "Canadian Refugee Policy for the Dogs," the conservative National Post columnist Diane Francis recounted the experiences of Vancouver physician Maria Hugi.[1] One night while staffing the emergency ward of a local hospital, Dr. Hugi was summoned to provide emergency medical treatment to a young man who had stopped breathing. Dr. Hugi successfully resuscitated her patient, but he would never recover; he died two weeks later from a full-blown case of tuberculosis (TB). As it turned out, Dr. Hugi had contracted this disease in the course of her treatment. She was understandably quite upset and traumatized by this turn of events. She waited anxiously for three months to find out whether this particular strain of TB could be treated, and when she found out that it could, she nonetheless suffered permanent liver damage from the medication. As Francis explained, however, what really irked Dr. Hugi was her belief that the Canadian state had failed in one of its basic responsibilities: to provide for her human security, not so much from the disease as from the class of person from whom she contracted TB.

Dr. Hugi's patient was a refugee: a twenty-six-year-old young man from Burma who was seeking asylum in Canada. While the immediate reason for his appearing in Dr. Hugi's life (i.e., his TB) had nothing to do with his status as a refugee claimant (i.e., his "well-founded fear of being perse-cuted"), this later subject-position nevertheless evoked a remarkable anxi-ety in Dr. Hugi—one strong enough to motivate her to go public with her story. Dr. Hugi's narrative of her experience (as well as Francis's editorial interventions) sharply criticized the Canadian state for failing to protect the "human security" of her and the general public of Vancouver. In this sense, Dr. Hugi's tale is but the most recent example of a rather long history of identifying diseased bodies as a danger to the health of the body politic.[2] The connection between domestic health and national security has taken on a renewed salience in Western states since the "broadening" of security agendas in the post–cold war era. Security is no longer interpreted solely in terms of the military capabilities of a particular state. Instead, diseases such as HIV/AIDS, SARS, TB, and Mad Cow have joined refugee movements, ethnic strife, environmental calamities, religious fundamentalisms, terror-ism, and a host of other developments in the rapidly expanding roster of threats to national and international security.

The fear of dangerous contagious diseases that can be transmitted through global population movements has taken a particularly prominent place in Canadian public discourse about security. When Dr. Hugi began to treat her refugee-patient, she was aware that he had recently traveled these networks of global movement. But she had also "assumed that he'd [been] screened for everything." Her rationale was simple and reasonable: "That would be what our government did and the responsible thing to do." The doctor's judgment was also reinforced by her own personal experience: when Dr. Hugi emigrated from Switzerland to Canada as a child, her fam-ily's application was delayed for three years because immigration officials were concerned about the severity of her father's medical condition (he had a spot on one of his lungs). In contrast to her experience as an "authentic" immigrant, Dr. Hugi protests that refugee policy in Canada has "gone to the dogs":

My dog has more protection at the border than I do. Pets are quarantined so that our dogs don't get dog diseases. They [the government border officials] do a good job of protecting us from imported disease when it involves life forms that can't talk. But when it comes to illegal aliens, the immigration and refugee lawyers who need to finance their children's orthodontics and to buy fancy houses with big fees corrupt the system.[3]

The rhetorical maneuvers employed in these criticisms are noteworthy and unpacking them will point to some of the central challenges involving the politics of refugeeness today.[4] Dr. Hugi's statements raise three interconnected themes: authenticity, speechlessness, and animality. When conjoined, these themes create a profound paradox for refugeeness, and one that potentially affects the life of every person seeking or assigned refugee status.

To begin, note how quickly Dr. Hugi subsumes her encounter with her refugee-patient into the general (and pejorative) discourse of "illegal aliens." Refugees here are subjected to a collective demonization with those who must resort to various forms of "irregular" migration.[5] Despite the various (yet diminishing) legal entitlements to which refugee claimants are eligible according to Canadian law (including, it should be stressed, emergency medical care), the refugee is considered inauthentic and dangerous. This is, of course, in stark contrast to Dr. Hugi's own status as a bona fide "official" immigrant. It seems that to be an authentic refugee, one must disappear from the public realm of civil society and—like Dr. Hugi's dog or a virus—remain detained, isolated, and monitored. And indeed, contemporary developments in Canada and elsewhere point to emergence of a "carceral age" for refugees.[6]

If the body of the refugee has yet to completely vanish from public space, the voice of the refugee nonetheless continues to silently exclaim a structured absence with respect to the political. Thus, a second theme—that of speechlessness—is raised in Dr. Hugi's testimony when she presents the refugee as a mute figure, incapable of speaking for himself, or acting in any kind of authoritative fashion. The refugee is not even capable of corrupting the system, a task reserved for lawyers, who both dominate as speaking subjects and allegedly profit from the situation. In terms of the refugee's capacity to speak and be heard in a political way, the refugee remains like the dog: "a life form that can't talk."

To claim that the refugee suffers from speechlessness is one thing, but to link this (alleged) silence to an animal nature has many disturbing consequences. Consequently, the assertion that refugees and animals share an incapacity for political talk raises a third theme, that of the refugee's relationship to animality. From Dr. Hugi's point of view, life—bare life—becomes indistinguishable at the border, or, rather, the distinctions between different forms of life become irrelevant. The appearance of a human being seeking refugee status or the appearance of, say, someone's dog should make no difference to those responsible (i.e., state officials) for protecting and sustaining the lives of both individuals and communities (human or dog). Obviously, the implications of this viewpoint go beyond concerns about public health and affect some fundamental debates about political authority, ethical responsibility, and the possibilities of hospitality. In this sense, Dr. Hugi's statements draw on and reinforce the theory of state sovereignty we have discussed in previous chapters. The theory of state sovereignty, it will be recalled, includes an ethical dimension whereby the securing of state borders simultaneously secures the possibility of being human. This involves a vision of responsibility that mirrors the strict (border) lines of the state, thus creating a hierarchy of humans between those who are inside and those who are outside. Take Dr. Hugi's summary: "I have no quarrel with looking after a Canadian, a homeless person. That's my social contract. But I expect my government to protect us from foreign invasion. That's the skinny. If we didn't think that way, then let's just stop pretending and eliminate the border."[7]

The increasingly restrictive and exclusive attitude toward refugee policy is making the world a less hospitable place for the forcibly displaced person. The "exilic bias" of refugee law that defined Western cultures of asylum during the cold war era has been systematically undermined in favor of a "source control bias" that focuses more on the "containment" of migration than on improving the protection offered to refugees.[8] Such an inhospitable climate, it needs to be emphasized in this era following September 11, 2001, is not the only option available to countries such as Canada. Derrida's writings on the topic of hospitality begin with the assumption that limited forms of hospitality are always aware of another way of relating with others, an approach that does not insist on conditions—such as proper documentation, state citizenship, or, as we shall see, even "humanity"—for hospitality. In fact, the fear of an unlimited hospitality nonetheless assumes the possibility of an unqualified welcome. By invoking the idea of unqualified hospitality, the entire question—and politics—of how to encounter the stranger is opened up. Such an opening, moreover, reveals that there is no settled meaning to the term hospitality. It is neither the universal law nor the categorical imperative that some make it out to be. Instead, hospitality is a concept whose meaning is entirely unsettled and, indeed, unsettling to established ways of thinking and acting both politically and ethically under contemporary conditions. For example, when Derrida interrogated the viability of an unconditional form of hospitality, he cast as wide a web as possible in terms of who will benefit from this affirmative ethos:

> Let us say yes to who or what turns up, before any determination, before any anticipation, before any identification, whether or not the new arrival is the citizen of another country, a human, animal, or divine creature, a living or dead thing, male or female.[9]

Derrida questioned whether hospitality is the sole property of the human world and suggested that it could be applicable to nonhumans as well. The idea of unconditional hospitality is immediately undermined if one imposes the conditionality of being human.

Such an understanding of hospitality is not without risk or its own specific dangers. As Derrida explained, "Pure, unconditional or infinite hospitality cannot and must not be anything else but an acceptance of risk. If I am sure that the newcomer that I welcome is perfectly harmless, innocent, that (s)he will be beneficial to me ... it is not hospitality. When I open my door, I must be ready to take the greatest of risks."[10] The point to be emphasized here is that while unconditional hospitality is always a risky endeavor, "hospitality without risk usually hides more serious violence."[11] The case of Dr. Hugi is case in point. She expected that an act of hospitality should come without risk or danger. Canada, from her perspective, should only grant asylum to individuals who have their official papers in order, who have been "screened for everything." Such preconditions on hospitality can lead to some profoundly inhospitable acts, such as detaining humans as if they were dogs. Hospitality, therefore, cannot be just another form of liberal accommodation. Too often the "host's" noble and high-minded toleration of the other conceals practices that try to efface all the dangers and risks that necessarily come with such engagements. Instead, Derrida underscored how hospitable relations always involve an element of enmity, remarking that "to be hospitable is to let oneself be overtaken ... in a fashion almost violent."[12] Hospitality, from this perspective, involves something much more complicated that merely offering a welcome or an open embrace. It is a question not just of embracing but also of accepting animosity, hostility, and antagonism as an unavoidable component of hospitality. Derrida introduced the neologism "hostipitality" to capture the violence that is constitutive of hospitality.

In this chapter, I examine how the practices of sovereignty place severe limits on the development of an unlimited form of hospitality. I examine the way the refugee's lack or failure of reasonable speech, examined in earlier chapters, has historically been deployed to discursively establish an animal quality to refugeeness. I argue that this animality poses a profound challenge for contemporary cultures of hospitality to refugees. The animal animosity facing refugees and asylum seekers is simultaneously a problem of human hospitality. This is demonstrated with regard to the ambiguous Canadian response to two major refugee crises in the summer of 1999. While the humanitarian pride over the emergency evacuation of almost five thousand Kosovar refugees seems to stand in sharp contrast to the xenophobic hysteria over the appearance of almost six hundred "boat people" from the Fujian province of China later that same summer, I argue in this chapter that the two cases share a number of disturbing commonalities. To demonstrate these similarities, I trace the overlapping dynamics of animality, speechlessness, and detention from the medieval institution of banishment all the way through to Microsoft's participation in cataloging the forcibly displaced.

Banished Voices: Language and Violence along the Human–Animal Divide

The characterization of refugees as dogs is not a new one, and their canine ancestry periodically emerges in the histories of forced migration. One way of reading Giorgio Agamben's recent intervention into the debate about the politics of sovereignty is that the figure of the "refugee" emerged as part of a larger bestiary of concepts. Agamben's analysis points to the medieval institution of banishment as one of the "origins" of refugeeness, structuring a relationship with the political that still holds relevance today. The practice of banishment is interesting to Agamben because he sees important links between the sovereign relation of the exception and the relation of the ban. In the hierarchy of medieval places, individuals who are banned from the city are not simply expelled from the city limits and asked never to return. They occupy a criminalized space and through their banishment they become bandits. In other words, to be condemned to a space outside the law has the effect of creating literal outlaws. For Agamben, those who have been banished are not simply outside the law but paradoxically included by virtue of their exclusion. To cast out, in this sense, is also to capture.

The outlaw status of banished individuals brought them into a close association with animality. Throughout medieval Europe, the bandit-outlaw was specifically associated with an animal–human hybrid of monstrous proportions. The Old Norse word for wolf (*vargr*) was also the legal term for "outlaw"—that is, the wolf is that person who is outside the law.[13] In ancient Germanic law, the term *wargus* was used to refer to both the outlaw and the wolf-man. Similarly, in England, the laws of Edward the Confessor (1030–35) equated the bandit with the werewolf.[14] The negative attitude toward the wolf-outlaw was also reinforced by medieval Christian iconography: Christ was associated with the figure of the lamb, whose eternal enemy, as everyone knew, was the wolf.[15]

The lack of authenticity suffered by those people who are classified as a "refugee" is, therefore, reinforced by their bandit-outlaw heritage. The wolf-man figure that was the medieval bandit also demonstrates the instability that strikes the category of "human" whenever one's life is no longer qualified by the political identity that comes with membership in a political community.[16] Agamben explains the implications of humanity's indeterminacy in such limit situations:

> He who has been banned is not, in fact, simply set outside the law and made indifferent to it but rather abandoned by it, that is, exposed and threatened on the threshold in which life and law, outside and inside, become indistinguishable. It is literally not possible

to say whether the one who has been banned is outside or inside the juridical order.[17]

The banished, therefore, occupy a "zone of indistinction" in which distinctions between inside and outside, self and other, animal and human become indistinguishable. The collapse of this last distinction is particularly relevant, as it demonstrates that at the limit of the political—that is, within the sovereign relation—animality is not a bounded condition separate and distinct from humanity. The distinction is less a stark contrast between two static conceptions of being (human being, animal being) than a complicated and immanent pattern of becoming, with each condition passing in and out of phase with the other. It is in this sense that Brian Massumi refers to so-called bounded spaces as "fields of variation." "Every boundary," Massumi argues, "is present everywhere, potentially. Boundaries are set and specified in the act of passage. The crossing actualizes the boundary—rather than the boundary defining something inside by its inability to cross. There is no transgression. Only a field of exteriority, a network of more or less regulated passages across thresholds."[18]

The "human" has been defined in a complicated reference to animals with a constancy that is truly striking. The Western tradition of political thought repeatedly contrasts humanity with animality, and this contrast is almost always negative and hierarchical.[19] Animal-being is presented as essentially different from human-being. For Aristotle, it was the human being's unique ability to make distinctions between good and evil, the just and the unjust, that distinguished him from animals.[20] For Hobbes, the basis of this division is language. For Rousseau, it is imagination. Hegel argued that animals lacked reflective capacity. Marx noted the absence of any consciousness on behalf of animals of their "species-being." The list can go on and on, but suffice to say, this tradition asserts that the political and ethical worlds belong to humans and cannot include animals. In short, animals are presented as incapable of reasoned speech and so possess no independent will (only nature's command), no intelligence (only the dictates of instinct), and no immortal soul (only mere existence).[21]

In the case of the refugee, it is the absence of speech that plays so negatively on the possibilities for a political subjectivity. The banished individual not only loses claim to a political community and identity but also is banished from the space where political speech is audible. This displacement from meaningful discourse also involves a dislodging of their claim to be human. As Akira Lippit explains, language—the ability to speak—plays a key role in this process of differentiating human beings from other creatures: "Arguably the most sensitive arena in which human subjectivity struggles for dominance is that of language in general, and speech in particular. Most surveys of Western philosophical thought affirm (with a few very important exceptions) the consensus that although animals undoubtedly communicate with one another, only human beings convey their subjectivity in speech.

That is, human speech exceeds its function as communication and actually performs, with each utterance, the subject."[22]

The writings of René Descartes are particularly relevant in this regard. Descartes provided the quintessential modern answer to the question "What makes a person human?" by focusing on what the human is not. Human beings, for Descartes, are neither animals nor machines. Informing this claim is a highly dualistic logic that Descartes employed to insist on a split between mind and body. This fundamental opposition, he argued, involves a hierarchical relation, whereby the mind (as the site of reason, intelligence, and consciousness) is privileged over the body (the locus of instinct, emotion, and machinic motions). While Descartes did admit that humans, animals, and machines all share a capacity for movement, only humans, in his estimation, are capable of engaging in genuine (i.e., rational) speech. The other two remain simple mimics, unconscious automata.[23] Descartes built on a Western tradition that posits a strict segregation between the world of humans and that of animals, sealing the two off with the adhesive of linguistic superiority. The economy of speech is thus highly restrictive and monopolized by humans to establish themselves as authentic subjects.

Like Descartes before him, Rousseau also considered the animal as automata, as an "ingenious machine."[24] Rousseau, however, conceded that animals, by virtue of their sensory capacity, do possess intelligence: "Every animal has ideas, since it has senses."[25] What animals lack is not so much intelligence as imagination. The fundamental difference between animals and humans lies in "the faculty of self-perfection, a faculty which, with the aid of circumstances, successively develops all the others, and resides among us as much in the species as in the individual."[26] For Rousseau, imagination is the means through which the uniquely human characteristic of self-perfection can be realized. However, Rousseau also stipulated that this can be accomplished only if imagination is linked with the human being's linguistic capacity. Like others in the Western tradition, Rousseau also considered the ability to speak as a key means through which humans are differentiated from animals. Animals are equipped with a vocal capacity to broadcast their cry, but they remain incapable of transforming this noise into intelligible speech.

As quickly as these divisions between humans and animals are established, they seem to fall apart. For example, in the following quotation, Rousseau quickly loses command over his own reasoned speech. The discursive divide separating human from animal can also be mistaken as a divide between nations.

> Speech distinguishes man among the animals; language distinguishes nations from each other; one does not know where a man comes from until he has spoken. Out of usage and necessity, each learns the language of his own country. But what determines that this language is that of his country and not of another? In order to

tell, it is necessary to go back to some principle that belongs to the locality itself and antedates its customs, for speech, being the first social institution, owes its form to natural causes alone.[27]

Rousseau, perhaps inadvertently, raises a crucial political problem with these statements. What separates an animal's grunt from the semantics of an unfamiliar tongue? What happens when human speech is mistaken for an animal utterance, when the language of the foreigner becomes Other, not speech but an inarticulate cry? Lippit suggests that what occurs in such circumstances is a subsumption of that foreign voice into a bodily state where all that remains is a kind of "naked" or "bare" life: "Without the semiosis that transforms sounds into words, animal utterances, like the nonsense of foreigners, can only portray the dynamic of affects and bodily states."[28]

Language has a performative aspect that can work toward stabilizing a properly human subjectivity through the identification of an animal-difference. In her examination of the contentious politics of language during the Bosnian war, Emily Apter draws attention to the violent fates suffered by categories of people defined by their incapacity for "authentic" speech. She notes that this was particularly the case when the criteria for qualifying as "human" relied on the deployment of terms that could easily and ambiguously slide between notions of humanity and animality. In the context of a general program of "ethnic cleansing," the discursive deployment of animality proved to be extremely hazardous to human life, as Apter explains in a succinct, yet harrowing manner:

> The use of "human" as a restrictive category can designate certain types of people. I'm thinking here of specific examples in Bosnia where very finite, small differences in Serbo-Croatian (or what used to be Serbo-Croatian) were used to determine whether you are animal or a human. As Michael Holquist has pointed out, everyone was assumed to be speaking some kind of language, but humans were speaking Serbian as it was understood in Bosnia, and so the others, then, were dismissed as animal, and could be shot like dogs.[29]

The technology by which human beings get "shot like dogs" is not simply a crude material one (firearms) but a discursive one as well. Indeed, the material practice (shooting a gun) relies on a prior discursive formation (uttering "animal") having already taken place. In other words, the human becomes a "restrictive category" in a political sense through the deployment of language. When the conditions of possibility for violence include a discursive construction of animality, paying attention to the politics of language therefore becomes of critical importance. Indeed, the stakes involved in these exclusionary utterances are tremendous, as Apter readily concedes: "Whether or not you can be shot like a dog thus becomes ominously entwined with intersubjective boundaries between dogginess and the human."[30]

We are confronted, then, with a paradox, and one that further complicates the refugee's relationship with his or her "humanity." On one hand, language is what makes humans distinct from animals. The discursive construction of "humanity" involves a simultaneous effacement of "animality" to bring about its presence. As Lippit notes, "The effort to define the human being has usually required a preliminary gesture of exclusion: a rhetorical animal sacrifice. The presence of the animal must first be extinguished for the human being to appear."[31] At the same time, however, language makes the distinction between humans and animals indistinct. As the examples from Rousseau and Apter make clear, the human–animal divide is not a chasm but rather an ambiguous, intersubjective, and dangerous discursive terrain.

Interned Identities

The connections between the refugee's animality and his or her incarceration, lack of authenticity, and missing political voice run very deep and constitute a very complicated politics. A key feature of these political relationships is the spatial and temporal ordering of the human–animal division. There is a temptation to conceive this division with an eye to segment the two worlds as opposites, each removed from the other. As we shall see in this section, however, the constitution of sovereign power (as the state of exception) requires that the human–animal relation be indeterminate, ambiguous, and indistinctive. While the modern state claims to provide the spatial conditions for citizens to realize their "humanity," at the limit of the state the sovereign relation passes in and out of phase with both animality and humanity. The practices of state sovereignty work to tame the contingency of these fluid relations by declaring them temporary and containing, reterritorializing them within the space of the camp. These practices place severe limitations on the hospitality available to refugees, as will become evident with reference to the Canadian state's responses to recent refugee crises.

To begin to understand the complexity of the human–animal relation, I want to consider the thoughts of Emmanuel Levinas on this matter. While not a refugee, Levinas speaks from the personal experience of someone who was incarcerated in a Nazi prisoner of war camp. We can learn much from his reflections on this experience. The seventy prisoners of war in this camp were all Jewish, but as Levinas explained, "the French uniform still protected us from Hitlerian violence."[32] He described the debilitating effect the gaze of human beings from outside the camp had on the prisoners. These people, whom Levinas called "free," possessed all of the rights of citizenship, thus making them fully human in the eyes of the inmates. Whenever the gaze of these people fell on the prisoners, Levinas declared that he and his fellow inmates found themselves propelled into a state of animality:

But the other men, called free, who had dealings with us or gave us work or orders or even a smile—and the children and women who passed by and sometimes raised their eyes—stripped us of our human skin. We were subhuman, a gang of apes. A small inner murmur, the strength and wretchedness of persecuted people, reminded us of our essence as thinking creatures, but we were no longer part of the world. Our comings and goings, our sorrow and laughter, illness and distractions, the work of our hands and the anguish of our eyes, the letters we received from France and those accepted for our families—all that passed in parenthesis. We were beings entrapped in their species; despite all their vocabulary, beings without language.[33]

Levinas explains how the experience of life outside the sovereign identity of citizenship makes one less than human. The lives of the prisoners exist in a state of exception; they were "no longer part of the world" of human beings. Instead, they lived their lives "in parenthesis" to an outside world where comings and goings, sorrow and laughter possessed meaning. Their interaction with an outside humanity had the paradoxical effect of removing their "human skin," revealing a bare life and forcing them to identify themselves as animal, as "a gang of apes," as "beings without language."

A curious contrast between human and animal emerges from Levinas's narrative, one that opposes articulate speech with meaningless verbiage. As we have seen, this division builds on a tradition of thought that considers animals not as they are but as a negative reference point to stabilize the meaning of humanity. What is significant here is that despite all of the pronouncements that insist on the essential difference between humans and animals, these divisions seem to dissolve at the limit of the camp. To the citizen-humans outside the camp, and certainly to the inmates, the camp fence was a borderline separating a full humanity from a naked life that was more animal than human. In Levinas's situation, it took a wandering dog—who, ironically enough, sought temporary refuge in the camp—to identify the humanity common to the French prisoners and German citizens alike. To this dog, given the exotic name "Bobby" by the inmates, such divisions were imperceptible. They were literally nonsensical, an imperceptible construction unique to the human world. Bobby—"the last Kantian in Nazi Germany"—had no difficulty recognizing a human being: "He would appear at morning assembly and was waiting for us as we returned, jumping up and down and barking in delight. For him, there was no doubt that we were men."[34]

Levinas's recollections reveal the great deal of confusion and anxiety that surrounds the humanity–animality nexus. He declared his puzzlement about the highly qualified form-of-life found within the camp: "How can we deliver a message about our humanity which, from behind the bars of quotation marks, will come across as anything other than monkey talk?"[35] His uncertain subject-position within the narrative (is he a human or an ape?) also points to how this unstable identity is closely connected to regimes of power and control. In this sense, "What makes us human?" is an incredibly political question. To inquire into the conditions of possibility for this human–animal (in)distinction, we must therefore establish its connection to the idea of the political. This means turning our attention once again to the practices of sovereign power.

The relationship between sovereignty and animality has often been presented as one of mutual exclusion. In the early modern era, when political theorists such as Hobbes, Bodin, and Pufendorf were working out the ontological conditions of sovereignty, the world of animals was considered outside the realm of the political and the civilized. The French historian of the *longue durée*, Fernand Braudel, emphasized this split at the very beginning of his three-volume history of capitalism and civilization in the early modern era. Braudel made the point that, from a global perspective, the demographic "weight of numbers" of animals far outreached the small inroads made by human settlements.[36] Despite their universal pretensions, human civilizations were relatively small players on the planet, the exception to the norm of vast, unpopulated lands devoid of sedentary human communities. For Braudel, to exit the "civilized" spaces of cities, states, and empires is to venture into a state of nature, animals, and "wild men." Whereas civilized space consists of highly differentiated social bodies, outside this space there was only "empty, echoing wastelands" in which "primitive life" lurked and where the "saga of man and the animals" was played out.[37] To encounter the forces of animality, therefore, is to reside in a space where one's capacity to remain "human" (rational, autonomous, cultured) is seriously undermined. Perhaps this is what Hobbes meant when he referred to life in the state of nature as a condition where "man is a wolf to men."[38]

Animality, therefore, is both spatially and temporally removed from humanity; it is a condition defined by being outside and before the political. However, despite Braudel's declaration that wild animals "are to be found wherever man is not,"[39] the line dividing the civilized and wild, the human and the animal, is both obscure and ambiguous. The two worlds intermingle and interact, with each transforming the other.[40] The "wild" and the "civilized" operate less like bounded entities than like qualities that are in constant variation with one another. For our present purposes, this "zone of indistinction" that marks the human–animal divide takes on a political importance whenever we are confronted with situations where we are motivated to relate to each other as humans (i.e., when the political category of citizen no longer applies). It is precisely in these situations that the human–animal distinction begins to collapse, exposing its woolly character to all those involved.

Canada was faced with such a situation in the spring and summer of 1999, when two refugee "crises" forced the nation to confront its capacity for hospitality. From all outward appearances, the hospitality Canada demonstrated toward the Kosovar refugees stands in stark contrast to the profoundly inhospitable treatment offered to the Chinese refugee claimants who appeared in four boats off the British Columbia coast later that summer. Indeed, to compare these two cases is to seemingly enter into a study of contrasts. On one hand, Canadians responded with great enthusiasm to the news that their government had agreed to participate in the international "humanitarian evacuation" program. The United Nations High Commissioner for Refugees (UNHCR) coordinated this project, which saw eighty-five thousand refugees airlifted to thirty-two countries outside the Balkan region. The Canadian government agreed to accept five thousand Kosovar refugees to relieve Balkan countries overwhelmed by the hundreds of thousands of forcibly displaced people during the NATO bombings of Kosovo and Serbia. This show of hospitality had great appeal, as it seemed to confirm a commonly held view among Canadians that their country acted like a "moral superpower" in world affairs.[41] For instance, Prime Minister Jean Chretien expressed his hope that Canadians will sponsor Kosovar refugees much in the same way they sponsored Vietnamese refugees in the 1970s: "I'd like that very much. The people of Canada are those type of people, that they want to welcome them and help them."[42] That type of people, of course, is a reference to Canada's self-conception as a hospitable culture and humanitarian nation.

Derrida's insights on hospitality are relevant here, for while he suggested that there exists an equivalence between hospitality and culture ("Hospitality—this is culture itself"),[43] the culture of hospitality articulated by the Canadian prime minister is severely limited in both its form and its content. As Derrida argued, "If the welcome is the simple manifestation of a natural or acquired disposition, of a generous character, of a hospitable habitus, there is no merit in it, no welcome to the other as other."[44] Like Janus, hospitality has two faces: "Hospitality as it exposes itself to the visit, to the visitation, and the hospitality that adorns and prepares itself in invitation."[45] Consequently, while the Kosovar refugees were in Canada by invitation, and welcomed as guests, the unexpected appearance of four ships carrying 599 people, mostly from China's Fujian province, elicited an entirely different response from Canadians. That nearly all the boat people claimed refugee status seemed to matter not. From the outset they were met with extreme hostility. "Go Home!" screamed the front-page headline of the Victoria *Times-Colonist* after the second boat reached British Columbia's shores. "Enough Already!" echoed the Vancouver *Province*.[46] The *Globe and Mail* gave front-page exposure to the views of the head of the British Columbia Royal Canadian Mounted Police (RCMP) immigration unit, who, with no firsthand knowledge of the details of their claims, declared that these asylum seekers were bogus refugees, queue jumpers, and liars.[47] By the time the third rusty, decrepit ship was spotted off the northern tip of Vancouver Island on August 31, 1999, public opinion polls were showing that 51 percent of Canadians wanted their country to "do no more or no less than what most other countries do to take in political refugees."[48] In other words, faced with the appearance of uninvited strangers, many Canadians wanted to seriously limit their hospitality and did not want to distinguish themselves as "humanitarian," as "that type of people."

Derrida's distinction between invitation and visitation aside, what is remarkable in both situations is that despite the apparent dissimilarity in official and public reaction, the two cases share many commonalities. These similarities are particularly apparent in terms of the spatial and temporal ordering of refugee identity. In both cases, the terms of hospitality demonstrated by the Canadian state had serious temporal and spatial qualifications: both groups of refugees were, from the outset, declared short-term strangers and both were detained within highly controlled spaces. The implications of this were that each group of refugees suffered a kind of ontological reduction as political beings by virtue of being conferred temporary and incarcerated identities.

In terms of the Chinese refugee claimants, they were deemed illegitimate and criminal from the start, and so their stay in Canada was to be both temporary and incarcerated. Upon their appearance on British Columbia's shores, they were subjected to representational practices that portrayed them as criminals. The asylum seekers were strip-searched, and they appeared in public only from behind fences, under hoods, shackled and handcuffed, and accompanied by heavy police guard—all of which implied serious wrongdoing and criminal activity. At first, the majority of the asylum seekers were housed in tents in makeshift detention camps; others were detained in an old military gymnasium at the Canadian Forces Base (CFB) in Esquimalt. As winter approached, they were transferred to prisons across British Columbia, a move that was often criticized, but only on the basis of the high costs of detention! The detained Chinese asylum seekers were cast as a financial burden on the Canadian taxpayer, and calls for their immediate deportation became more and more insistent.[49] Incredibly, the editorial writers of the *Globe and Mail* called on the federal Liberal government to invoke the "notwithstanding" clause of the Canadian constitution (essentially a codified form of the state of exception, as it allows for the government to suspend basic rights and freedoms "notwithstanding" their protection in the Constitution) to give the asylum seekers an "expeditious deportation to China."[50]

The official response to the public pressure was twofold: on one hand, the Citizenship and Immigration Minister reaffirmed her government's commitment to provide all refugee claimants with a hearing. Mass deportations were not an option: "Not while I am Minister. Not on my watch. That is guaranteed." At the same time, however, the refugee determination process for these refugees was accelerated to an unreasonable pace: "illegal migrants" would "be removed as quickly as possible."[51] Faced with incarceration and accelerated hearings, many of the asylum seekers participated in hunger strikes to protest their treatment. Chinese refugees held in a Burnaby prison for women, describe their situation in a letter to a local refugee advocacy group:

> This is a prison. We long to see the world outside. We dream of being like the people outside—welcoming and celebrating the millennium. We need the care and support of the well-informed people outside. We ask for your help. We are Chinese women who have fled here. We look forward to the day when we can live in freedom. We hope that you can extend your helping hand. Please come to visit and comfort us—we, the sisters from China who long for our freedom.[52]

Local refugee advocate groups such as Direct Action against Refugee Exploitation (DAARE) protested that the refugees were not getting a fair hearing, as they had been denied sufficient legal counsel and adequate interpreter services. A representative from the Vancouver Association of Chinese Canadians charged that the whole legitimacy of the refugee determination process was at risk: "These are lightning decisions. Adjudicators are not fully considering the cases. It's a sham, dressed up as a full hearing."[53]

If the Chinese asylum seekers were greeted with suspicion, distrust, and hostility, the Canadian response to the Kosovar refugee crisis was portrayed as magnanimous, generous, and hospitable. Canada, after all, is a member of NATO and was a participant in the military actions in Kosovo and Serbia. However, while Canada quickly responded to the UNHCR's request for participation in the Kosovar emergency humanitarian evacuation program, the hospitality demonstrated to the Kosovar refugees had remarkably similar spatial and temporal qualities that were later given to the Chinese refugees. In the first place, the nearly five thousand Kosovar refugees were housed not in the homes of individual sponsors, government housing, or motels as is usually the case but in military bases isolated from large population centers. The incoming Kosovars were first flown to either CFB Trenton in Ontario or CFB Greenwood in Nova Scotia's Annapolis Valley. From there, they were transferred to six other military bases in Ontario and the Maritimes.[54]

In addition to their encampment, the Kosovar refugees were given a highly qualified, temporary refugee status. The refugees were brought into Canada under the conditions outlined in a "temporary protection" arrangement with the UNHCR. The terms of this arrangement were such that the UNHCR conferred Convention refugee status to the Kosovars in advance of their departure for Canada. The immigration officials at the Canadian Refugee Board were thereby bypassed, and the Kosovar refugees were given speedy entrance into Canada. The origins of the temporary protection program lie principally in the European response to the refugee flows arising from the conflict in Bosnia-Herzegovina in the early 1990s. While not very well codified in law, temporary protection schemes nonetheless appear in a number of guises. In Europe, this category of refugee status is variously referred to as "B or C status," Duldung (tolerance), Aufenthaltsbefugnis (right to remain), "exceptional leave to remain," or "humanitarian status." In the United States, it is referred to as "temporary protected status."[55] The UNHCR explains the rationale of these programs: "Falling short of full refugee status, these alternative classifications allow asylum-seekers who might not qualify for refugee status to remain at the discretion of the authorities until it is deemed safe for them to return home."[56] In the case of the Kosovars, however, they were given temporary status even though UNHCR officials positively identified each individual as a bona fide Convention refugee. What's more, as was the case of the Bosnian refugees, the problem faced by the Kosovars with their temporary status was that they lacked sufficient protection from refoulement; that is, they were forced into a situation where their human security—let alone their human rights—could not be reasonably ensured.

Both the Kosovar refugees and the Chinese migrants had a peculiar relationship with Canadian society outside the walls of their confinement. The gaze conferred on them produced an animal effect not unlike the one described by Levinas. In both cases, the refugees were given not a civil refuge but a highly policed and militarized hospitality. The exceptional status endured by both the Kosovar refugees and the Chinese refugees in terms of their temporary status was reproduced spatially in terms of their housing. This remains the case even though it is true that their accommodations were unquestionably superior to their experiences in the overcrowded refugee camps in Macedonia and the cramped and dangerous conditions aboard the migrants' decrepit ships. To be sure, they both had all their basic needs (food, shelter, medicine) met in these comparatively comfortable conditions. However, the space of the camp is not limited to the kind of camp that Levinas found himself in—that is, the system of camps employed by the Nazi regime. The camp does not have to correspond to any specific historical, architectural, or topographical criteria. Rather, following Agamben, any space in which the "normal" rule of law is suspended can qualify as a camp.

> The soccer stadium in Bari in which the Italian police temporarily herded Albanian illegal immigrants in 1991 before sending them back to their country, the cycle-racing track in which the Vichy authorities rounded up the Jews before handing them over to the Germans, the refugee camp near the Spanish border where Antonio Machado died in 1939, as well as the zones d'attente in French international airports in which foreigners requesting refugee status are detained will have to be considered camps.[57]

For Agamben, the camp is the space that materializes whenever the state of exception becomes the rule.[58] It is a space that makes room for naked life, that which is barely human. Agamben described the paradoxes involved with analyzing the camp as a space of exception:

> The camp is a piece of territory that is placed outside the normal juridical order; for all that, however, it is not simply an external space. According to the etymological meaning of the term exception (*excapere*), what is being excluded in the camp is captured outside, that is, it is included by virtue of its very exclusion. Thus, what is being captured under the rule of law is first of all the very state of exception. In other words, if the sovereign power is founded on the ability to decide on the state of exception, the camp is the structure in which the state of exception is permanently realized.[59]

If the space of the camp is also a space of exception that, as we have seen, lies at the heart of the sovereign relation, then the animal–human hybrid identity that is produced by this space cuts to the heart of our conceptions of the political.

Becoming Human: Responding to the Refugee's Pitiful Cry

Hannah Arendt remarked on the curious connection between refugees, humanitarian action, and animality in *Imperialism*, the second volume of her trilogy *The Origins of Totalitarianism*. Her insights on this matter are first revealed in an observation about the acute identity crisis facing refugees:

> Only fame will eventually answer the repeated complaint of refugees of all social strata that "nobody here knows who I am"; and it is true that the chances of the famous refugee are improved just as a dog with a name has a better chance to survive than a stray dog who is just a dog in general.[60]

Arendt then went on to make a remarkable observation about the international efforts to provide humanitarian assistance to refugees and the stateless. She examined the constitutions of the voluntary humanitarian societies working to assist refugees—the precursors to present-day nongovernmental organizations (NGOs)—as well as their declarations of solidarity with the forcibly displaced. Arendt noted that these pronouncements all "showed an uncanny similarity in language and composition to that of societies for the prevention of cruelty to animals."[61] Arendt, of course, would go on to write some very strong words about the sovereign state's hegemony over humanity, noting how this monopoly puts severe limits on the type of ethical responsibility states have to humans lacking the political status of citizenship. However, she never directly expanded on the connection she established between refugeeness and animality. In this section, I attempt to make some of these connections by establishing the links between the humane treatment of animals and that of refugees.

The societies for the prevention of cruelty to animals to which Arendt referred have their origins in the early nineteenth century. In England, the Society for the Prevention of Cruelty to Animals (SPCA) was established in 1824, just two years after the Animal Protection Act made history by outlawing cruelty to cattle, horses, and sheep for the first time in a Western country. After Queen Victoria gave royal approbation to the SPCA in 1840, thus certifying the prestige of the now Royal SPCA, the movement to treat animals in a more humane fashion began to spread throughout Europe and across the Atlantic.[62] In Canada, the first humane society, the Canadian Society for the Prevention of Cruelty to Animals (CSPCA) was founded in Montreal in 1869.[63] Its stated mandate was "to provide effective means for the prevention of cruelty to animals throughout the Dominion of Canada." Its earliest campaigns focused on improving the conditions of workhorses, who suffered from regular beatings, overloading, starvation, and neglect. It was not long, however, before the activities of the CSPCA expanded to preventing cockfights and the killing of wild birds, as well as ensuring the humane treatment of dogs.

The emergence of humane societies coincided with historical developments that were radically calling into question the traditional distinctions made between animals and humans. In the nineteenth century, the writings of Charles Darwin introduced a profound rupture in humanity's relationship with animals. His theory on the evolution of humanity set out in *The Descent of Man* seeks to demonstrate that no fundamental difference exists in the mental faculties of humans and higher mammals. Darwin explicitly rejected the idea of an essential humanity; he refused to treat qualities such as reason, intellect, self-consciousness, and the ability to communicate as uniquely human attributes. These qualities are also shared by (some) animals, although to a lesser degree. The radical character of Darwin's ideas had a tremendous impact on Western conceptions of humanity and their relationship with animality. However, as Kay Anderson argues, despite—or perhaps, because of—the radical character of Darwin's theories, "certain ideas about the felt sense of 'human' stubbornly persisted."[64] The idea was that humans were divided beings, with a "physical" animal side and a "cultural-moral" human aspect. To be truly human was thus a pedagogical exercise of cultivating one's capacity to ascend out of instinct, savagery, and passion.[65]

Neither the CSPCA nor its English, French, and American counterparts were motivated by a vision of animal rights. At the time, the idea of human rights (or, more accurately, the Rights of Man) was still relatively new and there existed a huge discrepancy in the distribution of these rights, which were (to put it mildly) unequally allocated across gender, age, race, and class lines. In fact, in most jurisdictions, animal cruelty laws predated child protection legislation. Indeed, the children employed in English mines in the mid-nineteenth century often worked longer hours than the pit mules that were protected by animal cruelty laws. It took the initiative of the secretary of the RSPCA to establish the National Society for the Prevention of Cruelty to Children in 1884, sixty years after the establishment of the SPCA. Note, however, that the English Parliament ensured the security of working machines—making the Luddite campaign of machine-breaking a capital offense—in 1812, long before either the child laborer or the working animal enjoyed such protection. Humanitarianism indeed!

The public advocacy for the legal protection of animals was made not on the grounds of their inherent rights as living beings but rather because their suffering was an affront to the principles of humanity. Following the challenge posed by Darwin and others, the humane societies took the position that being human involves certain kinds of behavior, and abusing animals unnecessarily was not one of them.[66] Such behavior, it was declared, is not human but bestial. However, if a society's relationship with animals was judged as a measure of its civilized character, then the measure of "civilized" employed by the early humane societies was unmistakably a bourgeois determination. The early humane societies were an elite bunch, with aristocratic patrons, wealthy and influential leaders, and a solidly middle-class membership base. As for the working classes, James Turner argues that "there is no evidence of a significant presence of manual workers or artisans in any SPCA activity during the nineteenth century, with the exception of a few public meetings specifically drummed up to enlighten-while-entertaining teamsters, cab drivers, and the like."[67]

In this sense, it is not surprising to find that the early SPCAs did not limit their activities to the legal domain. The task of promoting a humane ethos throughout society required something more than advocating for new statutes and bylaws, however significant they may be. The task of educating society to behave in a humane manner was of paramount concern, especially with respect to the young and members of the lower classes. There was a strong belief that "training in kindness might yet root out the hatred, cruelty and anarchy thought to flourish in the lower classes. Public safety demanded that the people, wild animals in the nation's midst, be tamed."[68] It is in this spirit, to take but one example, that the CSPCA established the Ladies' Humane Education Committee, which was formed "for the promotion of the systematic education of the young in the principles of humanity, and by early training to inculcate in their minds the duty of kindness and consideration to all dumb creatures."[69] To support this education campaign, the society sponsored essay competitions and offered prizes and scholarships as well as published periodicals and calendars. From the perspective of humane societies, therefore, to be human is not simply to follow a biological imperative. Humanity, in their understanding, is not open to just any human-animal. Rather, to become human involves a disciplining of the self in accordance to hegemonic constructions of gender, racial, and class identities. To behave counter to these prevailing constructions risks one being conferred a bestial status.

Let us return to Arendt's observation of the animal character conferred upon individuals and groups who have lost everything (home, country, political identity) except their humanity. That the refugee had become subsumed within a discourse of animality is, at least in part, an effect of the success of the kind of discourses about human civilization promoted by humane societies. Referring to the problem of massive refugee flows, Arendt stated,

> The trouble is that this calamity arose not from any lack of civilization, backwardness, or mere tyranny, but, on the contrary, that it could not be repaired, because there was no longer any "uncivilized" spot on earth, because whether we like it or not we have really started to live in One World. Only with a completely organized humanity could the loss of home and political status become identical with expulsion from humanity altogether.[70]

As we have seen, to be outside of humanity is to be conferred animal status, one that is both prepolitical and speechless. Thus, the humanitarian societies responding to the suffering of refugees reacted not to an articulate appeal for assistance but to an inarticulate cry for help that precedes civilized discourse. The cry of the refugee, moreover, is closely connected to the cry of animals, the howl of the wolf. But as we saw earlier with respect to Rousseau and Apter, confusing human language with animal utterances can lead to serious problems.

From this perspective, refugees are precast to speak a language not too dissimilar to what Rousseau called the cry of nature—a primordial tongue that results from "a kind of instinct in pressing circumstances, to beg for help in great dangers, or for relief of violent ills."[71] To be sure, Rousseau's political writings offer some of the richest textual landscapes to witness the interaction between discourses on humanity and animality. In his *Discourse on the Origin of Inequality*, Rousseau offered a retrospective analysis of the origins of language. This venture led him to envision a prehistoric condition where animals and humans lived side by side, each equally residing within a state of nature: "In such a state as this man only knows himself; he does not see his own well-being to be identified with or contrary to that of anyone else; he neither hates anything nor loves anything; but limited to no more than physical instinct, he is no one, he is an animal."[72] In this situation, human language is purely affective, entirely animal: "Man's first language, the most universal, the most energetic and the only language he needed before it was necessary to persuade men assembled together, is the cry of nature."[73]

The linkage between the humanitarian responses to the suffering of refugees and the suffering of animals that Arendt spoke of in Imperialism lies in this incoherent yet unmistakable cry. The problem with being motivated to act in a humanitarian fashion by such cries is that the response is often propelled by feelings of pity. In *On Revolution*, Arendt offered a truncated critique of the morality of pity, arguing that this sentiment always involves the twin dimensions of detachment and generality.[74] Pity, she said, operates at a "sentimental distance" and relies on the deployment of generalizations to manage this detachment.[75] The key generalization here is that of a sharp, hierarchical distinction between those who suffer and those who do not. Luc Boltanski argues that what results from this generalized detachment is a kind of "spectacle of suffering."[76] This spectacle involves a series of spatial distinctions between here–there that closely follows the sovereign logic of inside–outside, safety–danger. Accordingly, those who suffer are elsewhere, "over there," where there is danger, violence, and bestial behavior. Those who do not suffer—the pitiers—are thus satisfied that here there is safety, civility, and humane behavior. In this sense, pity always involves a political relation. As Arendt explained,

> Pity does not look upon both fortune and misfortune, the strong and the weak, with an equal eye; without the presence of misfortune, pity could not exist, and it therefore has just as much vested interest in the existence of the unhappy as thirst for power has a vested interest in the existence of the weak. Moreover, by virtue of being a sentiment, pity can be enjoyed for its own sake, and this will almost automatically lead to a glorification of its cause, which is the suffering of others.[77]

Arendt is very pessimistic of the idea that pity is in any way a salvageable concept. "Pity," she said, "has proved to possess a greater capacity for cruelty than cruelty itself."[78] David Campbell makes a similar linkage in his identification of the "pitiful dimension" of contemporary humanitarian practice. Drawing on Nietzsche's critique of morality, Campbell points to how the morality of pity quickly becomes a politics of pity when people engage with the object of pity "as a means to increase their position and control." Campbell notes that "the object of pity would remain a victim regardless of the amount of attention directed their way, whereas the pitier would markedly increase their satisfaction and superiority. And if you think of Operation Provide Comfort in Iraq and Restore Hope in Somalia, the question is: whose comfort, whose hope?"[79]

Refugees do work hard to avoid the imposition of animal qualities into the expectations of refugeeness. During the period between the first and second world wars, for instance, refugees were eager to maintain the condition of national identity as a criterion for refugee status. Arendt argued that nationality, as the last vestige of a state identity, was considered by refugees as all that separated them from a "humanity" that was nothing short of an entirely bestial identity. Arendt noted that for refugees,

> the abstract nakedness of being nothing but human was their greatest danger. Because of it they were regarded as savages and, afraid that they might end by being considered beasts, they insisted on their nationality, the last sign of their former citizenship, as their

only remaining and recognized tie with humanity. Their distrust of natural, their preference for national, rights comes precisely from their realization that natural rights are granted even to savages.[80]

Today, the strict individualism of international refugee law removes the appeal to nationhood for refugees "afraid that they might end by being considered beasts." Instead, the humanity to which the modern refugee belongs condemns him or her to a bare life, lacking political qualification, that is at considerable risk of being indistinguishable from animal life.

The visual representations of the Kosovar and Chinese refugees reinforced the ontological reduction already imposed on them by their temporary, incarcerated identities. In the case of the Kosovars, the representations that dominated the mainstream media were of tragic sentimentalized images. One of the most widely distributed and discussed images was the cover photograph of the April 12, 1999, issue of *Time* magazine. In a cutting critique, Margaret Stetz analyzes to the social construction of the Kosovar woman refugee on the cover as "Woman as Mother in a Headscarf." Stetz described the cover image as

> a half-length photograph of a woman carrying an infant in her arms, with the headscarf encircling her face creating a visual echo of the swaddling cloth around the child. Indeed, the photograph was cropped to emphasize the inseparability of this pairing, for it cut off the woman's body at the waist, just at the point where the child's body ended, as though to render superfluous any part of the woman unconnected to support the child.[81]

The tragic and sentimental character of this photograph, Stetz argues, is not a neutral representation but rather an attempt to evoke feelings of pity among the viewing audience to support the so-called humanitarian bombing operations of their governments.

Stetz's reference to the cropping of the photograph is significant as it opens a space for interrogating the political dimensions of the image. Cropping, after all, undercuts the photojournalist's claim that she is merely showing us the world "as it is." Cropping necessarily involves exclusion; it consists of a variety of interventions on the part of the photographer, the developer, the editor, and so on to decide what will be included and what will be excluded. As such, cropping is an inherently political act. Understood this way, the cropping of the refugee woman involves a regime of power not dissimilar to the cropping of pornographic images. Kobena Mercer explains,

> The cropping and fragmentation of bodies—often decapitated, so to speak—is a salient feature of pornography, and has been seen from certain feminist positions as a form of male violence, a literal inscription of a sadistic impulse in the male gaze, whose pleasure thus consists of cutting up women's bodies into visual bits and pieces.[82]

In this case, the humanitarian gaze cuts the refugee body into "bits and pieces" in the sense that the refugee woman is presented in the barest terms. We don't know her name, her personal history, or anything else that would distinguish her as speaking human subject. Rather, these representations· imply that this refugee is a bare life, with only basic needs such as food, shelter, and medicine. Stetz establishes a connection between this bare life and animality when she notes that "the sentimentalized 'Woman as Mother in a Headscarf,' like a stray dog in an ASPCA poster, needs only scraps from your table and a corner on your floor. But real refugee women, as Virginia Woolf might have said, ask for a room of their own, just as you would."[83]

In the case of the nearly five thousand Kosovar refugees that Canada accepted under the UNHCR brokered "temporary protection" agreement, the politics of pity affected the type of welcome given to these refugees. In the May 17, 1999, issue of *Maclean's* magazine, an article titled "Flight from Terror" covered the events surrounding the arrival of the refugees. Two photographs, prominently placed on the first two pages of the article, capture the overall sentiment surrounding the Canadian government's offer of asylum. In each photograph, a smiling Canadian is portrayed demonstrating her hospitality toward a Kosovar refugee: one guides an exhausted and disoriented older "woman in a headscarf;" another poses with a small and bewildered boy holding a Canadian flag. Derrida noted that a culture of hospitality is inseparable from a culture of smile: "it is hard to imagine a scene of hospitality during which one welcomes without smiling at the other, without giving a sign of joy or pleasure."[84] This hospitality, as noted earlier, has two faces, and we should be careful to discern which face is smiling in this context. Here, it is important to note how both photographs bear an uncanny resemblance to familiar representations of people with domesticated animals, especially those employed by humane societies during adoption drives. The visual message in these representations encourages Canadians to think of sponsoring a refugee in the same way that they would consider adopting a pet. The shared caption offers a dialectical explanation of Canadian hospitality: "delight—and sadness." Here, the inside–outside borders of the sovereign relation firmly establish the space of "delight" as within the state while banishing "sadness" to the space of the international. For the Canadian hosts, while there is delight in meeting and hosting the Kosovar refugees, there is also sadness (i.e., pity) in contemplating their plight. For the Kosovars, there is delight in reaching a welcoming environment such as Canada and sadness in what they have lost to get there. In both cases, however, it is the Canadian citizen who claims that status of pitier; sadness, by contrast, is bare condition suffered by the refugees—the pitied.

The Chinese refugees, by contrast, would have only wished for as much hospitality as a dog would receive. Indeed, the second migrant ship that reached the shores of British Columbia included a dog among the passengers. The Victoria SPCA was overwhelmed by more than four hundred

offers from people all over the country to adopt the refugee-dog. One jour-
nalist writing for Vancouver magazine took a unique, if unscientific, approach to test public opinion on the issue by setting up a table outside a
local Vancouver drugstore and asking people to sign a petition in support
of the Chinese refugees. After twenty minutes, the petition was changed
to support the dog that was found among one of the migrants' ships. Steve
Burgess related the results of his experiment:

> That the dog garnered more support than the humans (8-to-1) was
> depressingly predictable. The surprising part was the starkness of
> the contrast. When I plumped for refugees, old ladies hissed at me.
> A bona fide white supremacist treated me to a finger-jabbing rant.
> Up went the dog sign, and suddenly it was a love-in. Best of all
> was the lady who entered the store while my refugee sign was up,
> and emerged only after I had switched over to the dog crusade.
> Evidently she had been stewing about my support for the boat
> people while she shopped, because upon leaving the store she im-
> mediately approached my table and began to berate me. "Oh no,
> look, ma'am," I protested, pointing to the sign. "We're working for
> dogs."
>
> "Oh!" she said, taken aback. "It's dogs you care about! Oh well, I
> agree with that. Sure I'll sign."[85]

In contrast to "man's best friend," there was nothing "domestic" about the
character of the Chinese migrants: they were presented as entirely foreign,
untrustworthy, and dangerous.

Microsoft Refugee?

Emergency situations are notorious for creating an atmosphere where "denunciations, gossip, innuendo, and rumours" proliferate, creating a climate
of suspicion where "no one can be sure who is who."[86] Is that person a genuine refugee or an economic migrant? Is she a helpless victim, fearful of being persecuted, and thus worthy of humanitarian assistance and protection?
Or is she a queue jumper, a bogus refugee, and thus unworthy of anything
except criminalization, incarceration, and an expedited deportation? This
chapter has thus far demonstrated how the discourse of animality influ-
ences such distinctions. Refugees are labeled human, but their relationship
to this concept is structured by an "inclusive exclusion" whereby they are
discursively and visually cast as animal. As we saw earlier with Descartes,
however, the modern conception of the human is also predicated on this
assumption that humans are not machines. Yet a machinic—or rather, cy-
bernetic—identity is increasingly being imposed on refugees in emergency
situations where it is difficult to determine "who is who."

Into this confusion around refugee identity enters the Microsoft Corporation. During the Kosovar refugee crisis, Microsoft led a consortium of international business interests to create a Refugee Field Kit for the electronic registration of refugees flowing into border regions of Albania and Macedonia. Microsoft supplied the software, Hewlett-Packard and Compaq supplied the hardware, and Securit World in London and ScreenCheck BV in the Netherlands provided their expertise in identification-card systems. Weighing only 45 kilograms, the portable and durable equipment consists of specially designed software, laptop computers, digital cameras, a power generator, and special identification-card printers. Humanitarian aid workers used the technology to enter the relevant biographical and demographic details of the refugees they interviewed into a database. An identification card with the refugee's photograph and signature could then be issued.

In her keynote address to Tech-Ed 2000 Europe, a Microsoft technology expo held in Amsterdam in June 2000, the then UN High Commissioner for Refugees Sadako Ogata explained why her agency was joining forces with Microsoft on this project:

> Let me explain why registration is so important. Becoming a refugee is a dehumanizing experience. A refugee identity card can represent the first important step toward restoring an individual's sense of self. A computerized registration database also enables distraught people to locate missing family members, including lost children, with great speed.[87]

In a world where refugee-dogs are given asylum while human-refugees are detained, Ogata claimed that our "common humanity" will be realized only once the "digital divide" is bridged. As a Microsoft press release stated, once the field kits were distributed, "in a short time, hundreds of thousands of refugees were given their identities back and reconnected with their lives."[88] A Microsoft employee who volunteered on the project echoed this connection between an authentic human self and technology: "When you see first-hand that it is possible to put computers to work in one of the hardest places on Earth—a refugee camp, in a war zone, without electricity or air conditioning—it makes you realize just how much technology can do. You can improve the human condition and restore to people their sense of self. That is a powerful thing."[89]

Microsoft's hospitality is not without its conditions. In the first place, companies such as Microsoft are always interested in expanding their global reach so that they can penetrate new markets. One UNHCR official reported that during the Kosovar refugee crisis the agency was "overwhelmed" by "dozens" of offers to provide electronic registration software and equipment. Smaller companies that placed bids on the project, such as Australia's LanCom Technologies, were simply overwhelmed by the resources available to the computer industry giant.[90] In addition to supplying the software and building a coalition of industry partners, Microsoft also donated

US$600,000 in cash and US$500,000 in services, and thirty-five Microsoft employees from nine countries volunteered on the project. Moreover, the William H. Gates Foundation donated an additional US$600,000.

Second, despite the rhetoric, it is unclear as to how much this technology lived up to its claim to bridge the "digital divide." The technology, after all, is most immediately useful to outside humanitarian actors, such as the UNHCR, and military actors providing humanitarian assistance, as NATO did during its intervention into Kosovo. As High Commissioner Ogata explained,

> For UNHCR, the registration database also allows us to develop a precise demographic profile of the refugee population, including the numbers and locations of separated children, isolated elderly people and other especially vulnerable persons. The result is more effective and efficient management, and the benefits flow to the refugees.[91]

This last statement turned out to be more hype than reality. While the UNHCR enjoyed the demographic data collected by the other four hundred thousand names entered into their database, fewer than fifty thousand identity cards were actually issued to refugees. Moreover, the information collected from the refugees was never made publicly available on the Internet to families and friends of the displaced so they could be "reconnected" as it were.[92]

In response to the "bugs" of the Kosovar operation, the UNHCR and its industry partners have refurbished the software, creating a now field-tested Refugee Field Kit 2000 (RFK-Y2K). The first post-Kosovar refugee situation in which the technology was employed was a refugee registration exercise in Senegal that began on January 31, 2000. Soon afterward the RFK-Y2K was used to register urban refugees in both New Delhi, India, and Lusaka, Zambia. In Kosovo, the technology was advertised as "restoring a sense of self" and "reconnecting families." The equipment Microsoft donated to the UNHCR in the Balkans was later handed over to Zambian authorities, who use the technology for the purposes of social control. Specifically, the technology has been employed to register the fifteen thousand refugees living and working in urban areas such as Lusaka. All refugees in Zambia's urban areas will be required to obtain and carry the electronic identification cards. The request came because Zambian authorities are suspicious that refugees are involved in criminal activities. The ID cards will be used to help police distinguish "genuine" refugees from "illegal migrants."[93] Refugees, in this situation, are not reconnected to their families and loved ones but instead digitally integrated into the surveillance and police apparatuses of the Zambian state. What was initially promoted as a technology of hospitality almost immediately became yet another technology of control. Refugees in this situation are cast in terms not dissimilar to how dogs and cats are treated in major urban areas in Western countries: both are allocated "electronic tags" to monitor and control their movement within public space.

Conclusion

A number of implications for refugees follow from the analysis of the human–animal relationship presented in this chapter. In the first place, humanity appears as a process, a pedagogical exercise that is inextricably connected to discourses of animality. Despite its universal appeal, the general category of humanity faces its constitutive limit at the threshold of animality. This limit is at once reinforced and made problematic by the sovereign relation. The logic of sovereignty is such that to lack the political identity of citizenship is to enter the domain of humanity. But this humanity—far from being a "neutral" category—is always already implicated in a relation of violence to the extent that its conceptual coherence relies on the exclusionary practices of the modern sovereign state. The sovereign and the refugee therefore form a couplet. The refugee is someone whose existence is constituted by his or her exposure to the state of exception. This existence is not a full humanity (full in the sense that he or she is cultured, capable of reasoned speech) but a thin humanity (a bare, naked life, an animal). To be identified as a part of humanity, therefore, is to be cast as someone whose capacity for credible speech has been reduced to an anguished cry, someone whose fundamental human right to mobility has been declared bogus, leading to criminalization and detention.

In the confusion of complex political and humanitarian emergencies today, the refugee finds her human identity intersecting with the exclusionary, marginal spaces of animality and the inclusive, controlling spaces of digital surveillance. This chapter traced how the ontology of sovereignty orders these slippages in identities, how it attempts to tame and discipline the contingencies that define the multiple identities that constitute refugeeness. The refugee, therefore, is in need of liberation from the "humanity" that declares her speechless, fearful, inauthentic, and animal. We need asylum from ways of thinking that create hierarchies and then segment their borders through acts of transgression that mark the violent limit. Such a humanity no one human deserves, and no dog deserves the obverse vision of animality. Human liberation, in this sense, may indeed be animal liberation.

5

Evasive Maneuvers: Refugee Warrior Communities Recast the Political

Return is struggle, not resignation!

—Slogan of returning Guatemalan refugees

Introduction: The Topsy-Turvy World of Refugee Warrior Communities

Conventional representations of refugeeness—both discursive and visual—cast the refugee as the mirror image of the citizen. This image, we have seen, appears only as an inverted reflection: the refugee's world is upside down, both out of place and out of sync with what are considered normal political identities, spaces, and practices. The space of citizenship, for example, is located inside the territorial boundaries of the sovereign state and is, therefore, said to be a secure and protected place. The space of the refugee, by contrast, is outside the protective sphere of the state and so is an insecure space of fear and danger—a state of emergency. The space of citizenship, moreover, defines belonging in relation to a common political community composed of fellow citizens. The refugee, by contrast, resides within a humanitarian space and so can only claim membership to the elusive moral community of "humanity." Citizens possess the capacity to voice their political views in a public space with the expectation of being heard; refugees are defined—no, erased—by their speechlessness. Citizens enjoy a "full" existence that comes from a politically qualified form-of-life, allowing them to participate in various social, cultural, and economic pursuits; refugees are allocated a bare life with minimal requirements, needing only the basics of food, shelter, and medical care to be sustained. Citizenship is a celebrated and much sought after identity; refugees are demonized, the "scum of the earth" as Hannah Arendt lamented.[1] In sum, from a political perspective, all that is present to the citizen is absent to the refugee.

The logocentric logic that structures the citizen–refugee relationship is equally present in what is commonly considered the limit activity of citizenship—that is, the sanctioned violence involved in state military service. Military service is a limit activity because it is a set of practices that are meant to forcefully defend the political community from external threats and dangers. As the sovereign territorial state serves as the condition of possibility not only for the citizen but for a politically qualified form-of-life as well, it is not surprising that the bodily danger involved in warring violence makes military service to be considered by many as the ultimate act of citizenship. Jean Elshtain summarized the ethos of war as the limit activity of citizenship:

> The plangent note sounds: the polity must be as one; the national will must not be divided; citizens must be prepared to defend civic autonomy through force of arms; whatever puts the individual at odds with himself is a threat to la nation une et indivisible. The body individual and the body politic must be driven by a single motor.[2]

It is no coincidence, therefore, that during the French Revolution universal suffrage for men was inaugurated at virtually the same time as universal military conscription. Modern conceptions of the political are, in short, thoroughly bound up with the idea of the citizen warrior.[3] The refugee, however, possesses a negative relation to citizenship and so is prohibited from engaging in political violence. The refugee cannot be a warrior.

Within the refugee studies literature there is a category of refugee that defies the traditional characteristics associated with refugeeness. Instead of being passive, these refugees take action. In place of voicelessness, they have clear objectives and demands. In defiance to the "humanitarian and nonpolitical" terms that define their status, they are unmistakably political actors engaged in the deployment of violence for political ends. Instead of being considered as individual refugees, as the UN Refugee Convention stipulates, they are attached to entire communities. Far from being a temporary phenomenon, they are a part of what are often long-standing social movements and political struggles, and many of these exile communities have existed for generations. What is being described here is the phenomenon of "refugee warriors" and "refugee warrior communities."

The regime of power/knowledge that governs the refugee's relationship to the political faces its greatest crisis with the emergence of refugee warrior

communities. It is, therefore, not surprising that the conventional literature on refugees condemns these individuals and communities not only on
moral grounds but on epistemological grounds as well. As we shall see, the
common consensus on the refugee warrior phenomenon is that this classification of refugees constitutes a misnomer, a category mistake. These refugees also constitute the greatest problem for the problem solvers. They pose
considerable challenges to humanitarian organizations intent on maintaining their neutrality, impartiality, and independence in refugee situations.
Refugee warrior communities make a mockery of these cherished principles and transform humanitarian space into something much more par-
tisan, biased, and dangerous—in short, political. Indeed, they undermine
the humanitarian discourse on refugees precisely because refugee warriors
have attained—and are recognized as possessing—political subjectivities.

The terms "refugee warrior" and "refugee warrior communities" were
first coined by Aristide Zolberg, Astri Suhrke, and Sergio Aguayo (hereafter
Zolberg et al.) in their influential 1989 study *Escape from Violence*. Zolberg
et al. defined refugee warrior communities as

> not merely a passive group of dependent refugees but … highly
> conscious refugee communities with a political leadership struc-
> ture and armed sections engaged in warfare for a political objec-
> tive, be it to recapture the homeland, change the regime, or secure
> a separate state.[4]

This commonly invoked definition raises a number of crucial questions,
namely, are refugees, as individuals or collectives, capable of being "highly
conscious" and "political" (and not just "passive" and "dependent") only
when they resort to armed violence?[5] Is making refugees an armed danger,
a threat to international peace and security the *only* way to bring political
presence to refugee subjectivity? What's more, even if this limited definition
is accepted, must this violence necessarily follow a statist trajectory? Is the
political action of refugee warriors to be aimed only at states? Are their objectives limited to recapturing a homeland, changing a regime, or securing
a separate state, as Zolberg et al. suggested? In sum, are all refugee warriors
"wannabe" citizen warriors?

To answer these questions about the refugee's relationship to warring
violence, we must consider once again the relationship between refugees
and the political. As we saw in chapter 2, refugees are typically thought to
reside within a humanitarian space that at once protects them from the violence of war and conflict while simultaneously excluding them from engaging in political relations. This exclusion, moreover, is in place irrespective
of whether these relations are based on the exercise of force. We also saw,
however, that this distinction between humanitarianism and politics cannot be maintained, as the two are in fact interrelated dynamics, defined not
by an external relationship but by an immanent relationship in which they

anticipate and cross over one another. As Daniel Warner points out, "Without war, there would be no humanitarian law; without war, there would be no humanitarian space."[6]

The official discourses on war tend to focus exclusively on the strategic dimensions of this phenomena; they are "overcoded with strategic rationales," as Michael Shapiro has complained.[7] As a consequence, such discourses fail to consider the significance of war as an ontological phenomenon—or rather, as part of the ontogenetic process of constituting sovereign spaces and identities. I demonstrated this earlier in chapter 2 with respect to Hegel's theory of the ethical state. Here, warring violence is considered to be an important part of an ongoing process of binding the body politic. War works to circumscribe the centrifugal forces emanating from a diverse and active civil society and thus brings unity to the state. From the Hegelian perspective, war is a "necessity" because it defends the autonomy and ensures the coherence of the modern state. To be sure, according to another tradition on the origin of the state—namely, that associated with Philip Toynbee and, more recently, Paul Virilio—fighting not only preserves the collectivity but also gives rise to the particular political collectivity of the city, the *polis*.[8] Political relations and relations of force are thus linked from the beginning within a discourse of sovereignty.

The paradoxes involved in the refugee's relationship to violence—but note, not limited only to warring violence—is at once the limit of humanitarian discourses on refugees and also the limit of political discourses on sovereign spaces and identities. Indeed, far from being a misnomer, category mistake, or oxymoron, the phenomenon of refugee warrior communities is, first and foremost, an expression of the limits of the discourses of humanitarianism and the political. In the first two sections of this chapter, I consider the way refugee warriors have been conceived of within the academic and policy literatures on refugee movements. The language of failure dominates this literature: the refugee warrior phenomenon is an example of failed refugees, failed states, and failed regimes. The first section examines the ontological dimension of the refugee warrior phenomenon, revealing that a great deal of consensus exists as to who qualifies as a refugee warrior (only failed refugees need apply). The second section considers the analytical debates on the phenomena, highlighting the controversy that exists over the "root causes" of this phenomenon (are refugee warriors the result of failed states or of a failed international refugee regime?). In each case, however, the failures can also be interpreted as a success of the sovereign relation of the exception. This relation, we have seen, involves some paradoxical performances, including the state power of capture. Here, the statist logic that informs conventional views on refugee warriors is at work trying to incorporate these "category mistakes" back into a state-centric world order.

How successful are these moves to overcode the refugee warrior phenomenon within the framework of a sovereign logic? I first address this question in the third section of this chapter, which considers recent initiatives by the United Nations High Commissioner for Refugees (UNHCR). In particular, I analyze the "Ladder of Options" policy for how it encourages the performance of sovereign practices around refugee identity, especially in conflict situations where the humanitarian–political relationship is being renegotiated. The fourth section demonstrates that, in spite of these efforts by the UN refugee agency, the case of Afghan Muhajirin refugee warrior communities demonstrates how difficult—indeed, how inherently problematic—it is to separate "authentic" refugees from "inauthentic" refugee warriors. These refugee warrior communities hold, at best, an ambivalent relationship to standard accounts of what it means to be a refugee. Indeed, members of such communities often interpret their refugeeness more in terms of Islamic traditions of forced migration (such as hijrah) than the conventional (Western liberal) terms outlined in the UN Refugee Convention.

Refugee warriors are, fundamentally, an example of refugees who attempt to escape the state of exception that defines the paradox of the refugee condition: he or she is always included within the sovereign relation by virtue of his or her exclusion. But such escapes are not always done by armed warriors intent on achieving strategic political objectives. Indeed, the humanitarian–political divide seems no longer to function in any meaningful way in states where the culture of asylum has been effectively criminalized. Accordingly, in the final section of this chapter, I consider the activities of refugees who are forced to engage in political activities—to become warriors, as it were—just to get the chance to be considered a bona fide refugee. In other words, refugees in places such as Australia, Canada, the United States, and Great Britain are being forced by circumstances to engage in inauthentic activities to be considered authentic refugees. In particular, I examine the case of refugee riots in Australia, demonstrating the lengths that refugees will take to secure a "human security" that does not trap them within the false options of "victim" or "criminal."

The refugee warrior phenomenon is the most recent example of the paradox of refugeeness. Their circumstances cause Walter Benjamin's words to ring forth once again as the exception has become the norm:

> The tradition of the oppressed teaches us that the "state of emergency" in which we live is not the exception but the rule. We must attain to a conception of history that is in keeping with this insight. Then we shall clearly realize that it is our task to bring about a real state of emergency.[9]

But what of this "real state of emergency" that Benjamin insists on? The position I take in this chapter is that the concept of the refugee warrior community must be expanded and cannot be predestined to only a statist trajectory. I argue that the term can be applied to refugees who strike out to reclaim their political identity, voice, and presence—and thus subverting traditional theories of the political based on the sovereign relation of the exception.

Who is a Refugee Warrior?

Examples of refugee warriors and refugee warrior communities abound, in spite of the regimes of classification that condemn them as misnomers. Zolberg et al. identified Palestinian refugees as the archetypical refugee warriors, referring to them as a "refugee nation" and noting that their "capacity for organized violence prefigured attempts by other refugees to take history in their own hands."[10] The Cuban exiles that used Florida as a base to attack the Castro regime in the early 1960s also qualify as refugee warriors.[11] Refugee warriors played a prominent role in Southern African conflicts in the 1980s.[12] In the 1990s, they include the Tutsis refugees who invaded Rwanda from Uganda in October 1990. They also include Afghans living in refugee camps in Pakistan, who first waged war against the Soviet-backed communist regime in Kabul and then against various successor regimes (many of which were made up of former refugee warriors).[13] The Khmer in Thailand, who waged war against the Vietnamese-backed government of Kampuchea qualify as refugee warriors, as do the Keren, who are waging war against the military regime of Myanmar from refugee camps in Thailand.[14] Kurds living in and around refugee camps in Iraq and Iran and who are in a military conflict with Turkey are also examples of refugee warriors. Tamils living in refugee camps in Sri Lanka are another example.[15]

While the situations and circumstances surrounding the refugee warrior phenomenon are as diverse as they are complicated, a great deal of consensus exists about them within the academic and policy literature on refugees. In particular, there are four identifiable points of convergence within this literature. First, there is a general agreement as to who actually qualifies as a refugee warrior. Second, there is a consensus that if the criteria for refugee warriorship is met, then what emerges is a "failed refugee" as the entire phenomena is essentially a contradiction in terms, a category mistake. Third, one of the consequences of this categorical failure is effacement of the traditional "humanitarian" terms that define refugeeness. Refugee warriors are unique among refugee populations in terms of the recognition they are given as political actors in their own right. Finally, the refugee warrior phenomenon is understood almost entirely in terms of how it represents both a danger and a threat to human, national, regional, and international security.

To begin, there is a great deal of coherence and unity in the academic and policy literature as to who actually qualifies as a refugee warrior. Howard Adelman established four conditions that must be met for an individual to be considered a refugee warrior:

1. The person is a refugee or is a descendant of people who fled their country of origin as refugees.
2. The person employs violence for political purposes, usually to overthrow a government or political regime.
3. The base from which this political violence is deployed is normally a refugee settlement, often camps, in neighboring states.
4. The refugees are not proxy forces for their host state. Instead, they are autonomous actors engaged trying to realize their own objectives.[16]

These conditions are in line with the criteria established by Zolberg et al., and together they have become widely cited reference points in academic discussions about the refugee warrior phenomenon. What these criteria affirm is that refugee warriors are to be considered a discrete category in and of themselves. On account of being warriors, they should not be confused with "genuine" or bona fide refugees. On account of being refugees, however, they should not be mistaken for internal rebel groups either. Indeed, even when recognition is given to how these identities and groups cross over with one another, the main point that refugee warriors are distinct because they are an international problem is underscored.[17]

As an international phenomenon, however, it should be noted that international law is unanimous in its prohibition of refugees from engaging in or actively supporting political violence. This leads us to the second commonality within the literature on refugee warriors—that is, to declare the concept of refugee warrior a category mistake. For example, Zolberg et al. stated in *Escape from Violence* that "refugee-warriors clearly are a contradiction in terms."[18] Adelman agreed, admitting,

> Strictly speaking, the phrase "refugee warrior" is a misnomer ... a refugee by definition cannot resort to violence. If a refugee resorts to violence, then that person no longer qualifies for refugee status. In law, a person may either be a refugee or a warrior, but he or she cannot be both.[19]

Consequently, to conjoin the two terms refugee and warrior is to attract considerable conceptual difficulties. After all, refugees—as the title of the Zolberg et al. book implies—are people who claim this identity precisely because they are escaping from violence and persecution, not engaging in such activities themselves. To be sure, while some refugees might have engaged in armed struggle against an oppressive state—the Hungarian freedom fighters cum refugees are an early, still classic, example—it was understood that they would leave such violent activities behind them once they made the decision to seek asylum abroad.

The legal coding of refugeeness in international law is unequivocal for how it prohibits refugees from engaging in political violence. While the UNHCR's founding statute affirms rather open-endedly that refugees should abide by the domestic laws of their countries of asylum, other international legal instruments are more direct in their prohibition of refugees from engaging in political violence. This is particularly the case in Africa, where a regional refugee regime has been established to respond to the unique problems associated with the process of decolonialization. The Organization of African Unity's (OAU) 1969 Convention on the Refugee Problems in Africa takes a very proactive stance in terms of discouraging refugees from becoming warriors. The preamble of the convention avows that the signatories are "determined to discourage" refugees from using their status to engage in activities that would be deemed subversive or criminal. Article II (6) invokes a spatial politics to reinforce the desire to eradicate the operations of refugee warriors, recommending "for reasons of security" that refugee populations shall be settled "at a reasonable distance from the frontier of their country of origin." Article III of the convention is even more forthright on the issue, as it is dedicated to the "Prohibition of Subversive Activities" by refugees. Article III (2) declares that host states must "prohibit refugees residing in their respective territories from attacking any State Members ... by use of arms, through the press, or by radio."[20] The wording of the last article is noteworthy, as the problem of refugees' relationship with the political is cast in much broader terms than mere physical violence. Here, there is a clear linkage between the prohibition of political violence ("use of arms") and the silencing of political voice ("through the press, or by radio").

The simultaneous effacement of violence and voice from refugee subjectivity outlined in the OAU Refugee Convention underscores a common anxiety held about the political status of refugee warriors. Thus, a third commonality emerges from the recognition allocated to refugee warriors as independent and authoritative political actors. Refugee warriors are, as both Adelman and Zolberg et al. independently declare, refugees who are distinguished by virtue of the fact that they "take history in their own hands."[21] But while the degree of recognition they are receiving as political actors in their own right is increasing, the terms of this recognition has remained committed to the prevailing frameworks of understanding refugeeness. Consider the following action proposal passed at a joint meeting of the OAU and UNHCR in Conakry, Guinea, in March 2000:

> In situations of armed conflict or similar situations, non-state actors should mutates mutandis: (i) respect protection principles, including non-refoulement and non-rejection at the border in regard to refugees and asylum seekers; (ii) comply with their obligations under international humanitarian law; (iii) observe any principles found in human rights and humanitarian instruments, which may provide additional protection; (iv) ensure the security of humanitarian workers and allow unhindered access to all civilians, including refugees, asylum-seekers and returnees, affected by the conflict; (v) maintain a secure environment in which humanitarian action can be carried out effectively.[22]

Notice how refugee warriors are treated by the two international refugee regimes. On one hand, the recognition they are allocated as political actors is considerable. Not only are they requested to follow the same rules and norms of warfare as state actors but the language employed here is distinctly political as well, with references to "obligations," "principles," and "international law." At the same time, however, this language refuses to speak of these "non-state actors" directly as "refugee warriors." Rather, through political recognition, refugee warriors are asked to reject their refugee status: they can be warriors, they can be political actors, but they cannot be refugees. It seems that in return for political recognition, the OAU and UNHCR want refugee warriors to concede to the international regime of power/knowledge that attempts to govern the allotment and meaning of refugeeness in Africa.

Finally, despite their recognition as authoritative actors—or perhaps, more accurately, because of it—refugee warriors are almost universally considered as a threat, as a source of insecurity, and as a destabilizing force to domestic peace, regional stability, and world order. As Adelman stated,

> Refugee warriors always come into conflict with those whose priority is the peaceful resolution of conflict, regional stability, and the provision of humanitarian aid exclusively to refugees. … Refugee warriors are a critical source of violence and instability in a region, in the countries in which they find refuge, and for the countries from which they have fled.[23]

As a dangerous threat, refugee warriors are a source of insecurity to a variety of populations. In particular, and irrespective of the level of support they receive within camps and other refugee-populated areas, the militarization inherent in refugee warrior communities inevitably creates a sense of profound insecurity for its refugee population, camp aid workers, and the local population. In extreme situations, these threats to human security include the outright bombing or shelling of camps, as was the fate of the militarized camps of Goma as well as those along the Thai–Cambodian border. Raids of refugee camps by refugee warrior groups to secure resources (e.g., food, vehicles, radio equipment), to take hostages, or to force conscription are also identified as a threat to human security. As one UNHCR humanitarian worker assessed the situation, "The AK-47 rifle is their version of the credit card. They can get anything they want with it, and they don't hesitate to do so."[24] Following this assessment, it is appropriate to inquire into the rate of interest and the terms of repayment. Sadly, the outlook looks good for neither. This is of particular concern when one considers the problem of forced conscription of children as well as gender-specific violence, such as rape and sexual assaults.[25] The severity of the violence within the camps is such that it may pose a threat that exceeds the local context and instead acts as a destabilizing force to international peace and security. The UNHCR has, therefore, brought the matter of refugee warrior communities to the attention of the UN Security Council, referring to the "proven danger" that "the militarization of refugee-populated areas can create or aggravate tensions between States, thereby posing a threat to regional peace and security."[26]

Assessing the Levels of Failure

While a great deal of consensus exists on the question of who qualifies as a refugee warrior, no such agreement exists on what causes this phenomenon in the first place. What conditions, processes, or structures give rise to refugee warrior activity? What enables refugee warriors to subvert the traditional terms of refugeeness and cultivate communities that will support their cause? What, in short, causes refugees to become warriors? These questions are hotly contested in both academic and policy literature on refugees. The terms of this debate, however, should be familiar to most students of international relations, as it has largely been framed in terms of determining which "level" of analysis is most significant in explaining the emergence of refugee warrior activity. The so-called levels of analysis debate applies whenever there is a dispute in resolving what Alexander Wendt called the "problem of explanation"—that is, "of assessing the relative importance of causal factors at different levels of aggregation in explaining the behaviour of a given unit of analysis."[27] In this section, I outline how the analytical "problem of explaining" the emergence of the refugee warrior phenomenon has become implicated within the discourse of "levels." Moreover, I explore the close relationship between the epistemological framework offered by the "levels of analysis" perspective and the (re)production of sovereign identities and spaces.

The sovereign logic of inside–outside also informs the levels of analysis schema when it is used for the purpose of explaining the emergence of refugee warrior communities. As we will see, the pervasiveness of sovereignty is such that even in situations of failure, the sovereign logic can maintain its presence. On one hand, there is the claim that local factors, internal to the states involved, are the most important causal factors. This is a position most often identified with Zolberg et al., as their study was the first to recognize the refugee warrior phenomenon as a "special problem of our time."[28] Here, it is the failure of states—or, more precisely, the failed state—that most directly fosters the conditions that allow for refugee warrior activity. On the other hand, there is the position, most provocatively asserted by Adelman, that factors external to states are the most relevant for explaining the emergence of refugee warrior communities. This position points to the international community (working within organizations such as the UNHCR) as the prime culprits for this violent breakdown in the management and control over refugee subjectivity and activity. In short, the level of analysis schema asks if the problem of refugee warriors comes from the inside (failed state) or outside (failed international community). However, it is one thing to recognize that this schema is structured by the logic of sovereignty and quite another to remember the exclusionary character of this logic. The relation of the exception, we have seen, defines the logic of sovereignty. This relation, Agamben has explained, thrives on a paradoxical power whereby all that it excludes is, in fact, included by virtue of its being expelled. As a consequence, regardless of whether the problem is said to lie at the level of the state (inside) or the international community (outside), the sovereign relation of inside–outside continues its powerful hold over contemporary imaginings on the location and character of all possible political spaces and practices.

To begin, let us consider the level of the state for explaining the emergence of refugee warrior activity. Here, it is worth remembering how commonplace it is to identify situations of forced displacement as a crisis or emergency situation. To be sure, in cases where refugee warrior communities are active, the conventional literature shifts the crisis vocabulary into overdrive. However, the terms of the crisis no longer are limited to refugees who fail to conform to the established norms of refugeeness but also are extended to sovereign states that have proved incapable of taking the necessary measures to repel the activities of refugee warriors. For instance, in their description of the "root causes" of refugee warrior communities, Zolberg et al. pointed to the level of the state to explain the emergence of this phenomenon. Indeed, they argued that a particular form of state—the so-called failed state—is largely responsible for the refugee warrior phenomenon:

> In the most extreme cases, a tenuously amalgamated national society can disintegrate into its component elements. With its existence externally ensured, the state is reduced to little more than an arena in which groups vie for survival, as if they were microstates in a contentious international system. Under these conditions, collective life is reduced to two fundamental activities, food production and war. Because cheap small weapons are widely available, and warriors are obviously in a position to secure their subsistence without engaging in their production themselves, war-making steadily gains the upper hand. The outcome is a proliferation of warrior bands, verging on a war of all against all.[29]

The language employed here is noteworthy. As Zolberg et al. described it, the situation within failed states is not unlike the condition of anarchy within the international system. Here, insecurity reigns as elements of a disintegrated order fight for survival and advantage. The only remaining collective practices involve the basics of life (food production) and death (the proliferation of warrior bands). From this perspective, the conclusion offered by Zolberg et al.—that is, that which emerges is a kind of Hobbesian situation of "war of all against all"—is neither surprising nor uncommon.

If the level of the failed state falls short of adequately explaining how refugee warrior groups might be considered as authentic political nonstate actors in themselves, the level of the international community hardly fares better. This position can be seen in the work of Adelman, who argues that the existence of the refugee warrior phenomenon cannot be principally attributed to state failure. For Adelman, the proliferation of refugee warrior communities is the result of a failure of the problem solvers to effectively manage the international refugee regime. "Refugee warriors," he contends, "are not so much a product of 'root causes' but of failures—sometimes deliberate—in the management of conflicts and, more specifically, the management of the plight of the refugees themselves, whatever their original causes."[30] Adelman offers the following summary of his position on the conditions of possibility for refugee warrior communities:

> Refugee warriors also result from the failure of the international community either to take any effective action in finding a permanent solution to the refugee problem, or from stemming the ability of the refugees to take up arms and resort to violence to solve their problems. Refugee warriors are more a product of international political and military relations, as well as the misuse of humanitarian aid, than the internal conflicts or the legitimacy crisis which produced the refugees in the first place.[31]

Put another way, what is at issue here is not a failed state but a failed international community, one that does not either adequately provide for durable solutions to forced migration or stem the flow of money and arms used to sustain refugee warrior groups.

The difficulty with this perpetual recourse to the language of levels—a recourse that one commentator has declared "all pervasive"[32]—has the effect of constraining international theory from appreciating conceptions of the political other than those informed by the sovereign relation of the exception. Indeed, as Jean Elshtain has argued, the levels of analysis approach "secures the domain of domestic politics (the reign of justice) as the world of, and for, political theorists, saving international politics for specialists in what 'states' do given the 'system' within which they must operate."[33] Rob Walker concurs, characterizing the levels of analysis approach as an effect of the constitutive practices of the sovereign relation: "it is strictly derivative from the principle of state sovereignty, and carries with it all those assumptions about the impossibility of any other resolution of fundamental political questions than that formalized by state sovereignty."[34] In this sense, the principle of state sovereignty formalizes a long historical struggle on the part of states to marginalize and deny legitimacy to any other form of community—be it a cosmopolitan, an ecumenical, a metropolitan, or even a refugee warrior community—as the site of serious political life.[35]

Reinscribing Sovereign Relations: The UNHCR's "Ladder of Options"

The way the UNHCR has responded to these kinds of challenges and criticisms is noteworthy, for it too is structured in many important respects by the sovereign logic of the exception. On one hand, the UNHCR, as indicated earlier, has given unprecedented recognition to refugee warrior groups as nonstate political actors in their own right. At the same time, however, the UNHCR refuses to name these "nonstate actors" as refugee warriors. These people, they say, are not bona fide refugees; their refugeeness is inauthentic. As a result, the recognition given to refugee warrior communities has always been viewed as an indication of a larger problem—that is, the failure of the sovereign identities and spaces to hold in any and all situations. Consequently, the UNHCR's response has been largely one of trying to reinscribe these identities, spaces, and relations according to a sovereign account of the political.

The UNHCR has been aware of the issue of (in)security among refugee populations since at least the late 1970s, when attacks by South African armed forces on refugee camps in Angola, Mozambique, and Zambia made international headlines.[36] The UNHCR's immediate response was to dispatch former High Commissioner Felix Schnyder to conduct a study on the matter.[37] While repeatedly noting its grave concern on the problem of refugee (in)security, the refugee agency nonetheless found it difficult throughout the 1980s to come to any consensus over how to respond to the problem.[38] Indeed, the position articulated in EXCOM Conclusion No. 48 (1987) was typical of this period. Here, the UNHCR called on all refugees and states to conform to the principles and assumptions that constitute their "authentic" identities. For refugees, they had the "duty" to remain nonpolitical subjects and were instructed to "abstain from any activity likely to detract from the exclusively civilian and humanitarian character of the camps and settlements."[39] Similarly, states were expected to perform as polities with "positive" sovereignty and were, therefore, asked to "do all within their capacity to ensure that the civilian and humanitarian character of such camps and settlements is maintained."[40]

By the late 1990s the UNHCR had changed its position on the matter of (in)security in refugee camps. The horrors of genocide in Rwanda and their complicated relationship with the hundreds of thousands of refugees that emerged from this conflict has convinced the refugee agency that not all states facing refugee crises possess the capacity to provide the necessary protection needed by refugees and international humanitarian staff. Consequently, at a regional Meeting on Refugee Issues in the Great Lakes held in Kampala, Uganda, in 1998, both the UNHCR and the OAU formally recognized the problems associated with "failed states" in the region. The UNHCR decided that it was no longer realistic to wait for these states to successfully perform the type of practices indicative of sovereignty. Indeed, from the perspective of the UNHCR, the state just doesn't seem to be there in any meaningful way during the massive refugee crises that have repeatedly marked the post–cold war era. The state is missing, absent, invisible; it is, at best, malfunctioning. The state is the victim of internal forces it can no longer control; its sovereignty is the product of norms (i.e., nonintervention) that come from without. In other words, what is occurring is a role reversal of dramatic proportions: it is now the refugee-subject who possesses political presence, while the political efficacy of the state is effaced.

In response to these developments, the UNHCR increasingly takes the position that it is the international community—and not local (failed) states—that will ensure the security and maintain the rule of law within refugee-populated areas, including camps. In a report titled The Security, and Civilian and Humanitarian Character of Refugee Camps and Settlements, the UNHCR spelled out in no uncertain terms the failed states and failed regimes that undermine the humanitarian and nonpolitical character of refugee identity and communities:

> In many cases, insecurity affecting refugee camps and refugee populated areas results from a failure to strictly respect the civilian and humanitarian character of refugee operations. In the aftermath of the genocide in Rwanda, the presence among refugees of former combatants and persons involved in grave crimes against humanity has been a tragic illustration of the failure of States hosting refugees and of the international community to ensure the neutrality of camps. Insecurity can also arise as a result of several other factors, such as conflict amongst different groups within the refugee population, conflict between refugees and the local population, common crime and banditry, and, in certain cases, the deployment of undisciplined police and security forces. In many instances, camps are located too close to international borders.[41]

This passage demonstrates the enormous challenges facing humanitarian organizations, such as the UNHCR, working in the context of refugee crises today. As we shall see, however, it also points toward a number of limitations to the international response.

The UNHCR's list of sources of insecurity in refugee-populated areas include individuals and groups that are the agents of some of the most notorious and horrific violence in recent history. For instance, the Rwandan *genocidaires* who hide among the refugee populations that they had recently tried to destroy should be considered as a problem to humanitarian organizations, as should anyone else who is accused of serious crimes against humanity. However, the other sources of insecurity identified in the previous list are much less straightforward. For instance, conflict within the refugee community and between refugees and the local community surely represent a qualitative difference than does the presence of agents of genocide. Even complaints about alleged criminal activity and "banditry" among refugees have to be made in the context of what is the uneven distribution of poverty, not wealth. Consequently, distinctions between these sources of insecurity are in order. How the UNHCR confronts the multiplicity of forces of insecurity and distinguishes between them is of considerable importance. However, the distinctions that are made, ironically, work to ignore or otherwise efface this multiplicity. The UNHCR takes the position that all of the activities previously outlined are inauthentic. Moreover, the UNHCR deals with them—and, it should be stressed, other, nonviolent political activities—in a single brushstroke by continually reasserting the primacy of sovereign codes and practices. As we shall see, however, this can be a self-defeating position with all sorts of contradictory effects.

In response to the kinds of concerns raised at the 1998 meeting of the UNHCR and OAU, the High Commissioner introduced the "ladder of options" concept to address the problem of (in)security in refugee-populated areas. As we shall see, this response may at times circumvent the authority of local states, but the importance of (re)inscribing sovereign relations and identities is affirmed. Indeed, the ladder of options policy is an attempt by the UNHCR to reinstate the traditional terms of humanitarian space (i.e., as nonpolitical). However, working within the context of "failed states" only highlights the immanent relationship shared between humanitarianism and the political, as the refugee agency is forced to take on many of the (violent, coercive) practices normally left to states.

The different levels of the UNHCR's ladder are referred to as soft, medium, and hard options, with each designating the varying degree of force that could be deployed in response to security problems within refugee-populated areas. At whatever level of intensity, these interventions involve a relationship to the political. The hard option is most obvious in this regard, as it involves the deployment of a UN Peacekeeping Operation or an international or regional force under Chapter VI or Chapter VIII of the UN Charter.[42] This is the most overt relationship, because it involves a public admission from states that they have failed in their quest for effectively realizing sovereignty: conditions within their territory are so insecure that the state's claim to a monopoly of violence no longer holds any legitimacy and so international forces are sent to maintain civil peace and perform the functions of order.

While the degree of militarization in the medium and soft options is reduced when compared with the hard option of military deployment, their relationship to the political is not at all diminished. The medium option involves a variety of measures but is essentially aimed at developing international capabilities to rapidly replace the "law and order" functions of a state during a refugee crisis or in situations involving heightened refugee warrior activity. Such measures can include the deployment of a multinational body of civilian observers to monitor the situation within refugee camps and settlements for signs of any refugee warrior activity. As well, this option also provides for the deployment of international police monitors as well as for an international police force, including the direct hiring of private security firms and personnel.[43] More recently, the UNHCR has

begun to develop a Humanitarian Security Assessment checklist to identify different types and sources of threats. As well, the refugee agency has
established a number of standby arrangements with states for the provision
of security personnel during refugee emergencies. These law and order experts are known as "Humanitarian Security Officers" (HSOs). They are to
be deployed within seventy-two hours of being notified by the UNHCR and
will have the responsibility to liaise with the various arms of local security
and police agencies to assess their capacity and willingness to police refugee
camps and settlements.

The ranks of the HSOs also include humanitarian security and "vulnerable populations" specialists. These officers provide expertise for the
prevention of sexual, gender-based, and domestic violence as well as work
toward protecting children younger than eighteen years of age from military recruitment.[44] The UNHCR has also responded to the problem of
sexual and gender violence within camps by developing and distributing
guidelines to humanitarian workers that outline how they can help pre-
vent and respond to such violence.[45] While these developments represent a
huge improvement over past practice, they are nonetheless problematic in
many respects.[46] In the first place, there are problems inherent in favoring
refugee camps on the basis of how they facilitate the work of humanitarian
workers. Camps, after all, have the benefit of gathering all aid recipients
into one place, thereby making the provision of food, shelter, and medical
care more efficient. However, this same "humanitarian space" also creates
the conditions whereby the risk of violence against women is heightened.
Security checklists aside, the refugee camp represents a disaster for refugees
in terms of increasing their vulnerability to violence and, in particular, to
sexual violence against refugee women.

Speaking specifically of the problem of sexual violence in camps,
Jennifer Hyndman has argued that, for the UNHCR, "better practices might
include ongoing discussions with refugees—women in particular—not simply of them, in an effort to bridge some of the social, cultural, and political
differences and discursive distance that is reproduced and managed under
the rubric of UN humanism."[47] The possibility that such consultation might
undermine the basic categories and behavioral expectations of refugees
made by humanitarian officials is a real possibility. Here, the most revealing perspective is found not in policy documents but in ethnographic accounts of how different people experience refugeeness in conflict zones. For
example, Julie Peteet, an anthropologist who studies the cultural politics of
violence within Palestinian refugee camps, has argued that the relationship
both women and children have to violence is not exclusively structured by
their victim status. They are not simply "womenandchildren," to borrow a
term from Cynthia Enloe, to be defended by international humanitarian
organizations.[48] Rather, Peteet's research has illustrated how the "activist
mother" living in a Palestinian refugee camp (the refugee warrior community par excellence) has a complicated and paradoxical relationship to the

conflict, one that is "simultaneously limiting and agential" and revealing of "previously ambiguous forms of subjectivity and creative agency."[49] Peteet made a related argument in her consideration of the male youth in the camps and in particular those participating in the intifada. She examined the experience of beatings and detention, noting how the male youth try to make sense of their suffering by interpreting this punishment as a ritual, a kind of "rite of passage" that is constitutive of a resistive form of masculinity. While Peteet highlights how the beatings become the basis of a "transformative experience that galvanizes one set of participants to unsettle power arrangements,"[50] the capacity for such a politicized masculinity to reaffirm and reproduce traditional gender hierarchies is nonetheless considerable. Because the UNHCR's established expectation of refugeeness is one where political subjectivities (even limited and paradoxical ones) have no place among refugees, the medium policy of sending in an international police force is unlikely to appreciate or recognize the significance and complexities of these subjectivities when they arise.

If the medium option is aimed toward securing a "normal" political order under exceptional circumstances so that a nonpolitical humanitarian space can be established, then the soft option attempts to defend the typical relationship between sovereignty and subjectivity found within these spaces. Indeed, despite its name, the soft option remains steadfast and firm in terms of enacting sovereign relations among refugee populations. It does so, in particular, by structuring relations of governance within refugee camps and settlements according to the logic of sovereignty. In the first place, this option insists that refugee populations, especially those within camps, should be located at a "reasonable distance" from international borders and their size should not exceed twenty thousand refugees. Border regions, it is thought, increase the level of confusion between authentic refugees and inauthentic refugee warriors, bandits, criminal groups, and other so-called irregular migrants that populate such zones of indistinction. Consequently, the placement of refugee camps is of intense political concern to the UN refugee agency. The agency is keen to domesticate these camps and not allow the dangerous forces of the international realm to contaminate this so-called humanitarian space.

The UNHCR is also unequivocal in its position that outside supervision of camps by international humanitarian staff is to be considered the norm. Furthermore, the refugee agency will take measures to cooperate with and offer training to local law enforcement agencies to ensure camp security. In terms of measures of self-governance by the refugees, the soft option places strict restrictions on how this may occur. This is significant because it comes at a time when the UNHCR is critical of donor states that place these kinds of restrictions on refugee self-governance. For example, in its 1998 report *The State of the World's Refugees: A Humanitarian Agenda,* the UNHCR stated,

The long-established notion that refugees should be active participants in the management of their camps and assistance programmes is quietly being set aside. Increasingly, donor states assess humanitarian organizations in terms of their capacity to deliver emergency relief, rather than their ability to empower marginalized populations and to bring a degree of dignity to their lives.[51]

Consequently, while the UNHCR chides states for funding humanitarian organizations to provide emergency relief (food, shelter, medicine: in other words, the basics to sustain bare life) but not finance community and social services programs, the agency does not seem willing to recognize its own involvement in the depoliticization of refugeeness. In particular, the soft option for dealing with the problem of (in)security in refugee camps does not prohibit the election of refugee representatives in camp governance outright, but it does insist that these representatives must be committed to camp neutrality. Moreover, the task of distributing aid to refugees will not be done through the elected camp leadership; aid will be given directly to individuals and families by international staff or military personnel.[52] The soft options, therefore, are very direct in insisting that refugee subjectivity be stripped not only of any violent characteristics but also of any political quality at all. Refugees remain as the OAU defined them more than three decades ago: prohibited from participating in any political relation—whether it be "by use of arms, through the press, or by radio"—that would grant them political voice or agency.

The Failure of Levels in Afghan Muhajirin Refugee Warrior Communities

The UNHCR insists that the integrity of the "humanitarian space" that defines refugee camps and settlements must be maintained to protect "bona fide" refugees from the threat posed by refugee warriors. Indeed, the ladder of options strategy for dealing with the refugee warrior phenomenon has at its core a desire to separate the "authentic" from the "inauthentic," the "bona fide" refugee from the refugee warrior. States and the international community, the agency argues, should work toward "separating bona fide refugees from those exiles who should be excluded from refugee status by virtue of their involvement in crimes against humanity, continued engagement in military activities or any other activity incompatible with refugee status under relevant conventions."[53] Refugees, moreover, are asked to reaffirm their commitment to the legal terms of their refugee status as well as to the normative dimensions of refugeeness. In other words, they should desist from participating in "inauthentic"—that is, political—activities.

The use of scare quotes around terms such as "authentic" and "bona fide" refugee in the context of refugee warrior activity is unavoidable. Refugee warriors, it needs to be stressed, are never simply individuals but always part of a refugee warrior community. In the refugee studies literature, these communities are grudgingly referred to as "mixed populations" of refugee warriors and genuine refugees. Such classifications are difficult to sustain, however, as Karen Jacobsen, a policy consultant for the UNHCR, has observed: "In most camp situations, non-combatants and combatants are related to each other (non-combatants are wives, children, parents of combatants). Under these circumstances, it is difficult to determine when a camp should be defined as militarized."[54] The kinship ties that bind the "authentic" refugee victim to the "inauthentic" refugee warrior are politically significant, as was demonstrated in the case of Afghan refugee warriors. These fighters resisted the Soviet intervention in their home country—and, later, the various successor regimes to the community government—from bases within or near refugee camps in Pakistan. Refugees actually engaged in armed fighting often used the camps as a kind of "family strategy" for collective survival. As Nazif Shahrani argued, "Most able-bodied males, having secured the safety of their families in the refugee camps, return to Afghanistan and participate in the armed resistance."[55]

The use of refugee camps as a family survival strategy, as with the refugee warrior activity among forcibly displaced Afghan populations, demonstrates how the effacement of authentic–inauthentic refugeeness can greatly benefit the populations in the region. From the UNHCR's perspective, this ambivalence is interpreted as cynicism toward its mandate to provide a "humanitarian space," and so it views such transgressions as a major problem. The charge of cynicism, however, misses how, for the refugees, the meaning of refugeeness is understood in very different terms from those provided for by the UN Refugee Convention. The slippage between authentic and inauthentic refugees, therefore, involves a complicated array of practices and assumptions about refugeeness. The confusion over refugee identity in circumstances where refugee warrior communities are active is not merely the product of various "failures." The failed states, failed regimes, and failed refugees that populate the conventional literature on refugee warriors is but an effect of a sovereign discourse that cannot bear refugee populations engaging in political activity of any sort, let alone political violence. Refugee warrior communities, however, hold a much more ambivalent relationship to the sovereign logic that defines refugeeness.

The case of the Afghan refugee warrior community is an interesting one, not least for how these refugees dramatically recast their interaction with both humanitarian space and their own refugeeness. In the refugee warrior communities of the region, refugeeness is interpreted as being consistent with a particular form of forced displacement found in the Islamic tradition. While the UN Refugee Convention includes a "well-founded fear of being persecuted" for religious beliefs to be a reasonable ground for the conferral of refugee status, this connection between exile and religion has been interpreted by Afghan refugee warrior communities in an altogether different manner. The way in which they interpret the interaction between their refugee status, their religious traditions, and their participation in armed violence has the effect of exploding not only traditional expectations of refugee behavior but also the received tradition of politics and ethics that informs the world order of nation-states and citizen-subjects. This world order, it should be recalled, is often referred to as the Westphalian system, after the 1648 treaty that established the principle that it would be the sovereign who would determine the religion of his or her state. This principle determined that international relations would be a secular and not sacred practice.[56] Refugee warriors in Central Asia, however, are forcefully reinterpreting their refugeeness in ways that blur the conventional distinctions made between the secular and the sacred, the religious and the political.

The term mujahidin is the most commonly invoked description of Muslim Afghan resistance fighters—the so-called "holy warriors."[57] However, this designation is most popular amongst the Western media and international organizations providing humanitarian assistance to the refugees in the region. Indeed, in the regional parlance, there are a number of terms used when referring to refugees. For instance, the Persian word *panahandah* is a relatively straightforward term, meaning "refugee, one seeking protection, one seeking political asylum."[58] On the other hand, another more pejorative term is also widely deployed: *awarah*, meaning "vagrant, homeless, tramp, refugee, evacuee, and vagabond."[59] As Nazif Shahrani explains, both of these terms "are used interchangeably primarily in reference to displaced peoples outside the Muslim world, whether caused by political violence or natural disasters."[60] However, the appellation most frequently used by the Afghan refugee warriors is the term *muhajirin*. While etymologically related to *mujahidin*, the meaning of *muhajirin* is nonetheless distinct and usually translated as "those who leave their homes in the cause of Allah, after suffering oppression."[61]

Prior to the 1978 communist coup in Kabul, the use of the term *muhajirin* was used by Turkmenistanis who took refuge in Afghanistan after their lands were incorporated within a consolidating Soviet Union in the early 1920s. A precedent for a political relation to be included in the practice of hijrah was therefore established by the time the communist coup in Kabul occurred in 1978. Shahrani has underscored the immanent relationship between politics and religion in this context: "The majority of Afghans who have made the often perilous journey into Pakistan and Iran view their decision simultaneously as a political act of resistance against Communist usurpation of state power in Kabul and as a moral act of faith in the sanctity of Islamic principles and their commitment to defend them."[62]

The phenomenon of forced migration, especially for reasons of religious persecution, is therefore one that is firmly rooted within the Islamic tradition. The Arabic word for such flights from persecution is *hijrah*. Even at the level of etymology, the theme of forced displacement is at the root of *hijrah*, as Zafar Ansari has explained:

> In Arabic, the root "h-j-r" denotes "to dissociate oneself, to separate, to keep away, to part company, to renounce, to leave, to aban-

don, to give up, to emigrate." (Hence, it is the antonym of the root "w-s-l" which means "to connect, to join, to unite, to combine, to link," etc.) Moreover, the root "h-j-r" also has the nuance of "dislike" as the motive for dissociating oneself from or leaving something or someone.[63]

Ansari continues by describing the fundamental features of *hijrah*: "The basic idea of *hijrah* is that if a Muslim finds that his environment makes it impossible for him to profess and practice Islam, and the situation in his homeland becomes irreparable, he should not allow either his instinctive love for his homeland or his material interests to stand in the way of migrating to an alien environment where he is likely to enjoy the freedom to practise his faith."[64]

From the perspective of the Islamic faith, all the major prophets—Noah, Abraham, Lot, and Moses—made a *hijrah* when they were forced to leave their native lands in search of a community more hospitable to their religious faith and practices. What makes the *hijrah* such a key Islamic virtue, however, is the fact that during the lifetime of the Prophet Muhammad, Muslims were twice forced to wander in search of hospitality. In one of these famous treks, moreover, Muhammad himself took part.[65] "In fact, in circumstances that warrant it, *hijrah* is looked upon as the supreme religious imperative. At times it assumes such an overriding importance that without making *hijrah* one may not be treated as a fully-fledged member of the Islamic body-politic."[66] Framed in this way, the status of being forcibly displaced does not automatically result in the same kind of absolute exclusion from political relations demanded by the secular, Western conception of refugeeness. On the contrary, if an individual or group identifies with membership in the "Islamic body-politic," as Ansari explained it, then being a "refugee"—or rather, making *hijrah*—is a crucial practice for membership in this community. When faced by this other regime of power–knowledge structuring the meaning of refugeeness, the UNHCR's demand for conformity to its model not surprisingly so often goes unheard.

In this context, it is difficult to see how the language of levels can hold any real degree of relevance, use, or legitimacy in situations where refugee warrior communities hold an ambivalent relationship to the standard expectations of refugeeness. The Afghani refugee warrior communities do not accept the ontology of sovereignty as the only precondition for living a politically qualified form-of-life. Rather, the religious significance of making *hijrah*, of being a *muhajir*, suggests that the level of culture and religion is at least as important for understanding the emergence of refugee warrior communities in Central Asia as any appeal to failed states, regimes, or refugees. While it is true that some adherents to the levels of analysis schema have developed perspectives that purport to account for the levels of culture or religion, such attempts usually end up reproducing the ontology of sovereignty. Indeed, the deployment of categories that claim to offer an alternative to the state-centric vision that dominates discussions about conflict and security should also be viewed with a critical eye. This is especially true of advocates of the level of "civilization" as a way of explaining the religious dimension of political phenomena such as refugee warrior communities. For instance, the novelty of the "Clash of Civilizations" thesis made popular by Samuel P. Huntington is, in the end, undermined by a rather crude take on civilizations that treats them as monolithic, territorially based geopolitical entities and thus reinforces the ontology of sovereignty as the only condition that will allow for political activity.[67] The result of such a move is a fairly conventional reproduction of a state-centric world order and a demonization of religiously informed refugee warrior groups as being agents of disorder to the Western liberal project of global governance and multilateralism.

When Refugees Riot: The Revenge of Bare Life

The case of Afghan muhajirin refugee warrior communities and their dramatic renegotiation of refugee identity in ways that recast the nature and location of political identity underscore the need to develop perspectives that do not reproduce the claustrophobic vision of the political promoted by the logic of sovereignty. The actions of refugee warrior groups can be understood as actively transgressing the terms and conditions that structure conventional sovereign accounts of refugeeness and political relations. At the same time, it should be stressed that not everyone fleeing Afghanistan is associated with a refugee warrior community. The country is home to a very diverse array of ethnic communities. The Taliban regime (1996–2001), for instance, was largely composed of ethnic Pushtuns. Their policies toward non-Pushtun minorities (in particular, the Hazara ethnic group)[68] have caused many individuals from this persecuted group to seek asylum abroad. The Taliban's notorious position on gender issues has also resulted in the attempt by many Afghan women from all ethnic groups to escape as refugees.[69] Many have chosen to avoid seeking asylum in neighboring countries such as Iran and Pakistan, fearing the violence associated with refugee warrior communities in those areas. Instead, a growing number of these asylum seekers have chosen Australia as their destination, as it is the closest state in the region that is a signatory to the UN Refugee Convention. As we shall see, however, their reception has been less than hospitable.

Eduardo Galeano wrote that in Latin America, "inequality before the law lies at the root of history, but official history is written by oblivion, not memory."[70] A half a world away, Afghan refugees making onshore applications in Australia find that inequality before the law is no longer an exception to the rule but a legally mandated norm that is increasingly casting them into oblivion. Since 1994, Australia refugee law has included a provision called "mandatory and non-reviewable detention," which prescribes immediate imprisonment to anyone who makes an onshore application for asylum and is *sans papiers*—that is, without any official papers establishing their identity. While the UNHCR, Amnesty International, and scores of other human rights organizations and refugee advocacy groups have repeatedly pointed out that many asylum seekers have good reason to be without official documentation, this advice has gone unheeded.[71] Thus, the reason for their incarceration is not because any of them had committed any crime other than having made a claim for asylum.

Refugees who have taken flight because of a well-founded fear of being persecuted find in Australia their lives further traumatized by the conditions of detention centers.[72] Refugees detained in these centers are faced with conditions that promote some of the most extreme negative aspects of refugeeness: they are constituted as a bare form-of-life and, therefore, made politically invisible, passive, temporary, and speechless. Their bare life is affirmed not only by the strip search that each refugee-prisoner is forced to endure but also by the (recently discontinued) practice by camp administrators to refer to the detained refugees not by name but by a series of letters and numbers.[73] Their invisibility is ensured by locating the detention centers in remote and isolated areas of the country, far away from communities that could provide them with much needed emotional, legal, and political support. Moreover, their invisibility is further advanced in places like the Woomera Detention Centre, where all mirrors have been removed from the site. The passive quality to refugeeness is also imposed on these refugees as any movements they make to and from the detention centers are done while under (involuntary) sedation and chemical restraints. Those refugees who are successful with their asylum claims nonetheless suffer from the temporary quality of refugeeness. Upon their release from detention, even refugees recognized as Convention refugees are given only three-year "Temporary Protection Visas," are prohibited from sponsoring spouses and children to join them, and cannot reenter Australia if they leave. Finally, in a provision that goes a long way to ensure that the voices of refugees will be literally silenced in the civil and political realms of society, refugees are prohibited from attending English-language classes funded by the national government.[74]

Faced with policies that are literally making them disappear from sight and remain out of earshot, refugees held within these detention centers are responding in a decidedly noncivil and nonhumanitarian manner. Their lives stripped bare—indeed, constituted as bare life—they have devised strategies of resistance that highlight the politics of their caged bodies. Camp inmates across Australia have regularly engaged in hunger strikes and endured solitary confinement. Some have taken the radical option of sewing their mouths shut to highlight their speechlessness. Others have engaged in self-immolation, setting their bodies ablaze to bring light to the collective outrage that is life within the camps. Still others have pushed their flesh against the razor wire that constitutes the violent perimeter of their interned identity. Indeed, this last strategy has culminated in a number of refugee riots at refugee detention centers across Australia.

The first of these actions took place on Thursday, June 8, 2000, when riots erupted at three remote refugee prisons in Australia in protest against these conditions and policies.[75] More than 750 asylum seekers escaped to experience life outside their internment for the first time in six months. After tearing down the barbwire perimeter fencing, refugees from the remote Woomera Detention Centre (the camp is 500 kilometers from Adelaide) headed toward the nearby town to stage a protest against the poor conditions of the camps. Their grievances included overcrowded living quarters, insufficient legal aid, no access to telephones and newspapers, and their general isolation from the outside world. Chanting "We want freedom!" the refugees occupied the town center, only to find that their interaction with civil society was once again constrained: this time not by razor wire fencing but by the bodies of riot police from the Australian Protective Services. These state agents operating at the limit of the sovereign relation erected a human wall to physically segregate the refugees from the general population: they actively discouraged local residents from talking to the refugees and also advised the public to keep their children home from school while the refugee-protestors were in town.

Fewer than three months after the June 2000 riots, a second refugee uprising took place in Woomera, this time repelled by tear gas and (for the first time in Australian history) a water cannon. Further riots and escapes have occurred, causing many refugee-advocacy groups to call on the government to repeal the policy of mandatory detention. To date, the Australian government's response has been to review the policy only in terms of strengthening it by expanding the armory of security officials at the camps. "We are not a soft touch," said Prime Minister John Howard, underlining how Australia is a real state, a strong state.[76] As such, the Australian state has been willing to deploy an effective police and detention system to detain all would-be asylum applicants, effectively criminalizing asylum. To be sure, when asked whether the ongoing refugee riots would initiate a policy review by the government, Immigration Minister Philip Ruddock responded by saying,

> Well, I'm not sure why one would argue that the policy of detention should be reviewed because detainees aren't prepared to observe normal standards of behaviour that we would expect in the Australian community. I mean, that would be like saying that you would close a jail because some people who had been convicted of offences didn't like being detained.[77]

These are, indeed, strong words, echoing a common sentiment propagated by the mainstream Australian media that casts these asylum seekers not only as a "problem" population but also more precisely as a "deviant" community that will only undermine the integrity and coherence of the Australian nation.

These rogue refugees (the vast majority from the so-called rogue states of Iraq and Afghanistan) were making a break from a state of exception, taking a line of flight from the political black hole of the camp that renders them voiceless, without rights, segregated from the lifeworld of civil society. Their segregation from the Australian public—both while in detention and while occupying public space for the purpose of a political action—is an indication of the powerful effect their identity as "refugee" has on their access to political space and voice.

Conclusion: The Criminalization of Sovereignty

From the perspective of the "levels of analysis" schema, the refugee warrior phenomenon is a decidedly international problem. Understood as a transversal phenomenon, however, refugee warrior activity becomes much more difficult to classify in the inside–outside logic of state sovereignty. Indeed, once we appreciate how ambiguous the sovereign relation is with regard to refugeeness, we can begin to recognize the variety of spaces and practices that might constitute a refugee warrior community. Sovereignty, we have seen, is defined not so much by a strict inside and outside as by the state of emergency that is its constitutive limit. The space of exception is more of a "zone of indistinction" than of a realm of strict distinctions between internal and external realms.

The conventional discourse on refugee warrior communities declares that this phenomenon is something that, from the perspective of Western states, happens over there. The dramatic reversal of the refugee's relationship to the political (i.e., when refugees become warriors) arises under conditions where failed states are the norm. The response of refugee claimants to their criminalization and incarceration by Australian authorities demonstrates that such a reversal is also occurring here—that is, in the advanced industrialized countries of the West, states that presumably possess "positive" sovereignty. Here, too, refugees are trying to make a break from the state of exception that defines their condition. While the policy of criminalizing asylum is objectionable for being inhospitable and unfair to refugee claimants (to put it mildly), it also presents some specific and unique dangers to the policy makers. The refugee, Agamben has shown, is not the only resident of the zone of indistinction. The sovereign, too, occupies this liminal space. To criminalize the refugee, to cast her as an adversary and exclude her from civil humanity is to risk having this designation turned around, turning the sovereign into a criminal. Agamben stated,

> What the heads of state, who rushed to criminalize the enemy with such zeal, have not yet realized is that this criminalization can at any moment be turned against them. There is no head of state on Earth today who, in this sense, is not virtually a criminal. Today, those who should happen to wear the sad redingote of the sovereignty know that they may be treated as criminals one day by

their colleagues. And certainly we will not be the ones to pity them. The sovereigns who willingly agreed to present themselves as cops or executioners, in fact, now show their original proximity to the criminal.[78]

The logic of sovereignty as the state of exception demonstrates that, at least with respect to activities at the limit of the political, all states are rogue states, all sovereigns are criminals. Therefore, how "refugee warriors"—the scare quotes are now necessary as the identity is no longer dependent on an armed state-centric violence being performed—are recasting the terms of their identities is one of the most significant sites for how the political is being transformed today.

Conclusion: Rethinking Refugeeness: Dangers and Prospects

The sans-papiers, the excluded among the excluded (though certainly not the only ones), have ceased to simply play the victims in order to become the actors of democratic politics. Through their resistance and their imagination, they powerfully help us give [politics] new life. We owe them this recognition, and to say it, and to commit ourselves ever more numerously at their side, until right and justice are repaid them.

—Étienne Balibar

A remarkable event took place on June 16, 2001. On that day—and that day only—the French National Assembly reconvened itself as the "Assembly of Refugees." The French parliamentarians invited 577 refugees representing seventy-one nationalities and, together, they passed the Paris Appeal. In it, they made a call to governments around the world to apply the principles of the UN Refugee Convention in a nonrestrictive way to their national refugee legislation.[1] This was a grand and important gesture, to be sure. The Assembly that approved the Rights of Man and the Citizen was now united in speaking about the Rights of the Refugee. But alas, the event lasted only a day. The refugees participated in a highly symbolic gathering that was never meant to endure. In the end, the Assembly of Refugees silently underscored the point that the refugee condition is only ever a temporary one. The refugee remains the aberrant counterpart of the normal(ized) national citizen.

The example of the French parliamentarians highlights the deep problems associated with how to include refugee voices into political discourses and institutional processes in a meaningful and effective manner. This is a problem that has been perplexing academics, policy makers, and refugee advocates for some time. The barriers that exist are quite formidable and extend well beyond the practical problems involved in communicating during crisis situations or in a situation of flight. "Giving" the refugee a voice is not just a practical problem of providing opportunities, especially when the hierarchies giver–receiver, helper–victim, listener–crier are left untouched, and it is not only a problem of rectifying unequal power relations. No, the problem of the refugee's voice is a deeply political problem, and one that cuts to the core of who counts as an authentic political subject.

The diversity and complexity in the causes, underlying dynamics, and effects of global refugee flows underscores how this phenomenon continues to pose some of the most pressing challenges facing modern political practice, analysis, and theory today. This study has explored the connections between the categorization of refugees as an "emergency" situation and the way in which "humanitarianism" has come to constitute a hegemonic discourse in which academics, policy makers, international organizations, and refugee advocates must formulate their arguments and actions. Humanitarianism is often portrayed as posing a challenge to the codes and practices of state sovereignty because it is a form of action that is purportedly motivated by a sense of obligation and responsibility to "humanity" that goes beyond the responsibility one feels for fellow citizens. By contrast, this study has argued that there is an intimate, interconnected, and immanent character to the relationship between coercion and altruism, violence and morality, the political and the ethical. The view advanced here is that a humanitarianism that presumes to possess an autonomous existence, separate and distinct from the vicissitudes of political life, is—and always has been—an impossibility. Instead, humanitarianism is an inherently political concept, and one that is always already implicated in a relation of violence and coercion.

Refugee identity, we have seen, is the site of a number of vexing paradoxes. Refugees belong to the "species of alterity"[2]—and yet they are constantly referred to by the most familial of terms: humanity. This humanity, however, is not a given but an identity that comes with a price. When refugees take flight from violence and persecution, their human life is stripped bare, with all political qualifiers (presence, voice, agency) erased from their identity. Refugees, therefore, are not so much human as the site "where the human stops."[3] It is testimony to the political character of humanitarianism that such strict limitations are placed around human identity. The effect of these exclusionary practices is the conflation of refugeeness with a "bare life" that is both consistent with and supportive of the practices of state sovereignty. From this perspective, framing the refugee phenomenon as a "humanitarian emergency" works to sustain constitutive practices that stabilize and reproduce sovereignty's resolution to questions of political identity, community, and world order.

The modern account of the location and character of the political spaces and subjectivities continues to be powerfully compelling. As this study has demonstrated, even actions residing on the limit of modern politics—such as humanitarian multilateral cooperation on the refugee problem—tend to be overdetermined by the statist prerogative to claim the authentic subjects and spaces of politics as its own. The humanitarian ethic in these cases is subsumed within the logic provided by state sovereignty, a logic that already posits a resolution between the moral obligations we feel toward the one and the many, the universal and the particular, humanity and citizen-subjects. Moreover, in the confusion of complex political and humanitarian emergencies today, refugees find their human identity intersecting with the exclusionary spaces of the state of exception—the camp, the detention center, the prison—as well as with the corresponding marginal identities of the victim, the fraud, the diseased body, the animal, the armed threat. This study has traced the various ways in which the relation of sovereignty has ordered these slippages in identities, attempting to tame and discipline the contingencies that define the multiple identities that constitute "refugeeness."

The prevailing humanitarian "solutions" to the refugee's plight both rely on and reproduce sovereign political relations when they focus on returning to refugees statist identities so as to restore the conditions under which they may once again enjoy a properly "human" life as citizens. This close link between humanity and sovereignty has the consequence that humanitarian actors today face the grave danger of maintaining what Agamben worries is "a secret solidarity with the very powers they ought to fight."[4] Reconceiving humanitarian action in ways that will both recognize and transform its political quality should, therefore, begin by considering the way such actions approach self–other relationships. In the case of humanitarian interaction with refugees and refugee communities, this means rethinking the assumptions made about refugee identity in both legal and cultural terms. Clearly, the pejorative qualities of refugeeness, whether they are seemingly benign (speechlessness, invisibility) or dangerous (animality, warriors), have to be transformed.

In many respects, these kinds of changes are already occurring, especially with respect to the refugee's voice. Promotion of the narratives that refugees construct to explain and make sense of their experience of persecution, flight, and asylum has gained momentum in recent years. These narratives are increasingly evident in the publications of humanitarian organizations, the popular media, and academic studies on refugees. For example, the UNHCR-50 Foundation, which organized the global celebrations to commemorate the fiftieth anniversary of the UN refugee agency, included cultural events involving poetry readings as well as musical and dance performances by refugees. In December 2000, the city of Geneva—the "birthplace" of the UNHCR—hosted a major musical event called "Refugee Voices: An Evening to Remember." This concert featured a variety of world-famous refugee musicians, such as Youssou N'Dour and Geoffrey Oryema from Africa, Horacio Duran from Chile, the Argentine duo Claudina and Alberto Gambino, the Burundi Drummers, and others. The UNHCR-50 Foundation Web site includes an ever-expanding Gallery of Prominent Refugees, which profiles hundreds of refugees from all over the world, highlighting their reasons for flight and their experiences in exile.

There has been a similar shift toward inclusiveness within the refugee studies literature, with a number of articles, working papers, and books incorporating the voices and narratives of refugees. While these kind of projects are to be regarded as an encouraging development, the impact of including refugee voices must nonetheless be qualified. After all, it is quite possible to include refugee testimonials and yet not challenge the tacit agreements that constitute conventional representations of refugeeness and sovereign political relations. For instance, it remains exceptionally rare within the academic and policy literature on refugees to seriously consider the possibility of including actual refugees as part of the decision-making process about "solutions" to their plight. This holds true even in what is otherwise an exemplary line of argument put forward by the renowned "subaltern" refugee scholar, B.S. Chimni. Chimni is a well-known critic of both the prevailing refugee regime and the practices of northern states that undermine the culture of asylum, thereby shifting the burden of refugees to countries in the South.[5] While Chimni has expressed his opinions and views as to what kinds of changes should occur at the level of states and regimes, he has also addressed the question of how these changes should occur. He proposed a "dialogic model," highlighting the multiple lines of communication that should occur to transform the refugee regime.[6] The dialogic model replicates neither the traditional bargaining tactics that occur between states nor the approach recently taken by the UNHCR in their Global Consultations. The former is more of an exclusive contest than of the inclusive conversation Chimni wants to encourage. The latter suffers from its ad hoc character, a one-time-only event organized around the occasion of the fiftieth anniversary of the UN Refugee Convention. Chimni proposed, instead, an ongoing dialogue based on the principles of deliberative democracy.

Where do refugees fit in this conversation? Here, it is worthwhile to note the actors that Chimni identified as crucial to this dialogue. The conversations will take place between states; between NGOs, academics, and the UNHCR; within the UNHCR; and between NGOs and governments.[7] However, immediately after outlining these interlocking and crosscutting dialogic relationships, Chimni presented an argument in favor of including the voices of refugees in determinations about solutions to their plight:

> In conducting the dialogue these actors must of course ensure that they do not always speak on behalf of, but in conversation with, refugees. The need to listen to refugee voices, and allow them to

participate in decisions which directly affect their lives, is of supreme significance in giving content to the concept of refugee protection.[8]

Despite these strong words, Chimni is lamentably silent throughout the rest
of his paper on how to provide political voice to refugees in this dialogue.
How can refugees be released from the (conceptual and increasingly real)
dungeons to which they are condemned and, instead, be included in dialogue? For all the use of emphasis and italics, the issue is dropped as soon
as it is brought up.

While Chimni met the problem of how to structure dialogical relationships with refugees with emphasized silence, others have been more proactive in these matters. This is especially true of international humanitarian
aid organizations, some of which have taken measures to at least listen to, if
not fully dialogue with, refugees. But here, too, the difficulty of reinforcing
the refugee's speechlessness through the very attempt to include his or her
voice is apparent. Oxfam (GB), for example, has recently made it a priority to listen to the forcibly displaced people to whom they provide aid and
development assistance. Accordingly, the organization commissioned a report, titled "Listening to the Displaced," with the aim of developing a methodology for how to listen to displaced people in conflict situations. The
ostensive purpose of this exercise is to "empower" people living in crisis
situations to have input into formulating the solutions to their plight. This
would allow Oxfam (GB) to respond to humanitarian emergencies in a way
that avoids "top-down solutions that do not always take the opinion of the
displaced refugees into account."[9]

In an incisive critique of the Listening project, Prem Kumar Rajaram
applauded Oxfam for recognizing the need to "listen to" refugees but seriously doubted what they are hearing. Rajaram has criticized the Oxfam
methodology for its failure to be self-reflexive about how the voices of the
displaced fit with the interests of this major international humanitarian
development agency. Rajaram's analysis suggests that the Listening project
"filters" voices to emphasize ones that can attest to the value of Oxfam's work
and thereby serves an institutional need for sustained funding. What results
is a kind of "violent reductionism"[10] that not only places severe limitations
on the range of experiences and views of the displaced but also presents a
severely decontextualized account of the refugee experience. In fact, the
director of Oxfam in Sri Lanka hints at this bias. In a review of the Listening
project, he noted Oxfam's failure in "translating" the concerns of displaced
people into a sustained policy development and advocacy strategy. What
was heard in the field was never to have an effective impact in the strategic
deliberations—other than financial—of the humanitarian agency. In fact,
after noting this concern over accountability, the director suggested the appropriate response would be for the Listening methodology to be altered so
as to counter any "unrealistic expectations" by refugees.[11]

Interventions into transforming refugeeness, therefore, must be approached with a great deal of caution. To be sure, proposals that have been met with some success are almost always subject to considerable qualifications, and the terms of their "success" often run contrary to the original intentions of the authors. This is well demonstrated in the case of James Hathaway and Alexander Neve's recent attempt to "reconceive" international refugee law.[12] Their motivation was to address the uneven character of contemporary refugee protection—a situation where northern states are protecting only 20 percent of the world's refugee population and yet allocate far greater resources to process and determine (and, indeed, deter) refugees at home than to assist the vast majority of refugees in the South.[13] The Hathaway and Neve proposal attempts to rectify this inequitable situation by brokering a compromise that proposes a "temporary protection" regime for northern states unwilling to make long-term commitments to vast numbers of asylum seekers. Hathaway and Neve justify this enhancement of the already temporary dimension of refugeeness by formulating a "burden sharing" agreement that would see northern states take greater responsibility and leadership in rectifying the global refugee crisis. The Hathaway and Neve proposal, therefore, involves a delicate balancing act between, on one hand, the political rights of sovereign states to control movement and manage populations and, on the other hand, the pressing human need for asylum faced by people fleeing situations of persecution and violence. As this study has demonstrated, however, this balancing act between the state and humanity is always tricky. Consequently, despite their desire to speak in "solution-oriented" terms, the Hathaway and Neve proposal inevitably confronts the force of the sovereign relation and its ongoing historical attempts to resolve this classic dilemma.

In the case of the Hathaway and Neve proposal, the real difficulty lay not in the fact that it was rejected out of hand or, as is more often the case, totally ignored but that, to the contrary, the proposal was taken seriously or—more to the point—some aspects of the proposal were accepted by states, while others were cast aside. In particular, the policy recommendations on "collectivized protection" measures under the banner of a "temporary protection" regime have been met with a positive reaction by Western states. At the same time, however, the so-called burden-sharing elements of the proposal have been largely ignored. In short, states took the proposals that augmented their power to establish increasingly restrictive terms of protection and asylum and left off all the concomitant protections. The end situation has been to promote an even greater temporary dimension to refugeeness than existed before.

To be open to ways in which refugees might be included in a dialogue about their fate nevertheless seems to be a necessary prerequisite for developing enduring solutions to this "problem" of world order. The first step to such a dialogue means dispensing with the classification scheme that condemns refugee identity as nonpolitical and, therefore, establishing the conditions under which refugees are made speechless, invisible, and dangerous. A number of promising studies have been made in this regard, with works by Nevzat Soguk, Jennifer Hyndman, Michael Dillon, Daniel Warner, and Liisa Malkki pushing the discourse on refugeeness to its limits.[14] In the realm of philosophy, too, thinkers such as Giorgio Agamben and Jacques Derrida have considered the problematic of the refugee from the perspective of recasting the political under current globalizing conditions.[15]

Nietzsche once wrote, "We are looking for words; perhaps we are also looking for ears."[16] Once we no longer expect to hear silence from refugees, then perhaps we will be ready to listen to how they are asserting themselves as political subjects, thereby recasting the terms on which the sovereign political relation has relied. For example, the role Guatemalan refugees played in negotiating the terms of return from settlements in Mexico in the late 1980s is indicative of how important it is to include refugees in these discussions. To be sure, these refugees actively resisted multilateral solutions to their plight that treated them as passive, voiceless, agentless victims. Instead, they organized themselves to become the first-ever international refugee community to "overcome the institutionally defined marginality of being 'spoken for' by international and refugee relief organizations [and] to represent itself directly during two years of internationally mediated talks aimed at specifying the terms of their own return."[17] This is demonstrated by the refusal of the Guatemalan refugees to abide by the 1986 UNHCR-negotiated voluntary repatriation agreement with the Mexican and Guatemalan governments. Instead, forty-five thousand refugees in southern Mexico elected members to a Permanent Commission (CCPP) to represent their interest in negotiating the terms of a communal return movement. "Return is struggle, not resignation" was the slogan of this movement, underlining the intensely political self-conception of these refugees. How they recast the political varied, but an important struggle in the return movement has been the personal and organized attempts by women returnees—many of whom were politicized during their exile in Mexico and through their active participation in the negotiation of the peace accords—to challenge the male-dominated decision-making structures and practices of their communities.[18]

The case of the Guatemalans is, unfortunately, the exception and not the rule. In an atmosphere of fear and paranoia following September 11, 2001, especially around allegedly "bogus" refugees-cum-terrorists, there is much cause for pessimism about future hospitality that can be shown toward refugees. Surely a more constructive and inclusive response is possible, and one that does not further contribute to the effacement of political subjectivity among refugees. The argument put forward in this study is that this effacement is indicative of a larger problem, one that is more fundamental than merely developing institutional mechanisms to amplify refugee voices. Indeed, giving recognition to political practices occurring in spaces and times that run counter to modern sovereign subjectivities runs the risk of opening up the entire architecture of our received conception of the political. Consequently, we are increasingly being forced to ask how the political is being recast under contemporary conditions. In addition, we must also inquire into who is doing the recasting (women or just men? children or just adults? believers or secular people? the poor or the affluent?) and where these practices are occurring (North or South? states, cities, or the countryside? parliaments or in the camps and in the streets?).[19]

The implication of the argument is that we should explore the ways in which the citizen–human dynamic of sovereignty is being recast by global–local practices. There are a number of possible directions that future research could take, but considering how the citizen–human dynamic is being renegotiated by "refugees," irrespective if they are "legitimate," is likely to be a fruitful strategy. For states and international humanitarian organizations, this means following the advice Chimni gave but never followed—that is, to resist the problem-solving mentality that effaces the political subjectivity of the refugee and to, instead, engage in a serious, equitable, and inclusive dialogue with refugees to determine the terms under which their lives will be conducted. For organizations such as the UNHCR, this means reconsidering the strict terms and qualifications imposed on refugee activities and self-governance in the camps. This would likely entail pursuing programs that would demand a greater emphasis on cultural translation for humanitarian staff. Indeed, the emphasis on the camp as the "humanitarian space" of choice might have to be reconsidered, especially for how camp life often precludes access to employment, mobility, and independence—activities that give refugees a real chance to move away from the minimal "bare life" of the zone of exception that is the camp.

In the countries of the North that had traditionally served as places of asylum, refugee activism is increasingly being organized against the trend toward allocating temporary status to refugees and using deportation and incarceration as "protection" measures. A number of social movements have emerged to work with refugees and oppose these developments. The antideportation movement qualifies as an especially interesting case for future research for how it pushes the sovereign logic to the limit.[20] While the activities and forms of action of this movement vary across time and space, they do share some commonalities with reference to their conception of refugeeness. Most dramatically, they insist that forcible displacement for economic reasons (a kind of "well-founded fear of poverty") are legitimate grounds for refugee status. In Germany and Australia, the movement is increasingly declaring its solidarity with the displaced through movement—in particular, through the organization of large caravans roaming across these countries to facilitate the political expression of refugee rights. In Germany, the Caravan for the Rights of Refugees and Migrants has, since 1998, organized an annual cross-country caravan that travels to forty-four German cities with the explicit purpose of bringing together refugees, migrants, and antiracist groups to express and organize themselves politically. Similarly, the Woomera 2002 Caravan in Australia converged on the site of the notorious refugee prison at the end of March 2002, with the purpose of revealing "the connections between dispossession and the enclosures" through a diversity of political and cultural practices that promise to "disrupt the present and create the future."[21]

While it is extremely difficult to predict the success or failure of a political movement, the transversal focus of the antideportation movement constitutes a very promising site where the political is being recast. The impact of this movement has perhaps been felt most directly in France, where the sans papiers movement has had a powerful effect on the political debates about the meaning of citizenship and the political in that country. The transformation of the National Assembly into the Assembly of Refugees is a dramatic example of how seriously refugees have affected that country's politics and self-conception of the political. With this event, the center of the state was momentarily taken over by the margins. The sovereign finally came clean and admitted that its power was derived through its "inclusive exclusionary" relationship with the bare life of the refugee. But as we have seen, the transformation lasted only for one day. This grand gesture on behalf of the French state, in the end, once again reaffirmed the temporary character of refugeeness.

Refugees, we have seen, are caught in a discursive web of power–knowledge relations that define them as human. But the "human" is not only to be interpreted as the bare life that dominates humanitarian practice today. Following Homi Bhabha, the human is to be

> identified not with a given essence, be it natural or supranatural, but with a practice, a task. The property of the human being is the collective or the transindividual construction of her or his individual autonomy; and the value of human agency arises from the fact that no one can be liberated by others, although no one can liberate herself or himself without others.[22]

To be prepared for this task, we need to be open to refugee politics, give support to it, and take direction from it. It is my hope that this study has contributed to understanding why taking such positions is crucial to our ethical and political life.

Notes

Introduction

1. David Held and Anthony McGrew, "Globalization and the Liberal Democratic State," in *Global Transformation: Challenges to the States System*, ed. Yoshikazu Sakamoto (Tokyo: United Nations University Press, 1994), 57–84.

2. David Harvey, *The Condition of Postmodernity* (Oxford: Basil Blackwell, 1990).

3. Doreen Massey, *Space, Place, and Gender* (Minneapolis: University of Minnesota Press, 1994), 149.

4. Brian Massumi, *Parables for the Virtual: Movement, Affect, Sensation* (Durham: Duke University Press, 2002), 8–9.

5. Lester Edwin J. Ruiz, "In Pursuit of the 'Body Politic': Ethics, Spirituality, and Diaspora," *Transnational Law and Contemporary Problems* 9, no. 2 (Fall 1999), 633–34. Emphasis in original.

6. Ibid., 634.

7. Elizabeth Grosz, *Volatile Bodies: Toward a Corporeal Feminism* (Bloomington: Indiana University Press, 1994).

8. Jenny Edkins, Nalini Persram, and Véronique Pin-Fat, eds., *Sovereignty and Subjectivity* (Boulder, CO: Lynne Rienner, 1999).

9. R.B.J. Walker, "International Relations and the Concept of the Political," in *International Relations Theory Today*, ed. Ken Booth and Steve Smith (University Park: Pennsylvania State University Press, 1995), 306.

10. R.B.J. Walker, *Inside/Outside: International Relations as Political Theory* (Cambridge: Cambridge University Press, 1993).

11. Friedrich Nietzsche, *On the Genealogy of Morals* (New York: Vintage Books, 1969), II, §17.

12. Thomas J. Biersteker and Cynthia Weber, eds., *State Sovereignty as Social Construct* (Cambridge: Cambridge University Press, 1996).

13. Warren Magnusson, *The Search for Political Space* (Toronto: University of Toronto Press, 1996), 293. Emphasis in original.

14. Carl Schmitt, *Political Theology: Four Chapters on the Concept of Sovereignty*, trans. George Schwab (Cambridge, MA: MIT Press, 1985), 5.

15. Walter Benjamin, "Critique of Violence," in *Reflections*, trans. Edmund Jephcott (New York: Schocken Books, 1978), 277–300.

16. For an elaboration on this point, see Eric L. Santner, "Some Reflections on States of Exception," in *Social Insecurity: Alphabet City* No. 7, ed. Len Guenther and Cornelius Heesters (Toronto: Anansi, 2000), 154.

17. Bonnie Honig, *Democracy and the Foreigner* (Princeton, NJ: Princeton University Press, 2001).

18. Giorgio Agamben, *Homo Sacer: Sovereign Power and Bare Life*, trans. Daniel Heller-Roazen (Stanford, CA: Stanford University Press, 1998), 18.

19. Gilles Deleuze and Félix Guattari, *A Thousand Plateaus: Capitalism and Schizophrenia*, trans. Brian Massumi (Minneapolis: University of Minnesota Press, 1987), 386.

20. Ibid., 360. See also Paul Patton, *Deleuze and the Political* (New York: Routledge, 2000).

21. David Campbell, "Political Excess and the Limits of the Imagination," *Millennium: Journal of International Studies* 23, no. 2 (1994), 365–75.

22. Giorgio Agamben, "Beyond Human Rights," in *Radical Thought in Italy: A Potential Politics*, ed. Paolo Virno and Michael Hardt (Minneapolis: University of Minnesota Press, 1996), 159.

23. Examples of this emerging literature include Liisa Malkki, *Purity and Exile: Violence, Memory, and National Cosmology among Hutu Refugees in Tanzania* (Chicago: University of Chicago Press, 1995), Nevzat Soguk, *States and Strangers: Refugees and Displacements of Statecraft* (Minneapolis: University of Minnesota Press, 1999), Jennifer Hyndman, *Managing Displacement: Refugees and the Politics of Humanitarianism* (Minneapolis: University of Minnesota Press, 1999), Aihwa Ong, *Buddha Is Hiding: Refugees, Citizenship, the New America* (Berkeley: University of California Press, 2003), and Didier Bigo, "Security and Immigration: Towards a Critique of the Governmentality of Unease," *Alternatives* 24, supplement (2002), 63–92.

24. Liisa H. Malkki, "National Geographic: The Rooting of Peoples and the Territorialization of National Identity among Scholars and Refugees," *Cultural Anthropology* 7, no. 1 (1992), 37.

25. Liisa H. Malkki, "Speechless Emissaries: Refugees, Humanitarianism, and Dehistoricization," *Cultural Anthropology* 11, no. 3 (1996), 377–404.

Chapter 1

1. Sadako Ogata, "Foreword," in *The State of the World's Refugees: The Challenge of Protection*, ed. UNHCR (New York: Penguin, 1993), iii. Emphasis added.

2. Carl Schmitt, *Political Theology: Four Chapters on the Concept of Sovereignty*, trans. George Schwab (Cambridge, MA: MIT Press, 1985), 5.

3. Jenny Edkins, *Poststructuralism and International Relations: Bringing the Political Back In* (Boulder, CO: Lynne Rienner, 1999), 2.

4. Liisa H. Malkki, "Speechless Emissaries: Refugees, Humanitarianism, and Dehistoricization," *Cultural Anthropology* 11, no. 3 (1996), 386.

5. Soren Jessen-Petersen, "Statement to the Security Council by Soren Jessen-Petersen, UNHCR," *Refugee Survey Quarterly* 17, no. 1 (1998), 65.

6. These statistics on refugees and other forcibly displaced persons are drawn from the UNHCR Web site, http://www.unhcr.ch/cgi-bin/texis/vtx/home?page=statistics.

7. See Pierre Bourdieu, *Distinction: A Social Critique of the Judgement of Taste*, trans. Richard Nice (Cambridge, MA: Harvard University Press, 1984).

8. Bernard Husson, André Marty, and Claire Pirotte, "Observations on Crises," in *Responding to Emergencies and Fostering Development: The Dilemmas of Humanitarian Aid,* ed. Claire Pirotte, Bernard Husson, and François Grunewald (London: Zed Books, 1999), 12.

9. Daniel Warner, "Review of Constructing a Productive Other," *International Journal of Refugee Law* 7, no. 2 (1995), 372.

10. United Nations, General Assembly, 42nd Session, Executive Committee of the High Commissioner's Programme, *A Study of UNHCR Emergency Preparedness and Response: Preliminary Conclusions from the Persian Gulf*, December 11, 1991 (A/AC.96/788), 1

11. Ibid., 2.

12. Ibid., 3.

13. Robert W. Cox, "Social Forces, States and World Order: Beyond International Relations Theory," in *Neorealism and Its Critics*, ed. Robert O. Keohane (New York: Columbia University Press, 1986), 208.

14. Sandra Whitworth, "Where Is the Politics in Peacekeeping?" *International Journal* 50, no. 2 (1995), 434.

15. Michel Foucault, *The Archaeology of Knowledge*, trans. A.M. Sheridan Smith (New York: Pantheon Books, 1972).

16. Michel Foucault, "The Order of Discourse," in *Language and Politics*, ed. Michael J. Shapiro (New York: New York University Press, 1985), 108–38.

17. Zygmunt Bauman, *Modernity and Ambivalence* (Cambridge: Polity Press, 1991), 14.

18. It is in this sense that distinctions between a state of emergency and an ordered state of affairs correspond to a culturally specific form of discriminations that Jacques Derrida labeled logocentric. Derrida described logocentric distinctions as hierarchically arranged binary oppositions in which one privileged term (logos) provides the orientation for interpreting the meaning of the subordinate term. In his many writings, Derrida has repeatedly shown that for all its accomplishments, for all its great variety and diversity, the Western tradition of modern thought relies on some very simple dichotomies: for example, masculine–feminine, good–evil, reason–force, here–there, order–crisis, and so on. For Derrida, our received traditions of thought work according to a logic of Identity, a metaphysics striving for Unity. It is a way of thinking that describes the world, or aspects of it such as social life, as an ontological whole. However, this desire for unity, ironically, generates a logic of separateness or hierarchical oppositions. The resulting binaries are, therefore, arranged in a pattern of what Jonathan Culler called "unequal dependence." Logocentric interpretations of these dichotomous oppositions always

involve a hierarchy: there is a superior term and an inferior term; "the superior term belongs to the logos and is a higher presence; the inferior term marks a fall." The superior term has a pure and incorruptible identity; the inferior term can be understood only in a negative, unequal relation to the first. See Jonathan Culler, *On Deconstruction: Theory and Criticism after Structuralism* (Ithaca, NY: Cornell University Press, 1982), 93.

19. Husson et al., "Observations on Crises," 11.

20. United Nations, *UNHCR Emergency Preparedness and Response*, 2.

21. Giorgio Agamben, *Homo Sacer: Sovereign Power and Bare Life* (Stanford, CA: Stanford University Press, 1998).

22. Jutta Weldes, "The Cultural Production of Crises: US Identity and Missiles in Cuba," in *Cultures of Insecurity: States, Communities, and the Production of Danger*, ed. Jutta Weldes, Mark Laffey, Hugh Gusterson, and Raymond Duvall (Minneapolis: University of Minnesota Press, 1999), 40.

23. R. Yewdall Jennings, "Some International Law Aspects of the Refugee Question," *The British Yearbook of International Law* 20 (1939), 98. Emphasis added.

24. Andrew Vincent, *Theories of the State* (Oxford: Basil Blackwell, 1987), 21.

25. Liisa H. Malkki, "National Geographic: The Rooting of Peoples and the Territorialization of National Identity among Scholars and Refugees," *Cultural Anthropology* 7, no. 1 (1992), 24–44.

26. Paul Virilio, "Is the Author Dead? An Interview with Paul Virilio," in *The Virilio Reader*, ed. James Der Derian (Oxford: Blackwell, 1998), 20.

27. For a study that moves the accident from the margins to the centre of IR theory, see James Der Derian, "Global Events, National Security, and Virtual Theory," *Millennium: Journal of International Studies* 30, no. 3 (2001), 669–90.

28. Lal Jayawardena, "Foreword," in *Mistrusting Refugees*, ed. E. Valentine Daniel and John Chr. Knudsen (Berkeley: University of California Press, 1995), viii.

29. For different readings on the "modern" nature of refugees, compare Michael Marrus, *The Unwanted: European Refugees in the Twentieth Century* (New York: Oxford University Press, 1985), Gil Loescher, *Beyond Charity: International Cooperation and the Global Refugee Crisis* (New York: Oxford University Press, 1993), Nicholas Xenos, "Refugees: The Modern Political Condition," *Alternatives* 18, no. 4 (1993), 419–30.

30. Marrus, *The Unwanted*, 92. See also, John Torpey, *The Invention of the Passport: Surveillance, Citizenship and the State* (Cambridge: Cambridge University Press, 2000).

31. Claudena M. Skran, *Refugees in Inter-War Europe: The Emergence of a Regime* (Oxford: Clarendon, 1995), 13–14.

32. Marrus, *The Unwanted*, 15.

33. Ibid., 20.

34. Aristide R. Zolberg, Astri Suhrke, and Sergio Aguayo, *Escape from Violence: Conflict and the Refugee Crisis in the Developing World* (New York: Oxford University Press, 1989), 11. The practices of "incarceration–transportation–massacre" have by no means been eliminated from the lives of the forcibly displaced. For an excellent history, see William Walters, "Deportation, Expulsion, and the International Police of Aliens," *Citizenship Studies* 6, no. 3 (2002), 265–92.

35. Giorgio Agamben, "Beyond Human Rights," in *Radical Thought in Italy: A Potential Politics*, ed. Paolo Virno and Michael Hardt (Minneapolis: University of Minnesota Press, 1996), 161.

36. Hannah Arendt, *Imperialism: Part II of the Origins of Totalitarianism* (New York: Harvest, 1968), 147.

37. Ibid., 161.

38. Zolberg et al., *Escape from Violence*, 19–20.

39. Loescher, *Beyond Charity*, 37.

40. Nevzat Soguk, *States and Strangers: Refugees and Displacements of Statecraft* (Minneapolis: University of Minnesota Press, 1999), 110.

41. Loescher, *Beyond Charity*, 46.

42. This limitation on financial control continued to haunt the UNHCR throughout its five decades of operation. The widening gap between assessed needs and likely sources of resources reached a crisis point in the late 1980s when the UNHCR registered a $40 million deficit. In 1989, member states refused for the first time to approve the UNHCR budget. These financial difficulties affected the UNHCR's ability to secure stable leadership. In October 1989, High Commissioner Jean Pierre Hocke resigned, and his successor Thorval Stoltenberg resigned only thirteen months later. See Alex Cunliffe, "The Refugee Crisis: A Study of the United Nations High Commission for Refugees," *Political Studies* 43, no. 2 (1995), 278–90.

43. L. Holborn, *Refugees: A Problem of Our Time: The Work of the United Nations High Commissioner for Refugees, 1951–1972* (Metuchen, NJ: Scarecrow Press, 1975), 101.

44. Randy Lippert, "Governing Refugees: The Relevance of Governmentality to Understanding the International Refugee Regime," *Alternatives* 24, no. 3 (1999), 302. Emphasis added.

45. Soguk, *States and Strangers*, 111. Emphasis added.

46. Xenos, "Refugees," 422.

47. Malkki, "Speechless Emissaries," 386.

48. See http://www.unhcr.ch/images/images.htm.

49. Note that by focusing on the lack of proper clothing and shelter, this photograph implies a relatively thin "normal" existence. This (arguably) reinforces a bias toward the most basic and visible forms of humanitarian emergency relief (e.g., shelter, food, medicine). Other relief activities such as education, recreation, counseling, skills training, and so forth are deemed secondary and so are left to last or are not addressed at all. In chapter 2 I explore this theme with reference to Giorgio Agamben's concept of "bare life" and its relationship to sovereign power.

50. UNHCR, *The State of the World's Refugees: A Humanitarian Agenda* (New York: Oxford University Press, 1998).

51. David Levi Strauss, "Epiphany of the Other," *Artforum* 29 (February 1991), 98. There is, of course, a large market for photographs of this nature. As Eduardo Galeano observed, "Poverty is a commodity that fetches a high price on the luxury market." Eduardo Galeano, ed., "Salgado: Light Is a Secret of Garbage," in *We Say No* (New York: Norton, 1992), 248.

52. Malkki, "Speechless Emissaries," 388. Emphasis in original.

53. Soguk, *States and Strangers*, 8.

54. Malkki, "Speechless Emissaries," 388–89. Emphasis in original.

55. Etienne Balibar, "Propositions on Citizenship," *Ethics* 98 (1988), 724.

56. Arendt, *Imperialism*, 174.

57. Ibid., 176.

58. Warren Magnusson, *The Search for Political Space* (Toronto: University of Toronto Press, 1996).

59. Gilles Deleuze and Félix Guattari, *A Thousand Plateaus: Capitalism and Schizophrenia*, trans. Brian Massumi (Minneapolis: University of Minnesota Press, 1987), 360.

60. Richard K. Ashley and R.B.J. Walker, "Reading Dissidence/Writing the Discipline: Crisis and the Question of Sovereignty in International Studies," *International Studies Quarterly* 34, no. 3 (1990), 367–416.

61. Cynthia Weber, *Simulating Sovereignty: Intervention, the State and Symbolic Exchange* (Cambridge: Cambridge University Press, 1995), 3. See also Thomas J. Biersteker and Cynthia Weber, eds., *State Sovereignty as Social Construct* (Cambridge: Cambridge University Press, 1996), Cynthia Weber, "Performative States," *Millennium: Journal of International Studies* 27, no. 1 (1998), 77–95.

62. Sebastião Salgado, *Workers: An Archaeology of the Industrial Age* (New York: Aperture, 1990).

63. Arjun Appadurai, "Disjuncture and Difference in the Global Cultural Economy," *Public Culture* 2, no. 2 (1990), 1–24.

64. While the analysis presented here is primarily based on my viewing of the Parisian exhibit in June 2000, the photographs of the exhibit have been collected in two companion volumes: Sebastião Salgado, *Migrations: Humanity in Transition* (New York: Aperture, 2000), and Sebastião Salgado, *The Children: Refugees and Migrants* (New York: Aperture, 2000).

65. Strauss, "Epiphany of the Other," 96.

66. Galeano, "Salgado," 248.

67. Strauss, "Epiphany of the Other," 98.

68. Ibid.

69. Jan Jindy Pettman, "Border Crossings/Shifting Identities: Minorities, Gender, and the State in International Perspective," in *Challenging Boundaries: Global Flows, Territorial Identities*, ed. Michael Shapiro and Hayward Alker (Minneapolis: University of Minnesota Press, 1996), especially 264–67.

70. Emphasis added. In chapter 3, I consider at length the interrelation of fear and reason in the UN refugee definition, emphasizing their role in constituting both refugee and sovereign identities.

71. R.B.J. Walker, *Inside/Outside: International Relations as Political Theory* (Cambridge: Cambridge University Press, 1993).

72. UNHCR, "Focus: Ethnic Conflict," *Refugees* 93 (1993), 48.

73. It is disconcerting that Salgado's exhibition participates in foisting an aura of voicelessness on refugees. The entire exhibit, for example, names only one photographic subject: Alberto Cairo. He is, tellingly, not a refugee at all but rather an international humanitarian aid worker working on the ICRC's Orthopaedic Project for Afghanistan.

74. Maison Européenne de la Photographie, "Sebastião Salgado: Exodes," *Mots Ecrans Photos* no. 8 (April 2000).

75. David Campbell, "Disaster Politics and the Politics of the Disaster: Exploring 'Humanitarianism,' " in *The Politics of the Emergency: Intervention, Peacekeeping, Humanitarianism, Development: Report of an Interdisciplinary Research Workshop*, ed. Jenny Edkins (University of Manchester Papers in Politics, no. 2, 1997), 17. Emphasis in original.

76. R.B.J. Walker, "International Relations and the Concept of the Political," in *International Relations Theory Today*, ed. Ken Booth and Steve Smith (University Park: Pennsylvania State University Press, 1995), 306–27.

77. Paolo Virno, "Virtuosity and Revolution: The Political Theory of Exodus," in *Radical Thought in Italy: A Potential Politics*, ed. Paolo Virno and Michale Hardt (Minneapolis: University of Minnesota Pres, 1996), 189–210.

78. Mario Tronti, "The Strategy of Refusal," in "Autonomia: Post-political Politics," *Semiotexte*(e) no. 3 (1980), 28–34.

79. Virno, "Virtuosity and Revolution," 197.

80. Virno and Hardt, "Glossary of Concepts," *Radical Thought in Italy*, 262.

81. Paolo Virno, "The Ambivalence of Disenchantment," in *Radical Thought in Italy*, 33.

82. Homi Bhabha, *The Location of Culture* (New York: Routledge, 1994), 41.

83. David Campbell, "Political Excess and the Limits of the Imagination," *Millennium: A Journal of International Studies* 23, no. 2 (1994), 368.

Chapter 2

1. Quoted in Mark Cutts, "Politics and Humanitarianism," *Refugee Survey Quarterly* 17, no. 1 (1998), 10.

2. Cornelio Sommaruga, "Address to the UN General Assembly, 20 November 1992," *International Review of the Red Cross* no. 292 (1993), 52.

3. Cutts, "Politics and Humanitarianism," 3–5.

4. Chris Brown, *International Relations Theory: New Normative Approaches* (New York: Columbia University Press, 1992).

5. Jim George, "Realist 'Ethics,' International Relations, and Post-modernism: Thinking Beyond the Egoism-Anarchy Thematic," *Millennium: Journal of International Studies* 24, no. 2 (1995), 195–223.

6. Fiona Robinson, "Globalizing Care: Ethics, Feminist Theory, and International Relations," *Alternatives* 22, no. 1 (1997), 114–15.

7. For a helpful discussion that points to a way out of this Eurocentric maze, see David Blaney and Naeem Inayatullah, *International Relations and the Problem of Difference* (New York: Routledge, 2003).

8. Robinson, "Globalizing Care," 117.

9. R.B.J. Walker, "Norms in a Teacup: Surveying the 'New Normative Approaches,' " *Mershon International Studies Review* 38 (1994), 268.

10. The phrase is from Michael J. Shapiro, "The Ethics of Encounter: Unreading, Unmapping the Imperium," in *Moral Spaces: Rethinking Ethics and World Politics*, ed. David Campbell and Michael J. Shapiro (Minneapolis: University of Minnesota Press, 1999), 57.

11. Robert H. Jackson, "Armed Humanitarianism," *International Journal* no. 48 (1993), 581.

12. Cutts, "Politics and Humanitarianism," 2.

13. Ibid.

14. Nicholas Leader, "Proliferating Principles; Or How to Sup with the Devil without Getting Eaten," *Disasters* 22, no. 4 (1998), 288–308.

15. UN General Assembly resolution 46/182 (December 19, 1991).

16. Quoted in Adam Roberts, *Humanitarian Action in War: Aid, Protection and Impartiality in a Policy Vacuum*, Adelphi Paper 305 (Oxford: International Institute for Strategic Studies, 1996), 51.

17. Peter Aeberhard, "A Historical Survey of Humanitarian Action," *Health and Human Rights* 2, no. 1 (1996), 36.

18. Skran, for example, squarely identified "sovereignty" and "humanitarianism" to be the two "basic principles [that] underpinned the international refugee regime that existed in the inter-war years." Claudena M. Skran, *Refugees in Inter-War Europe: The Emergence of a Regime* (Oxford: Clarendon, 1995), 67.

19. Quoted in ibid. Further evidence to how the various interwar international refugee organizations distanced themselves from "political" considerations can be seen in the October 1933 decision of the Assembly of the League of Nations to refer the issue of refugees from Germany to the Second Committee (Technical Organizations) rather than to the Sixth Committee (Political Questions). Ibid., 36.

20. Leader, "Proliferating Principles," 290.

21. Fiona Terry, *Condemned to Repeat? The Paradox of Humanitarian Action* (Ithaca, NY: Cornell University Press, 2002).

22. Roberts, Humanitarian Action, 51–54. The qualification "so-called" is necessary because as the Bosnian case tragically demonstrated, the absence of policy can be the result of a direct strategic action. On this point, see Michel Feher, *Powerless by Design* (Durham: Duke University Press, 2000).

23. Larry Minear and Thomas G. Weiss, *Humanitarian Action in Times of War: A Handbook for Practitioners* (Boulder, CO: Lynne Rienner, 1993), 18–41.

24. Leader, "Proliferating Principles."

25. Andrew Linklater, *The Transformation of Political Community: Ethical Foundations of the Post-Westphalian Era* (Cambridge: Polity, 1998), 5.

26. Andrew Linklater, *Men and Citizens in the Theory of International Relations*, 2nd ed. (London: Macmillan, 1990).

27. R.B.J. Walker, "Gender and Critique in the Theory of International Relations," in *Gendered States: Feminist (Re)Visions of International Relations Theory*, ed. V. Spike Peterson (Boulder, CO: Lynne Rienner, 1992), 189.

28. Linklater, Transformation of Political Community. For a critical analysis of "primordialism," see Arjun Appadurai, *Modernity at Large: Cultural Dimensions of Globalization* (Minneapolis: University of Minnesota Press, 1996).

29. R.B.J. Walker, "The Hierarchicalization of Political Community," *Review of International Studies* 25 (1999), 154. Emphasis in original.

30. Ibid.

31. Mervyn Frost, *Ethics and International Relations: A Constitutive Theory* (Cambridge: Cambridge University Press, 1996), 76.

32. Ibid., chaps. 2 and 4.

33. Ibid., 141–59.

34. An important exception is Shlomo Avineri, *Hegel's Theory of the Modern State* (Cambridge: Cambridge University Press, 1974), especially chapter 10.

35. Michael Shapiro, *Violent Cartographies: Mapping Cultures of War* (Minneapolis: University of Minnesota Press, 1997), 41–47.

36. Michael Shapiro commented on Hegel's "advocacy" of war, noting that Hegel considers war a "necessity" because it is a "consequence of his philosophically constructed commitments to the state, to the organic connection between the individual and the state, and, most crucially, to the dynamics of negation in the maintenance of both." Ibid., 42.

37. "In peace civil life continually expands: all its departments wall themselves in, and in the long run men stagnate. Their idiosyncrasies become continually more fixed and ossified. But for health the unity of the body is required, and if its parts harden themselves into exclusiveness, that is death." G.W.F. Hegel, *Philosophy of Right*, trans. T.M. Knox (Oxford: Oxford University Press, 1967), Addition #188 to §324, p. 295.

38. Hegel stated, "War has the higher significance that by its agency, as I have remarked elsewhere, 'the ethical health of peoples is preserved in their indifference to the stabilization of finite institutions; just as the blowing of the winds preserves the sea from the foulness which would be the result of a prolonged calm, so also corruption in nations would be the product of prolonged, let alone "perpetual," peace.' " Ibid., §324, p. 210.

39. Frost, *Ethics*, 143.

40. See, for example, Charles Tilly, *Coercion, Capital, and European States, AD 990–1992* (Cambridge: Blackwell, 1992).

41. Pierre Hassner, "Refugees: A Special Case for Cosmopolitan Citizenship?" in *Re-imagining Political Community: Studies in Cosmopolitan Democracy*, ed. Daniele Archibugi, David Held, and Martin Kohler (Stanford, CA: Stanford University Press, 1998), 273–86.

42. Thomas Keenan, "Humanism without Borders," in *Social Insecurity*, ed. Len Guenther and Cornelius Heesters, Alphabet City No. 7 (Toronto: Anansi, 2000), 41.

43. Hannah Arendt, *Imperialism: Part II of the Origins of Totalitarianism* (New York: Harvest, 1968), 179.

44. Jean-François Lyotard, "The Other's Rights," in *The Politics of Human Rights*, ed. The Belgrade Circle (London: Verso, 1999), 181–88.

45. Giorgio Agamben, "Beyond Human Rights," in *Radical Thought in Italy: A Potential Politics*, ed. Paolo Virno and Michael Hardt (Minneapolis: University of Minnesota Press, 1996), 151.

46. Jacques Rancière, "Ten Theses on Politics," *Theory and Event* 5, no. 3 (2001), §23.

47. Ibid.

48. In chapter 3, I discuss in detail the relationship between reason, fear, and the (contested) process of refugee subjectification.

49. Michel Foucault, *The History of Sexuality: Vol. I An Introduction*, trans. Robert Hurley (New York: Vintage, 1978), 143.

50. Ibid., 140.

51. The gendered implications of this distinction are discussed in Jenny Edkins, "Sovereign Power, Zones of Indistinction, and the Camp," *Alternatives* 25, no. 1 (2000), especially 20–21.

52. Giorgio Agamben, *Homo Sacer: Sovereign Power and Bare Life*, trans. Daniel Heller-Roazen (Stanford, CA: Stanford University Press, 1998), 4.

53. Carl Schmitt, *Political Theology: Four Chapters on the Concept of Sovereignty*, trans. George Schwab (Cambridge: MIT Press, 1985), and Carl Schmitt, *The Concept of the Political*, trans. George Schwab (Chicago: University of Chicago Press, 1996).

54. Michael J. Shapiro, "Literary Geography and Sovereign Violence: Resisting Tocqueville's Family Romance," *Alternatives* 25, no. 1 (2000), 40.

55. Agamben, *Homo Sacer*, 3.

56. Ibid., 185.

57. Ibid., 106.

58. Agamben, "Beyond Human Rights," 161.

59. Agamben, *Homo Sacer*, 131.

60. Ibid., 133.

61. Edkins, "Zones of Indistinction," 18.

Chapter 3

1. A number of periodicals on refugees have taken the occasion of the UNHCR's fiftieth anniversary to devote special issues to consider these questions: *International Migration Review* 35, no. 1 (2001), *Refuge: Canada's Periodical on Refugees* 20, no. 1 (2001), *Forced Migration Review* no. 10 (April 2001).

2. The Global Consultations were organized around three themes: protection of refugees in mass influx situations; protection of refugees in the context of individual asylum systems; and the search for protection-based solutions. Judith Kumin, "Revitalizing International Protection: The UNHCR's Global Consultations," *Refuge: Canada's Periodical on Refugees* 19, no. 4 (February 2001), 5–7.

3. Ruud Lubbers, UN High Commissioner for Refugees (presentation made to the Informal Meeting of the European Union Ministers for Justice and Ministers for Home Affairs, Stockholm, February 8, 2001).

4. Lubbers (presentation to European Union Ministers). Emphasis added.

5. Quoted in "When Is a Refugee Not a Refugee?" *The Economist*, March 3, 2001, 23.

6. Lubbers (presentation to European Union Ministers).

7. Erika Feller, "The Convention at 50: The Way Ahead for Refugee Protection," *Forced Migration Review* no. 10 (2001), 6.

8. There is an important continuity between this line of argument and feminist and postcolonial scholarship that has highlighted how women and non-Western people have been (negatively) defined by their emotions or so-called base drives. For a classic treatment, see Edward Said, *Orientalism* (New York: Vintage, 1978).

9. Kay Anderson, "The Beast Within: Race, Humanity, and Animality," *Environment and Planning D: Society and Space* 18 (2000), 302.

10. Brian Massumi, "Preface," in *The Politics of Everyday Fear*, ed. Brian Massumi (Minneapolis: University of Minnesota Press, 1993), ix.

11. Michael Dillon, "The Scandal of the Refugee: Some Reflections on the 'Inter' of International Relations and Continental Thought," in *Moral Spaces: Rethinking Ethics and World Politics*, ed. David Campbell and Michael J. Shapiro (Minneapolis: University of Minnesota Press, 1999), 94–95.

12. The wording here is significant, for Hobbes considered the "political" as coming after sovereignty. This point is often underemphasized in the literature on sovereignty. Hobbes does not consider sovereignty as political. Rather, sovereignty is the condition of possibility for modern forms of political space, identity, and practice. As Karena Shaw commented, "Sovereignty itself—the establishment of a common ontology—is not political for Hobbes. It is, rather, the precondition for the political. Whatever violences it may involve, sovereignty must be rendered natural and necessary rather than contingent." Karena Shaw, "Feminist Futures: Contesting the Political," *Transnational Law and Contemporary Problems* 9, no. 2 (Fall 1999), 578.

13. UNHCR, *The State of the World's Refugees: The Challenge of Protection* (New York: Penguin Books, 1993), 169–70. As originally conceived, the UNHCR had no limitations placed on its mandate. However, the Convention obliged its signatory nations to a much narrower commitment. The Convention applied only to individuals who were refugees "as a result of events occurring in Europe before 1 January 1951." Despite the strong objections voiced by delegates from non-Western countries (in particular, Mexico, India, and Pakistan), the narrow Eurocentric view prevailed up until 1967, limiting mandatory international protection to pre-1951 European refugees. The 1967 Protocol Relating to the Status of Refugees eliminated these time and space limitations. In addition, two regional arrangements have further modified the Convention definition of the refugee in Africa and Latin America. In 1968, the Organization of African Unity established the Convention Governing the Specific Aspects of Refugee Problems in Africa, which granted refugee status to people who have been forced to flee across an international border because of any "man-made disaster" and not just fear of persecution. Similarly, the Organization of American States' Cartagena Declaration of 1984 embraced the many involuntary migrants who had fled their countries not because of individualized persecution but because they feel threatened by "generalized violence, foreign aggression, internal conflicts, massive violations of human rights or other circumstances which have seriously disturbed public order."

14. Gil Loescher, *Beyond Charity* (New York: Oxford University Press, 1993), 6.

15. Ibid.

16. Arati Rao, "Home-Word Bound: Women's Place in the Family of International Feminism," *Global Governance* 2, no. 2 (1996), 241–60.

17. Jacqueline Bhabha, "Legal Problems of Women Refugees," *Women: A Cultural Review* 4, no. 3 (1993), 242.

18. These difficulties are further augmented at the level of national refugee determination, where the private–public distinction can dangerously interact with cultural power dynamics. As Bhabha's review of refugee case law demonstrates, a dangerous paradox exists with decisions that focus on persecution emanating from the "private" sphere of other cultures: "decisions upholding an asylum applicant's claim of persecution may contain culturally arrogant, even racist

descriptions of the state of origin's policies; conversely judgments that dismiss the asylum application may adopt the language of cultural sensitivity or respect for state sovereignty as a device for limiting refugee admission numbers." Jacqueline Bhabha, "Embodied Rights: Gender Persecution, State Sovereignty, and Refugees," *Public Culture* no. 9 (1996), 11.

19. Universal Declaration of Human Rights, United Nations General Assembly Resolution 217 A(III), December 10, 1948, Preamble.

20. Ibid., Article 14.

21. The IRO Constitution was passed by the United Nations General Assembly on December 15, 1946. This citation appears at Section C(1)(a)(i). Emphasis added.

22. James C. Hathaway, *The Law of Refugee Status* (Toronto: Butterworths, 1991), 67. For a good general introduction to the debates over the refugee definition and the establishment of the UNHCR, see Louise Holborn, *Refugees: A Problem of Our Time* (Metuchen, NJ: Scarecrow Press, 1975).

23. For a classic representation of this argument, see Friedrich A. Hayek, *The Road to Serfdom* (Chicago: University of Chicago Press, 1944).

24. Bhabha, "Embodied Rights," 8.

25. Loescher, *Beyond Charity*, 69. Emphasis added.

26. Linda Green, "Fear as a Way of Life," *Cultural Anthropology* 9, no. 2 (1994), 230.

27. Quoted in Martin Heidegger, *Being and Time*, trans. John Macquarrie and Edward Robinson (New York: Harper and Row, 1962), §342, p. 392.

28. Quoted in Michael Taussig, *The Nervous System* (New York: Routledge, 1992), 2.

29. Ibid., 3.

30. Quoted in Massumi, "Preface," x.

31. Thomas L. Dumm, *Democracy and Punishment: Disciplinary Origins of the United States* (Madison: University of Wisconsin Press, 1987), 148. Emphasis in original.

32. Thomas L. Dumm, "Fear of Law," *Studies in Law, Politics, and Society* 10 (1990), 47.

33. Thucydides, *The Peloponnesian War*, trans. Richard Crawley (New York: Modern Library, 1982), 44.

34. Machiavelli, *The Prince*, chap. 17, in Peter Bondanella and Mark Musa, eds., *The Portable Machiavelli* (New York: Penguin, 1979), 130–33.

35. Thomas Hobbes, *Leviathan*, ed. C.B. Macpherson (London: Penguin Books, 1968), 262: "Feare and Liberty are consistent; as when a man throweth his goods into the Sea for feare the ship should sink, he doth it neverthelesse very willingly, and may refuse to doe it if he will."

36. When comparing fear and courage, Hobbes defined the first term as primary and active (fear is the "expectation of evil") and the latter term as secondary and passive (courage is "the absence of fear"). Thomas Hobbes, *Body, Man, Citizen*, ed. Richard S. Peters (New York: Collier Books, 1962), 216–17.

37. Hedley Bull, "Hobbes and the International Anarchy," *Social Research* 48, no. 4 (1981), 720–21.

38. See R.B.J. Walker, *Inside/Outside: International Relations as Political Theory* (Cambridge: Cambridge University Press, 1993).

39. Darwin emphasized the ancient quality of fear when he wrote that "fear was expressed from an extremely remote period in almost the same manner as it now is

by man." Quoted in Rush W. Dozier Jr., *Fear Itself: The Origin, Nature, and Reality of Our Most Primal Emotion* (New York: Thomas Dunne Books, 1998), 5.

40. Hobbes, *Leviathan*, 187.

41. David Campbell, *Writing Security: United States Foreign Policy and the Politics of Identity* (Minneapolis: University of Minnesota Press, 1992), 66.

42. For a critique of Hobbes's political anthropology, see Pierre Clastres, *Archeology of Violence*, trans. Jeanine Herman (New York: Semiotext[e], 1994), especially 87–92 and 139–67.

43. David Johnston, *The Rhetoric of "Leviathan": Thomas Hobbes and the Politics of Cultural Transformation* (Princeton, NJ: Princeton University Press, 1986).

44. Dumm, "Fear of Law," 46.

45. William E. Connolly, *Political Theory and Modernity*, 2nd ed. (Ithaca, NY: Cornell University Press, 1993), 30.

46. Ibid., 29.

47. Hobbes, *Leviathan*, 124.

48. Ibid., 105.

49. In chapter 6 of *Leviathan*, Hobbes offered this definition of fear: "Aversion, with opinion of Hurt from the object, FEARE." Ibid., 123.

50. Ibid.

51. William W. Sokoloff, "Politics and Anxiety in Thomas Hobbes's Leviathan," *Theory and Event* 5, no. 1 (2001), §13. Available at http://muse.jhu.edu/journals/theory_&_event.

52. Shaw, "Feminist Futures," 578–79.

53. Green, "Fear as a Way of Life," 227.

54. Richard Bernstein, *Beyond Objectivism and Relativism: Science, Hermeneutics, and Praxis* (Philadelphia: University of Pennsylvania Press, 1983), 18.

55. This emphasis on the individual refugee is of great significance, however. Arguably, this individualism goes a long way in explaining why refugees are spoken of in emergency terms whenever they appear as a mass phenomenon. As Giorgio Agamben commented, "What is essential is that each and every time refugees no longer represent individual cases but rather a mass phenomenon (as was the case between the two World Wars and is now once again), these organizations as well as the single States—all the solemn evocations of the inalienable rights of human beings notwithstanding—have proved to be absolutely incapable not only of solving the problem but also of facing it in an adequate manner." Giorgio Agamben, "Beyond Human Rights," in *Radical Thought in Italy: A Potential Politics*, ed. Paolo Virno and Michael Hardt (Minneapolis: University of Minnesota Press, 1996), 161.

56. Dillon, "The Scandal of the Refugee."

57. Jean-Yves Carlier, "General Report," in *Who Is a Refugee?: A Comparative Case Law Study*, ed. Jean-Yves Carlier, Dirk Vanheule, Klaus Hullmann, and Carlos Pena Galiano (The Hague: Kluwer Law International, 1997), 696.

58. Ibid., 696–97.

59. UNHCR, *Handbook on Procedures and Criteria for Determining Refugee Status under the 1951 Convention and the 1967 Protocol Relating to the Status of Refugees* (Geneva: Office of the United Nations High Commissioner for Refugees, 1988), 11.

60. Ibid., 11.

61. Ibid., 12.

62. Ibid., 11–12. Emphasis added.

63. In his analysis of the UN Convention definition of the refugee, James Hathaway argued that the "well-founded fear of being persecuted" standard is designed to highlight the importance of a future-oriented risk. "The use of the term 'fear' was intended to emphasize the forward-looking nature of the test, and not to ground refugee status in an assessment of the refugee's state of mind." As a consequence, Hathaway argued that the UNHCR's claim of an "objective" and "subjective" element to the definition is misleading. The Convention is nothing more than "an objective test to be administered in the context of present or prospective risk for the claimant." Hathaway, *Law of Refugee Status*, 69.

64. UNHCR, *Handbook*, 12. Emphasis added.

65. Ibid., 13.

66. Ibid., 14.

67. Peter Andreas, "Borderless Economy, Barricaded Border," *NACLA: Report on the Americas* 33, no. 3 (1999), 14–21.

68. Daniel Warner, "Voluntary Repatriation and the Meaning of Return to Home: A Critique of Liberal Mathematics," *Journal of Refugee Studies* 7, no. 2/3 (1994), 160–74.

69. E. Valentine Daniel and John Chr. Knudsen, eds., *Mistrusting Refugees* (Berkeley: University of California Press, 1995).

70. UNHCR, *Handbook*, 49–50.

71. Ibid., 13.

72. Aristide Zolberg and his coauthors made an earlier version of this argument when they argued that refugees should be defined not according to their "fear of persecution" but rather from a more general "fear of violence." Aristide Zolberg, Astri Suhrke, and Sergio Aguayo, *Escape from Violence: Conflict and the Refugee Crisis in the Developing World* (Oxford: Oxford University Press, 1989).

73. UNHCR, *The State of the World's Refugees: A Humanitarian Agenda* (Oxford: Oxford University Press, 1998), 11. Emphasis added.

74. See, for example, Assembly of Refugee, "Paris Appeal," Article 9: "Asylum seekers should enjoy living conditions reflecting due regard for human dignity, which comprise in particular accommodation, social protection, the right for adults to exercise a professional activity and schooling for children."

75. The importance of the culture of exile is discussed in special issues of *Forced Migration Review* no. 6 (December 1999) and *Network News: National Network for Immigrant and Refugee Rights* (Summer 1999). More generally, compare Iain Chambers, *Migrancy, Culture, Identity* (New York: Routledge, 1994), Arjun Appadurai, *Modernity at Large: Cultural Dimensions of Globalization* (Minneapolis: University of Minnesota Press, 1996).

76. Helen Scott-Danter, "Theatre for Development: A Dynamic Tool for Change," *Forced Migration Review* no. 6 (December 1999), 22–24.

77. Nazim Akhundov, "Psychosocial Rehabilitation of IDP Children: Using Theatre, Art, Music and Sport," *Forced Migration Review* no. 6 (December 1999), 20–21. See also Ditty Dokter, ed., *Arts Therapists, Refugees and Migrants: Reaching across Borders* (London: Jessica Kingsley, 1998).

78. David Parkin, "Mementoes as Transitional Objects in Human Displacement," *Journal of Material Culture* 4, no. 3 (1999), 304.

79. Roland Bleiker, "Editor's Introduction," *Alternatives* 25, no. 3 (2000), 271.

80. Costas M. Constantinou, "Poetics of Security," *Alternatives* 25, no. 3 (2000), 289.

81. Aissaoui's poem was part of the Refugee Council of England's ongoing campaign of promoting a more positive image of refugees. During Refugee Week 1999, the poetry of refugees living in Brixton and Leeds (including Aissaoui's) was read on BBC Radio Four and was published in the Council's magazine *In Exile* (Summer 1999).

82. This poem appears in *Forced Migration Review* no. 3 (December 1998), 44.

83. Donna Haraway, "A Manifesto for Cyborgs: Science, Technology, and Socialist Feminism in the 1980s," in *Feminism/Postmodernism*, ed. Linda J. Nicholson (New York: Routledge, 1990), 190.

84. Kathy Ferguson explained that irony "can appear as the slippage between what is said and what is meant, or between what is said and what can be understood, or between what is indicated and what is implied or evaded, or between stability and motion." Kathy E. Ferguson, *The Man Question: Visions of Subjectivity in Feminist Theory* (Berkeley: University of California Press, 1993), 30.

85. Ibid. 178.

86. I discuss the concept of "refugee-becoming" in detail in chapter 4. For an accessible introduction to the idea of "becoming," see Gilles Deleuze, *Negotiations, 1972–1990*, trans. Martin Joughin (New York: Columbia University Press, 1995).

87. On the paradox of modern attempts to find alternatives to sovereignty-politics, see R.B.J. Walker, "After the Future: Enclosures, Connections, Politics," in *Reframing the International: Law, Culture, Politics*, ed. Richard Falk, Lester Ruiz, and R.B.J. Walker (New York: Routledge, 2002).

Chapter 4

1. Diane Francis, "Canadian Refugee Policy for the Dogs," *National Post*, August 14, 1999, D3.

2. David Campbell, *Writing Security: United States Foreign Policy and the Politics of Identity* (Minneapolis: University of Minnesota Press, 1992), 94–99.

3. Francis, "Canadian Refugee Policy for the Dogs," D3.

4. For a discussion of the rhetoric on migration and danger, especially in terms of how migrants are cast as agents of a "biological invasion," see Banu Subramaniam, "The Aliens Have Landed! Reflections on the Rhetoric of Biological Invasions," *Meridians: Feminism, Race, Transnationalism* 2, no. 1 (2001), 26–40.

5. In another article, Francis again linked refugeeness with a lack of authenticity: "('Refugees' are not people who have been displaced and are brought in for humanitarian reasons into Canada. Only a few are in that category. Most are smuggled in or are queue-jumpers who lie their way into the country by pretending they cannot go home and get all the entitlements they need immediately. There is no proper adjudication process, they are not even held pending a medical examination, most disappear before their first refugee hearing and even if found to be dangerous or fraudulent they are rarely deported.)" Note that Francis wrote all of this in parentheses, as an aside. Her prejudice is asserted as common sense

and as fact. Note too that in her script, the term refugee cannot be expressed outside the prison bars of scare quotes. The refugee, for Francis, is a general category that does not live up to its principles in practice. Diane Francis, "Cities Fight for Fair Refugee Policy," *National Post*, May 15, 2001.

6. Jonathan Simon, "Refugees in a Carceral Age: The Rebirth of Immigration Prisons in the United States," *Public Culture* 10, no. 3 (1998), 577–607.

7. Francis, "Canadian Refugee Policy for the Dogs," D3.

8. T. Alexander Aleinikoff, "State-Centered Refugee Law: From Resettlement to Containment," in *Mistrusting Refugees*, ed. E. Valentine Daniel and John Chr. Knudsen (Berkeley: University of California Press, 1995), 257–78.

9. Jacques Derrida, *Of Hospitality: Anne Dufourmantelle Invites Jacques Derrida to Respond*, trans. Rachel Bowlby (Stanford: Stanford University Press, 2000), 77. Emphasis in original.

10. Derrida quoted in Mireille Rosello, *Postcolonial Hospitality: The Immigrant as Guest* (Stanford, CA: Stanford University Press, 2001), 11–12.

11. Ibid., 173.

12. Jacques Derrida, "Hostipitality," in *Acts of Religion* (New York: Routledge, 2002), 361. Emphasis added.

13. Adam Douglas, *The Beast Within* (London: Chapmans, 1992), 67. This association of the outlaw with the wolf has survived in the modern term vagrant.

14. Giorgio Agamben, *Homo Sacer: Sovereign Power and Bare Life*, trans. Daniel Heller-Roazen (Stanford, CA: Stanford University Press, 1998), 104.

15. Douglas, *The Beast Within*, 94–95.

16. For a sustained discussion of the relationship between Agamben's political philosophy and animality, see Giorgio Agamben, *The Open: Man and Animal*, trans. Kevin Attell (Stanford, CA: Stanford University Press, 2002).

17. Agamben, *Homo Sacer*, 28–29.

18. Brian Massumi, "Everywhere You Want to Be: Introduction to Fear," in *The Politics of Everyday Fear*, ed. Brian Massumi (Minneapolis: University of Minnesota Press, 1993), 27.

19. It is true that most cultures and societies—and not just Western ones—draw some kind of distinction between humans and other animals. However, the difference, I suggest, is that not all cultures and societies draw such a strict separation between the human and the nonhuman as does the Western Judeo-Christian tradition.

20. The sexist language here is, of course, unavoidable as Aristotle's patriarchal world order is well known. Aristotle's functional and hierarchical thinking does not end at the nature–human divide but extends into the human world, with propertied men ruling at the top, and women, children, slaves, and barbarians occupying the lower levels.

21. James J. Sheehan, "Introduction," in *The Boundaries of Humanity: Humans, Animals, Machines*, ed. James J. Sheehan and Morton Sosna (Berkeley: University of California Press, 1991), 29. See also Paul Clarke and Andrew Linzey, eds., *Political Theory and Animal Rights* (London: Pluto Press, 1990).

22. Akira Mizuta Lippit, *Electric Animal: Toward a Rhetoric of Wildlife* (Minneapolis: University of Minnesota Press, 2000), 14.

23. René Descartes, "Discourse on the Method," in *Descartes: Selected Philosophical Writings*, trans. John Cottingham, Robert Stoothoff, and Dugald Murdoch (Cambridge: Cambridge University Press, 1988), 44.

24. Jean-Jacques Rousseau, "Discourse on the Origin of Inequality," in *The Basic Political Writings*, trans. and ed. Donald A. Cress (Indianapolis: Hackett, 1987), 44.

25. Ibid., 45.

26. Ibid.

27. Quoted in Lippit, *Electric Animal*, 30.

28. Ibid., 30. Emphasis in original.

29. Emily Apter, "Clinging to the Animal Relation," in *Social Insecurity*, 53. See also Emily Apter, "Balkan Babel: Translation Zones, Military Zones," *Public Culture* 13, no. 1 (2001), 65–80.

30. Apter, "Clinging to the Animal Relation," 53.

31. Lippit, *Electric Animal*, 8.

32. Emmanuel Levinas, "The Name of a Dog, or Natural Rights," in Emmanuel Levinas, *Difficult Freedom: Essays on Judaism*, trans. Seán Hand (Baltimore: Johns Hopkins University Press, 1990), 152.

33. Ibid., 152–53.

34. Ibid., 153.

35. Ibid.

36. Fernand Braudel, *The Structures of Everyday Life: The Limits of the Possible, Vol. I, Civilization and Capitalism, 15th–18th Century*, trans. Siân Reynolds (London: Fontana Press, 1981), 64–70.

37. Ibid., 64.

38. Thomas Hobbes quoted in Agamben, *Homo Sacer*, 106.

39. Braudel, *Structures of Everyday Life*, 64.

40. For instance, Braudel distinguished different types of "wild men" on the basis of their spatial relation to the grand civilizations. The "wild people" of China and India, for instance, were mostly "confined and encircled by disapproving civilizations." By contrast, the "real savages" were found elsewhere, on the "appalling land," the "vast and hostile spaces" of Siberia, and so on. There, condition was one of "complete freedom" as they lacked any notion of the political and the constraining forms of power exclusive to it. Ibid., 65.

41. Tess Chakkalakal, "Canada: The Moral Superpower," *This Magazine* 33, no. 1 (July–August 1999), 30–33.

42. *Globe and Mail*, April 8, 1999, 1. Emphasis added.

43. Jacques Derrida, "Hostipitality," 361.

44. Ibid.

45. Ibid., 362.

46. For a critique of British Columbia's media coverage of this issue, see Roma Luciw, Gray Miles, Peter Wall, and Brian Lin, "The Media versus the Migrants," *Thunderbird: UBC Journalism Review* 2, no. 1 (November 1999). More generally, see Gillian Creese and Laurie Peterson, "Making the News: Racializing Chinese Canadians," *Studies in Political Economy* no. 51 (Fall 1996), 117–45; Alan Smart and Josephine Smart, "Monster Homes: Hong Kong Immigration to Canada, Urban Conflicts, and Contested Representations of Space," in *City Lives and City*

Forms: Critical Research and Canadian Urbanism, ed. Jon Caulfield and Linda Peake (Toronto: University of Toronto Press, 1996), 33–46.

47. The views of this official are treated as credible even though he admits that his "analysis" is based entirely on what he could glean from television news clips. Jane Armstrong, "Smuggled Chinese Aren't Real Refugees, Mountie Says," *Globe and Mail*, August 6, 1999, 1.

48. Jeff Sallot, "Migrants Not Owed Free Ride, Poll Says," *Globe and Mail*, August 31, 1999, 1.

49. Such complaints ignore the "head tax" that, since 1995, the Canadian government levies on all adult immigrants and refugees coming to Canada. The levies included a C$975 Right of Landing Fee, plus a C$500 application fee, bringing the total cost for a refugee claimant to C$1475. While the Canadian government actively collects fees from those who can least afford it (indeed, as a prohibitive act), business-class immigrants regularly violate the terms of their entrepreneur visas. Indeed, between 1994 and 1997 more than seven thousand of these "business-class" migrants failed to open businesses in Canada. Mike Byfield, "Business Immigrants Scoff at the Law," *Report Newsmagazine*, October 25, 1999, 47. For a critical analysis of Canada's policy to encourage the rapid entry of wealthy entrepreneurs (especially from East Asia) and its relation to neoliberal forms of governance and economics, see Katharyne Mitchell, "Trans-nationalism, Neoliberalism, and the Rise of the Shadow State," *Economy and Society* 30, no. 2 (May 2001), 165–89.

50. "Boat People Who Need a Return Ride: Sad as Their Economic Lives May Be, Illegal Chinese Don't Belong Here," *Globe and Mail*, July 23, 1999.

51. Elinor Caplan, "Asylum Seekers on Dangerous Ships Won't Be Turned Back without a Hearing," Speech to the Canadian Society for Yad Vashem, Toronto, November 8, 1999. Available in *Canadian Speeches* 13, no. 5 (1999), 67–70.

52. "Letter to Storefront Orientation Services (S.O.S.) from Fujianese Women in the Burnaby Correctional Centre for Women, November 1999," English translation printed in Direct Action against Refugee Exploitation (DAARE), *Movement across Borders: Chinese Migrant Women in Canada*, pamphlet, April 2001.

53. Rod Mickleburgh, "27 Boat People See Refugee Claims Rejected," *Globe and Mail*, November 10, 1999.

54. The military encampment of the Kosovar refugees was not unique to Canada. Both the United States and Australia, who took in twenty thousand and four thousand refugees, respectively, also transferred the Kosovars to isolated military bases. In fact, the United States placed a large proportion of the refugees in the middle of the Pacific Ocean, at their military base in Guam.

55. Jean-Yves Carlier et al., *Who Is a Refugee? A Comparative Case Law Study* (The Hague: Kluwer Law International, 1997), 692–93.

56. UNHCR, *The State of the World's Refugees 1993: The Challenge of Protection* (New York: Penguin, 1993), 41.

57. Giorgio Agamben, *Means without End: Notes on Politics*, trans. Vincenzo Binetti and Cesare Casarino (Minneapolis: University of Minnesota Press, 2000), 42.

58. Ibid., 39.

59. Ibid., 40. Emphasis in original.

60. Hannah Arendt, *Imperialism: Part II of The Origins of Totalitarianism* (New York: Harvest, 1968), 167.

61. Ibid., 172.

62. James Turner, *Reckoning with the Beast: Animals, Pain, and Humanity in the Victorian Mind* (Baltimore: Johns Hopkins University Press, 1980), 39–52.

63. The Montreal SPCA was quickly followed by animal protection societies in Quebec City (1870), Ottawa (1871), and Toronto (1873). By 1874, more than thirty such societies had been established in cities and towns across the United States. Ibid., 158, n. 53.

64. Kay Anderson, "The Beast Within: Race, Humanity, and Animality," *Environment and Planning D: Society and Space* 18 (2000), 309. This is especially the case in the humanities and the social sciences: "Whereas zoologists and biologists have been pursuing the specificity of the kind of animal that humans are, the point of departure for the humanities and social sciences has been that which makes humans categorically different from animals" (p. 302).

65. Ibid., 309.

66. The qualification is important here, because humane societies are notorious for their support of a variety of practices, such as hunting and agriculture, which bring harm to animals. "As animal welfare organizations and their advocates take pains to point out, they are most definitely not animal rights supporters by any definition of the term. Their ranks comfortably include farmers, hunters, trappers, researchers, and all sorts of people who make their living using animals. This is a part of the animal world in which an associate of the Mackenzie Institute, the Toronto research organization obsessed with 'terrorists,' can happily run the country's largest Humane Society." Charlotte Montgomery, *Blood Relations: Animals, Humans, and Politics* (Toronto: Between the Lines, 2000), 42.

67. Turner, *Reckoning with the Beast*, 53.

68. Ibid., 55.

69. The Canadian Society for the Prevention of Cruelty to Animals, pamphlet, Montreal 1873.

70. Arendt, *Imperialism*, 177.

71. Rousseau, "Origin of Inequality," 49.

72. Quoted in Michael C. Williams, "Rousseau, Realism, and Realpolitik," *Millennium: Journal of International Studies* 18, no. 2 (1989), 190.

73. Rousseau, "Origin of Inequality," 49.

74. Hannah Arendt, *On Revolution* (New York: Penguin Books, 1973), 59–114.

75. Ibid., 89. Arendt contrasted her negative judgment of pity with a more positive appraisal of compassion. Compassion, she argued, is directed to specific individuals and depends on the social proximity of face-to-face encounters. Such proximity allows for an appreciation of specific contexts, thus making it difficult to generalize about the condition of the sufferer. To be compassionate, moreover, is to forego loquacity: the display of compassion involves a "curious muteness" as its language "consists in gestures and expressions of countenance rather than in words." Ibid., 85–86.

76. Luc Boltanski, *Distant Suffering: Morality, Media and Politics*, trans. Graham Burchell (Cambridge: Cambridge University Press, 1999).

77. Arendt, *On Revolution*, 89.

78. Ibid.

79. David Campbell, "Disaster Politics, and the Politics of Disaster: Exploring 'Humanitarianism,'" in *The Politics of Emergency*, ed. Jenny Edkins (Manchester: University of Manchester Papers in Politics, 1997), 22.

80. Arendt, *Imperialism*, 180.

81. Margaret D. Stetz, "Woman as Mother in a Headscarf: The Woman War Refugee and the North American Media," *Canadian Woman Studies* 19, no. 4 (December 1999–February 2000), 66–70.

82. Kobena Mercer, *Welcome to the Jungle: New Positions in Black Cultural Studies* (New York: Routledge, 1994), 183.

83. Stetz, "Woman as Mother in a Headscarf," 70.

84. Derrida, "Hostipitality," 358.

85. Steve Burgess, "The Evil That Dogs Do," http://www.salon.com/people/feature/1999/11/13/dogs.

86. Linda Green, "Fear as a Way of Life," *Cultural Anthropology* 9, no. 2 (1994), 227.

87. Sadako Ogata, "Making a Difference for Refugees: Opening Keynote Address by Mrs. Sadako Ogata; United Nations High Commissioner for Refugees, for Microsoft Tech-Ed 2000 Europe," Amsterdam, July 4, 2000, www.unhcr.ch/refworld/unhr/hcspeech/000704.htm.

88. Microsoft Press Release, "How Goodwill, Good People and Great Software Can Help Make the World a Better Place," www.microsoft.com/presspass.

89. Microsoft Press Release, "Reaching Refugees across the Digital Divide," www.microsoft.com/presspass.

90. Nathan Cochrane, "War Breaks Out over Kosovo Aid Agency Information Services," I.T. News from the World of Information Technology, May 17, 1999, http://www.it.fairfax.com.au/software/19990517/A27961-1999May17.html. See also the report of the Kosovo Refugee Information Systems and Network (KRISYS.NET), an initiative of the Chicago-Kent College of Law, Illinois Institute of Technology, on their efforts to implement a Central Refugee Registration System in Tirana, Albania, http://pbosnia.kentlaw.edu/projects/kosovo/tripreports/june99_albania.htm.

91. Ogata, "Making a Difference for Refugees."

92. See the report compiled by the Advocacy Project, "The Internet and the Kosovo Humanitarian Crisis," www.advocacynet.org.

93. UN Office for the Coordination of Humanitarian Affairs, "Zambia: Electronic ID Cards for Refugees," www.reliefweb.int.

Chapter 5

1. Hannah Arendt, *Imperialism: Part II of the Origins of Totalitarianism* (New York: Harvest, 1968), 147.

2. Jean Bethke Elshtain, *Women and War* (New York: Basic Books, 1987), 60.

3. On the gendered character of the citizen warrior, see J. Ann Tickner, *Gender in International Relations: Feminist Perspectives on Achieving Global Security* (New York: Columbia University Press, 1992), 39–41.

4. Aristide R. Zolberg, Astri Suhrke, and Sergio Aguayo, *Escape from Violence: Conflict and the Refugee Crisis in the Developing World* (New York: Oxford University Press, 1989), 275.

5. Gil Loescher also referred to refugee warriors as being "highly conscious" in his definition of this phenomenon: "While refugees are often pawns or victims in relations between states, they are by no means always passive political actors. Frequently, they are part of highly conscious communities with armed leaders engaged in warfare for political objectives, such as to recapture their homeland, to destabilize the ruling regime, or to secure a separate state." Gil Loescher, *Beyond Charity: International Cooperation and the Global Refugee Crisis* (New York: Oxford University Press, 1993), 27. Emphasis added.

6. Daniel Warner, "The Politics of the Political/Humanitarian Divide," *International Review of the Red Cross* no. 833 (March 13, 1999), 109.

7. Michael J. Shapiro, *Violent Cartographies: Mapping Cultures of War* (Minneapolis: University of Minnesota Press, 1997), 45.

8. Paul Virilio and Sylvère Lotringer, *Pure War*, rev. ed., trans. Mark Polizzotti (New York: Semiotext[e], 1997).

9. Walter Benjamin, "Theses on the Philosophy of History," in *Illuminations*, trans. Harry Zohn (New York: Schocken Books, 1968), 257.

10. Zolberg et al., *Escape from Violence*, 241.

11. Ibid., 189.

12. Karen Jacobsen, "Refugees as Security Threats in Sub-Saharan Africa," in *International Migration and Security*, ed. Myron Weiner (Boulder, CO: Westview, 1993).

13. Randolph Martin, "Regional Dynamics and the Security of Afghan Refugees in Pakistan," *Refugee Survey Quarterly* 19, no. 1 (2000), 71–78.

14. Courtland Robinson, "Refugee Warriors at the Thai–Cambodian Border," *Refugee Survey Quarterly* 19, no. 1 (2000), 23–37.

15. Joke Schrijvers, "Fighters, Victims and Survivors: Constructions of Ethnicity, Gender and Refugeeness among Tamils in Sri Lanka," *Journal of Refugee Studies* 12, no. 3 (1999), 307–33.

16. Howard Adelman, "Why Refugee Warriors Are Threats," *Journal of Conflict Studies* 18, no. 1 (Spring 1998), 50.

17. Ibid., 52.

18. Zolberg et al., *Escape from Violence*, 276.

19. Adelman, "Why Refugee Warriors Are Threats," 50.

20. The text of the Charter of the Organization of African Unity can be found in Ian Brownlie, *Basic Documents in International Law*, 4th ed. (Oxford: Oxford University Press, 1995), 77–86.

21. Zolberg et al., *Escape from Violence*, 241; Adelman, "Why Refugee Warriors Are Threats," 52.

22. Special OAU and UNHCR Meeting of Government and Non-Government Technical Experts on the Thirtieth Anniversary of the 1969 OAU Refugee Convention: Report, Conakry, Guinea, March 27–29, 2000. Action No. 10. Emphasis added. (CONF.P/OAU30TH/REPORT.) For a copy of this report and for critical reflections on the accomplishments of the OAU Refugee Convention, see the special issue of *Refugee Survey Quarterly* 20, no. 1 (2001).

23. Adelman, "Why Refugee Warriors Are Threats," 50, 64.

24. Quoted in Ray Wilkinson, "We Are Very Close to the Limit," *Refugees* 4, no. 121 (2000), 7.

25. A study conducted by the International Rescue Committee in 1996 in Kibondo District, Tanzania, determined that 27 percent of women between the ages of twelve and forty-nine had been sexually assaulted since becoming refugees. Moreover, the danger posed to UNHCR staff and other humanitarian aid workers is also considerable. During the Great Lakes refugee crisis, for instance, thirty-six UNHCR staff and workers were killed. "Security for Women," *Forced Migration Review* no. 5 (August 1999), 34; Frances T. Pilch, "Security Issues and Refugees: Dilemmas, Crises, and Debates," *Refuge: Canada's Periodical on Refugees* 19, no. 1 (July 2000), 27.

26. EXCOM, *The Security and Civilian and Humanitarian Character of Refugee Camps and Settlements: Operationalizing the "Ladder of Options."* Doc. No. EC/50/SC/INF.4 (June 27, 2000), §1.

27. Alexander Wendt, "Bridging the Theory/Meta-theory Gap in International Relations," *Review of International Studies* 17 (1991), 387.

28. In the concluding pages of *Escape from Violence*, Zolberg et al. listed a variety of issues related to refugee movements that they considered to qualify as "special problems of our time." Refugee warrior communities top this list (see pp. 275–78).

29. Zolberg et al., *Escape from Violence*, 44.

30. Adelman, "Why Refugee Warriors Are Threats," 52.

31. Ibid.

32. R.B.J. Walker, *Inside/Outside: International Relations as Political Theory* (Cambridge: Cambridge University Press, 1993), 131.

33. Jean Bethke Elshtain, "International Politics and Political Theory," in *International Relations Theory Today*, ed. Ken Booth and Steve Smith (University Park: Pennsylvania State University Press, 1995), 265.

34. R.B.J. Walker, "Security, Sovereignty, and the Challenge of World Politics," *Alternatives* 15, no. 1 (1990), 17.

35. Warren Magnusson, "The Reification of Political Community," in *Contending Sovereignties*, ed. R.B.J. Walker and Saul Mendlovitz (Boulder, CO: Lynne Rienner, 1990), 45–60.

36. Elly-Elikunda Mtango, "Armed Attacks on Refugee Camps," in *Refugees and International Relations*, ed. Gil Loescher and Laila Monahan (Oxford: Clarendon, 1990), 92–94.

37. EXCOM, Report by Ambassador Felix Schnyder on Military Attacks on Refugee Camps and Settlements in Southern Africa and Elsewhere. UN Doc. No. EC/SCP/26 (March 15, 1983).

38. For examples of the UNHCR's indecision on the matter of military or armed attacks on refugee camps and settlements, see EXCOM Conclusion No. 27 (1982), EXCOM Conclusion No. 32 (1983), EXCOM Conclusion No. 45 (1986).

39. EXCOM, *Military or Armed Attacks on Refugee Camps and Settlements*, Conclusion No. 48 (1987), §4(a). UN Doc. No. A/AC.96/702.

40. Ibid., §4(b).

41. EXCOM, *The Security and Civilian and Humanitarian Character of Refugee Camps and Settlements.* Doc. No. EC/49/SC/INF.2 (January 14, 1999), §2. Emphasis added.

42. These options are given further consideration in EXCOM, *Strengthening Partnership to Ensure Protection also in Relation to Security* (September 14, 1999), www.unhcr.ch/refworld/unhcr/excom/reports/923e.htm.

43. EXCOM, *The Security and Civilian and Humanitarian Character of Refugee Camps and Settlements* (January 14, 1999), §15.

44. See EXCOM, *The Security and Civilian and Humanitarian Character of Refugee Camps and Settlements: Operationalizing the "Ladder of Options"* (June 27, 2000).

45. UNHCR, *Sexual Violence against Refugees: Guidelines on Prevention and Response* (Geneva: UNHCR, 1995).

46. For a discussion of past practices, see Hilkka Pietilä and Jeanne Vickers, *Making Women Matter: The Role of the United Nations* (London: Zed Books, 1996).

47. Jennifer Hyndman, *Managing Displacement: Refugees and the Politics of Humanitarianism* (Minneapolis: University of Minnesota Press, 1999), 84.

48. Cynthia Enloe, "The Gendered Gulf," in *Collateral Damage: The "New World Order" at Home and Abroad*, ed. Cynthia Peters (Boston: South End Press, 1992).

49. Julie Peteet, "Icons and Militants: Mothering in the Danger Zone," *Signs* 23 (Autumn 1997), 103.

50. Julie Peteet, "Male Gender and Rituals of Resistance in the Palestinian Intifada: A Cultural Politics of Violence," *American Ethnologist* 21, no. 1 (1994), 31.

51. UNHCR, *The State of the World's Refugees: A Humanitarian Agenda* (Oxford: Oxford University Press, 1997), 67.

52. EXCOM, *The Security and Civilian and Humanitarian Character of Refugee Camps and Settlements* (January 14, 1999), §§10–14.

53. Ibid., §4.

54. Karen Jacobsen, "A Framework for Exploring the Political and Security Context of Refugee Populated Areas," *Refugee Survey Quarterly* 19, no. 1 (2000), 9.

55. M. Nazif Shahrani, "Afghanistan's Muhajirin (Muslim 'Refugee-Warriors'), Politics of Mistrust and Distrust of Politics," in *Mistrusting Refugees*, ed. E. Valentine Daniel and John Chr. Knudsen (Berkeley: University of California Press, 1995), 194.

56. See the special issue on "Religion and International Relations," *Millennium: Journal of International Studies* 29, no. 3 (2000).

57. It should be noted that the term jihad, while usually interpreted in Western media and scholarship as "holy war" also has another meaning as "holy struggle." It is, therefore, not an exclusively violent concept or practice.

58. Shahrani, "Afghanistan's Muhajirin," 189.

59. Ibid.

60. Ibid.

61. This definition is drawn from a passage in the Qur'an (XVI: 41), the full citation of which reads, "To those who leave their homes in the cause of Allah after suffering oppression—We will assuredly give a goodly home in this world; but truly the reward of the Hereafter will be greater."

62. Shahrani, "Afghanistan's Muhajirin," 192.

63. Zafar Ishaq Ansari, "Hijrah in the Islamic Tradition," in *The Cultural Basis of Afghan Nationalism*, ed. Ewan W. Anderson and Nancy Hatch Dupree (New York: Pinter, 1990), 9.

64. Ibid., 10.

65. Ibid., 4.

66. Ibid. Emphasis added.

67. Samuel Huntington, "The Clash of Civilizations," *Foreign Affairs* 72, no. 3 (1993), 22–49.

68. Sayed Askar Mousavi, *The Hazaras of Afghanistan: An Historical, Cultural, Economic, and Political Study* (New York: St. Martin's, 1998).

69. Physicians for Human Rights, *The Taliban's War on Women: A Health and Human Rights Crisis in Afghanistan* (Boston: Physicians for Human Rights, 1998).

70. Eduardo Galeano, *Upside Down: A Primer for the Looking Glass World* (New York: Metropolitan Books, 2000), 201.

71. See, for example, UNHCR, *Handbook on Procedures and Criteria for Determining Refugee Status under the 1951 Convention and the 1967 Protocol Relating to the Status of Refugees* (Geneva: Office of the United Nations High Commissioner for Refugees, 1988), 13–16.

72. For a study that examines the traumatic effects of detention by asylum seekers, see Derrick Silove, Zachary Steel, and Charles Watters, "Policies of Deterrence and the Mental Health of Asylum Seekers," *Journal of the American Medical Association* 284, no. 5 (August 2, 2000), 604–11.

73. The letters refer to the first three letters from the ship that brought them to Australia, and the numbers are those assigned to them by Australian immigration officials.

74. Maley, "Security, People-Smuggling, and Australia's New Afghan Refugees," 358.

75. For an excellent online selection of reports, analyses, and information on border crossings and border policing in Australia, see www.xborder.net.

76. Quoted in Kerry O'Brien, "UNHCR Goes Up against Government in Plight of Refugees," Australian Broadcasting Corporation, 7:30 Report (June 19, 2001), http://www.abc.net.au/7:30/s315568.htm. On the masculine practices of statism, see Charlotte Hooper, *Manly States: Masculinities, International Relations, and Gender Politics* (New York: Columbia University Press, 2001).

77. "Refugee Riot: Australian Broadcasting Corporation (ABC) Radio Interview with Immigration Minister Philip Ruddock" (May 12, 2001), www.abc.net/au/am/s295268.htm. Emphasis added.

78. Giorgio Agamben, *Means without End: Notes on Politics*, trans. Vincenzo Binetti and Cesare Casarino (Minneapolis: University of Minnesota Press, 2000), 106.

Conclusion

1. Assembly of Refugees, "Paris Appeal," reprinted in *Refugee Survey Quarterly* 20, no. 3 (2001), 130–35.

2. Gayatri Chakravorty Spivak, "Imperatives to Re-imagine the Planet," in *Social Insecurity: Alphabet City No. 7*, ed. Len Guenther and Cornelius Heesters (Toronto: Anansi, 2000), 268.

3. Hortense Spillers, "Where the Human Stops," in ibid., 52.

4. Giorgio Agamben, *Homo Sacer: Sovereign Power and Bare Life*, trans. Daniel Heller-Roazen (Stanford, CA: Stanford University Press, 1998), 133.

5. B.S. Chimni, "The Geopolitics of Refugee Studies: A View from the South," *Journal of Refugee Studies* 11, no. 4 (1998), 350–74.

6. B.S. Chimni, "Reforming the International Refugee Regime: A Dialogic Model," *Journal of Refugee Studies* 14, no. 2 (2001), 151–68.

7. Ibid., 152.

8. Ibid. Emphasis in original.

9. Kerry Demusz, *Listening to the Displaced: Action Research in the Conflict Zones of Sri Lanka* (Oxford: Oxfam Working Papers, 2000), 46.

10. Prem Kumar Rajaram, "Humanitarianism and Representations of the Refugee," *Journal of Refugee Studies* 15, no. 3 (2002), 248.

11. Simon Harris, "Listening to the Displaced: Analysis, Accountability and Advocacy in Action," *Forced Migration Review* no. 8 (August 2000), 21. Rajaram, by contrast, called for a transformation in identities for both aid worker and refugee. "A sense of identity as ongoing and dialogical may lead to more significant 'empowering': one that recognizes that development must be a collaborative exercise between aid worker and refugee, it must systematically challenge the hierarchies that exist." Rajaram, "Representations of the Refugee," 263.

12. James C. Hathaway and R. Alexander Neve, "Making International Refugee Law Relevant Again: A Proposal for Collectivized and Solution-Oriented Protection," *Harvard Human Rights Review* 10 (1997), 115–211.

13. For example, in the year 2000 Canada contributed US$37.5 million to international refugee aid agencies (UNHCR, IOM, UNRWA) while allocating C$645 million to the Department of Citizenship and Immigration and more than C$80 million to the Immigration and Refugee Board. The statistics are from Displaced Persons, Worldwide and in Canada, a statistical document produced by the Centre for Refugee Studies, York University (January 2002).

14. Nevzat Soguk, *States and Strangers: Refugees and Displacements of Statecraft* (Minneapolis: University of Minnesota Press, 1999), Jennifer Hyndman, *Managing Displacement: Refugees and the Politics of Humanitarianism* (Minneapolis: University of Minnesota Press, 1999), Michael Dillon, "The Scandal of the Refugee: Some Reflections on the 'Inter' of International Relations and Continental Thought," in *Moral Spaces*, ed. David Campbell and Michael J. Shapiro (Minneapolis: University of Minnesota Press, 1999), 92–124; Daniel Warner, "Voluntary Repatriation and the Meaning of Return to Home: A Critique of Liberal Mathematics," *Journal of Refugee Studies* 7, nos. 2–3 (1994), 160–74; Liisa H. Malkki, *Purity and Exile: Violence, Memory, and National Cosmology among Hutu Refugees in Tanzania* (Chicago: University of Chicago Press, 1995). See also the special issue of *Refuge: Canada's Periodical on Refugees* 17, no. 5 (1998), titled "Critical Perspectives on Refugees" and edited by Nevzat Soguk.

15. Giorgio Agamben, *Homo Sacer*; Jacques Derrida, *On Cosmopolitanism and Forgiveness*, trans. Mark Dooley and Michael Hughes (New York: Routledge, 2001).

16. Friedrich Nietzsche, *The Gay Science*, trans. Walter Kaufmann (New York: Vintage, 1974), §346.

17. Michael Peter Smith, "The Disappearance of World Cities and the Globalization of Local Politics," in *World Cities in a World-System*, ed. Paul L. Knox and Peter J. Taylor (Cambridge: Cambridge University Press, 1995), 259.

18. Roman Krznaric, "Guatemalan Returnees and the Dilemma of Political Mobilization," *Journal of Refugee Studies* 10, no. 1 (1997), 61–78; Anita Rapone and Charles R. Simpson, "Women's Response to Violence in Guatemala: Resistance and Rebuilding," *International Journal of Politics, Culture and Society* 10, no. 1 (1996), 115–40.

19. For a recent engagement with these questions, see Engin F. Isin, *Being Political: Genealogies of Citizenship* (Minneapolis: University of Minnesota Press, 2002).

20. Peter Nyers, "Abject Cosmopolitanism: The Politics of Protection in the Anti-deportation Movement," *Third World Quarterly* 24, no. 6 (2003), 1069–93.

21. For an overview of the various cultural and political actions organized, see www.woomera2002.com.

22. Homi K. Bhabha, "On Minorities: Cultural Rights," *Radical Philosophy* no. 100 (March–April 2000), 6.

Bibliography

Adelman, Howard. "Why Refugee Warriors Are Threats." *Journal of Conflict Studies* 18, no. 1 (1998): 49–69.

Aeberhard, Peter. "A Historical Survey of Humanitarian Action." *Health and Human Rights* 2, no. 1 (1996).

Agamben, Giorgio. "Beyond Human Rights." In *Radical Thought in Italy: A Potential Politics*, ed. Paolo Virno and Michael Hardt. Minneapolis: University of Minnesota Press, 1996.

———. *Homo Sacer: Sovereign Power and Bare Life*. Trans. Daniel Heller-Roazen. Stanford, CA: Stanford University Press, 1998.

———. *Means without End: Notes on Politics*. Trans. Vincenzo Binetti and Cesare Casarino. Minneapolis: University of Minnesota Press, 2000.

———. *The Open: Man and Animal*. Trans. Kevin Attell. Stanford, CA: Stanford University Press, 2002.

———. *State of Exception*. Trans. Kevin Attell. Chicago: University of Chicago Press, 2005.

Akhundov, Nazim. "Psychosocial Rehabilitation of IDP Children: Using Theatre, Art, Music and Sport." *Forced Migration Review* 6 (1999): 20–21.

Aleinikoff, T. Alexander. "State-centred Refugee Law: From Resettlement to Containment." In *Mistrusting Refugees*, ed. E.V. Daniel and J. Chr. Knudsen. Berkeley: University of California Press, 1995.

Anderson, Kay. "The Beast Within: Race, Humanity, and Animality." *Environment and Planning D: Society and Space* 18, no. 3 (2000): 301–20.

Anderson, Perry. *Lineages of the Absolutist State*. London: Verso, 1974.

Andreas, Peter. "Borderless Economy, Barricaded Border." *NACLA: Report on the Americas* 33, no. 3 (1999): 14–21.

Ansari, Zafar Ishaq. "Hijrah in the Islamic Tradition." *In The Cultural Basis of Afghan Nationalism*, ed. Ewan W. Anderson and Nancy Hatch Dupree. New York: Pinter, 1990.

Appadurai, Arjun. "Disjuncture and Difference in the Global Cultural Economy." *Public Culture* 2, no. 2 (1990): 1–24.

———. *Modernity at Large: Cultural Dimensions of Globalization*. Minneapolis: University of Minnesota Press, 1996.

Apter, Emily. "Balkan Babel: Translation Zones, Military Zones." *Public Culture* 13, no. 1 (2001): 65–80.

———. "Clinging to the Animal Relation." In *Social Insecurity: Alphabet City* No. 7, ed. Len Guenther and Cornelius Heesters. Toronto: Anansi, 2000.

Arendt, Hannah. *Imperialism: Part II of the Origins of Totalitarianism*. New York: Harvest, 1968.

———. *On Revolution*. New York: Penguin Books, 1973.

Aristotle. *De Anima*. Trans. Hippocrates G. Apostle. Ginnell, IA: Peripatetic Press, 1981.

———. *Ethics*. Trans. J.A.K. Thomson. New York: Penguin, 1976.

———. *The Politics*. Trans. T.A. Sinclair. New York: Penguin, 1962.

Armstrong, Jane. "Smuggled Chinese Aren't Real Refugees, Mountie Says." *Globe and Mail,* August 6, 1999, 1.

Ashley, Richard K. "Untying the Sovereign State: A Double Reading of the Anarchy Problematique." *Millennium: Journal of International Studies* 7, no. 2 (1988): 227–62.

Ashley, Richard K., and R.B.J. Walker. "Reading Dissidence/Writing the Discipline: Crisis and the Question of Sovereignty in International Studies." *International Studies Quarterly* 34, no. 3 (1990): 367–416.

Assembly of Refugees. *Paris Appeal: Fiftieth Anniversary of the Geneva Convention of 28 July 1951*. Reprinted in Refugee Survey Quarterly 20, no. 3 (2001): 130–35.

Augustine, Saint. *The City of God against the Pagans*. Trans. and ed. R.W. Dyson. Cambridge: Cambridge University Press, 1998.

Avineri, Shlomo. *Hegel's Theory of the Modern State*. Cambridge: Cambridge University Press, 1974.

Ayoob, Mohammed. "Defining Security: A Subaltern Realist Perspective." In *Critical Security Studies: Concepts and Cases*, ed. Michael C. Williams and Keith Krause. Minneapolis: University of Minnesota Press, 1997.

———. "The Security Problematic of the Third World." *World Politics* 43, no. 2 (1991): 257–83.

Balibar, Étienne. "Propositions on Citizenship." *Ethics* 98 (1988): 723–30.

———. "What We Owe to the Sans-Papiers." In *Social Insecurity: Alphabet City* No. 7, ed. Len Guenther and Cornelius Heesters. Toronto: Anansi, 2000.

Bartelson, Jens. *The Critique of the State*. Cambridge: Cambridge University Press, 2001.

Bauman, Zygmunt. *Modernity and Ambivalence*. Cambridge: Polity, 1991.

Benjamin, Walter. *Illuminations*. Ed. Hannah Arendt. New York: Schocken Books, 1968.

———. *Reflections*. Trans. Edmund Jephcott. New York: Schocken Books, 1978.

Bernstein, Richard. B*eyond Objectivism and Relativism: Science, Hermeneutics, and Praxis*. Philadelphia: University of Pennsylvania Press, 1983.

Bhabha, Homi K. *The Location of Culture*. New York: Routledge, 1994.

————. "On Minorities: Cultural Rights," *Radical Philosophy* no. 100 (March–April 2000): 6.

Bhabha, Jacqueline. "Embodied Rights: Gender Persecution, State Sovereignty, and Refugees." *Public Culture* 9 (1996): 3–32.

————. "Legal Problems of Women Refugees." *Women: A Cultural Review* 4, no. 3 (1993).

Biersteker, Thomas J., and Cynthia Weber, eds. *State Sovereignty as Social Construct.* Cambridge: Cambridge University Press, 1996.

Bigo, Didier, "Security and Immigration: Towards a Critique of the Governmentality of Unease." *Alternatives* 24, supplement (2002): 63–92.

Blaney, David, and Naeem Inayatullah. *International Relations and the Problem of Difference.* New York: Routledge, 2003.

Bleiker, Roland. "Editor's Introduction," *Alternatives* 25, no. 3 (2000): 269–84.

————. *Popular Dissent, Human Agency and Global Politics.* Cambridge: Cambridge University Press, 2000.

Boltanski, Luc. *Distant Suffering: Morality, Media and Politics.* Trans. Graham Burchell. Cambridge: Cambridge University Press, 1999.

Bourdieu, Pierre. *Distinction: A Social Critique of the Judgement of Taste.* Trans. Richard Nice. Cambridge, MA: Harvard University Press, 1984.

Braudel, Fernand. *The Perspective of the World. Vol. III, Civilization and Capitalism, 15th–18th Century.* Trans. Siân Reynolds. New York: Harper and Row, 1984.

Brown, Chris. *International Relations Theory: New Normative Approaches.* New York: Columbia University Press, 1992.

Bull, Hedley. "Hobbes and the International Anarchy." *Social Research* 48, no. 4 (1981): 717–38.

Calarco, Matthew. "On the Borders of Language and Death: Agamben and the Question of the Animal." *Philosophy Today* 44 (2000): 91–97.

Campbell, David. "Disaster Politics, and the Politics of Disaster: Exploring 'Humanitarianism.' " In *The Politics of Emergency,* ed. Jenny Edkins. Manchester: University of Manchester Papers in Politics, 1997.

————. *National Deconstruction: Violence, Identity, and Justice in Bosnia.* Minneapolis: University of Minnesota Press, 1998.

————. "Political Excess and the Limits of Imagination." *Millennium: Journal of International Studies* 23, no. 2 (1994): 365–75.

————. "Why Fight: Humanitarianism, Principles, and Post-structuralism." *Millennium: Journal of International Studies* 27, no. 3 (1998): 497–521.

————. *Writing Security: United States Foreign Policy and the Politics of Identity.* Minneapolis: University of Minnesota Press, 1992.

Campbell, David, and Michael J. Shapiro, eds. *Moral Spaces: Rethinking Ethics and World Politics.* Minneapolis: University of Minnesota Press, 1999.

Caplan, Elinor. "Asylum Seekers on Dangerous Ships Won't Be Turned Back without a Hearing" (speech to the Canadian Society for Yad Vashem, Toronto, November 8, 1999). *Canadian Speeches* 13, no. 5 (November–December 1999): 67–70.

Carlier, Jean-Yves, Dirk Vanheule, Klaus Hullmann, and Carlos Pena Galiano, eds. *Who Is a Refugee?: A Comparative Case Law Study.* The Hague: Kluwer Law International, 1997.

Chakkalakal, Tess. "Canada: The Moral Superpower." *This Magazine* 33, no. 1 (July–August 1999): 30–33.

Chambers, Iain. *Migrancy, Culture, Identity.* New York: Routledge, 1994.

Cheah, Pheng, and Bruce Robbins, eds. *Cosmopolitics: Thinking and Feeling Beyond the Nation.* Minneapolis: University of Minnesota Press, 1998.

Chimni, B.S. "The Geopolitics of Refugee Studies: A View from the South." *Journal of Refugee Studies* 11, no. 4 (1998): 350–74.

———. "Reforming the International Refugee Regime: A Dialogic Model." *Journal of Refugee Studies* 14, no. 2 (2001): 151–68.

Chin, Christine B.N. *In Service and Servitude: Foreign Female Domestic Workers and the Malaysian "Modernity" Project.* New York: Columbia University Press, 1998.

Chitty, Andrew. "On Humanitarian Bombing." *Radical Philosophy* 96 (July–August 1999): 2–5.

Chomsky, Noam. *The New Military Humanism: Lessons from Kosovo.* Vancouver: New Star Books, 1999.

Citizenship and Immigration Canada. "Immigration and Refugee Protection Act Introduced." *News Release.* February 21, 2001.

Clarke, Paul, and Andrew Linzey, eds. *Political Theory and Animal Rights.* London: Pluto Press, 1990.

Clastres, Pierre. *Archaeology of Violence.* Trans. Jeanine Herman. New York: Semiotext[e], 1994.

Connolly, William E. *Political Theory and Modernity, 2nd ed.* Ithaca, NY: Cornell University Press, 1993.

Constantinou, Costas M. "Poetics of Security." *Alternatives* 25, no. 3 (2000): 287–306.

Coutin, Susan Bibler. "From Refugees to Immigrants: The Legalization Strategies of Salvadoran Immigrants and Activists." *International Migration Review* 32, no. 4 (1998): 901–25.

———. "The Oppressed, the Suspect, and the Citizen: Subjectivity in Competing Accounts of Political Violence." *Law and Social Inquiry* 26, no. 1 (2001): 63–94.

Cox, Robert W. "Social Forces, States and World Order: Beyond International Relations Theory." In *Neorealism and Its Critics,* ed. Robert O. Keohane. New York: Columbia University Press, 1986.

Creese, Gillian, and Laurie Peterson. "Making the News: Racializing Chinese Canadians." *Studies in Political Economy* 51 (Fall 1996): 117–45.

Culler, Jonathan. *On Deconstruction: Theory and Criticism after Structuralism.* Ithaca, NY: Cornell University Press, 1982.

Cunliffe, Alex. "The Refugee Crisis: A Study of the United Nations High Commission for Refugees." *Political Studies* 43, no. 2 (1995): 278–90.

Cutts, Mark. "Politics and Humanitarianism." *Refugee Survey Quarterly* 17, no. 1 (1998): 1–15.

Daniel, E. Valentine, and John Chr. Knudsen, eds. *Mistrusting Refugees.* Berkeley: University of California Press, 1995.

Deleuze, Gilles. *Bergsonism.* Trans. Hugh Tomlinson and Barbara Habberjam. New York: Zone Books, 1988.

———. *Negotiations.* Trans. Martin Joughin. New York: Columbia University Press, 1995.

Deleuze, Gilles, and Félix Guattari. *A Thousand Plateaus: Capitalism and Schizophrenia.* Trans. Brian Massumi. Minneapolis: University of Minnesota Press, 1987.

Der Derian, James, and Michael J. Shapiro, eds. *International/Intertextual Relations: Postmodern Readings of Word Politics.* Lexington, MA: Lexington Books, 1989.

Derrida, Jacques. *Acts of Religion.* New York: Routledge, 2002.

———. "The Force of Law: 'The Mystical Foundation of Authority.'" In *Deconstruction and the Possibility of Justice,* ed. Drucilla Cornell et al. New York: Routledge, 1992.

———. *Of Hospitality: Anne Dufourmantelle Invites Jacques Derrida to Respond.* Trans. Rachel Bowlby. Stanford, CA: Stanford University Press, 2000.

———. *Politics of Friendship.* Trans. George Collins. London: Verso, 1997.

Derrida, Jacques with Penelope Deutscher and Paul Patton. "A Discussion with Jacques Derrida." *Theory and Event* 5, no. 1 (2001).

Descartes, René. "Discourse on the Method." In *Descartes: Selected Philosophical Writings,* trans. John Cottingham, Robert Stoothoff, and Dugald Murdoch. Cambridge: Cambridge University Press, 1988.

Dillon, Michael. "The Scandal of the Refugee: Some Reflections on the 'Inter' of International Relations and Continental Thought." In *Moral Spaces: Rethinking Ethics and World Politics,* ed. David Campbell and Michael J. Shapiro. Minneapolis: University of Minnesota Press, 1999.

———. "Sovereignty and Governmentality: From the Problematics of the 'New World Order' to the Ethical Problematic of the World Order." *Alternatives* 20, no. 3 (1995): 323–68.

Doty, Roxanne Lynn. "The Double-Writing of Statecraft: Exploring State Responses to Illegal Immigration." *Alternatives* 21, no. 2 (1996): 171–89.

Douglas, Adam. *The Beast Within.* London: Chapmans, 1992.

Dozier Jr., Rush W. *Fear Itself: The Origin, Nature, and Reality of Our Most Primal Emotion.* New York: Thomas Dunne Books, 1998.

Dumm, Thomas L. *Democracy and Punishment: Disciplinary Origins of the United States.* Madison: University of Wisconsin Press, 1987.

———. "Fear of Law." *Studies in Law, Politics, and Society* 10 (1990): 29–57.

Edkins, Jenny. *The Politics of Emergency: Intervention, Peacekeeping, Humanitarianism, Development; Report of an Interdisciplinary Research Workshop.* Manchester: University of Manchester Papers in Politics, No. 2, 1997.

———. *Poststructuralism and International Relations.* Boulder, CO: Lynne Rienner, 1999.

———. ed. "Sovereign Power, Zones of Indistinction, and the Camp." *Alternatives* 25, no. 1 (2000): 3–25.

Edkins, Jenny, Nalini Persram, and Véronique Pin-Fat, eds. *Sovereignty and Subjectivity.* Boulder, CO: Lynne Rienner, 1999.

Elshtain, Jean Bethke. *New Wine and Old Bottles: International Politics and Ethical Discourse.* Notre Dame: University of Notre Dame Press, 1998.

———. *Women and War.* New York: Basic Books, 1987.

Enloe, Cynthia. "The Gendered Gulf." In *Collateral Damage: The "New World Order" at Home and Abroad,* ed. Cynthia Peters. Boston: South End Press, 1992.

Farr, Grant M., and John G. Merriman. *Afghan Resistance.* Boulder, CO: Westview, 1987.

Feher, Michel. *Powerless by Design: The Age of the International Community.* Durham: Duke University Press, 2000.

Feller, Erika. "The Convention at 50: The Way Ahead for Refugee Protection." *Forced Migration Review* 10 (2001): 6.

Ferguson, Kathy. *The Man Question: Visions of Subjectivity in Feminist Theory.* Berkeley: University of California Press, 1993.

Ferris, Elizabeth. *Beyond Borders: Refugees, Migrants and Human Rights in the Post–Cold War Era.* Geneva: WCC Publications, 1993.

———. ed. *Refugees and World Politics.* New York: Praeger, 1985.

Fitzpatrick, Peter. "Bare Sovereignty: Homo Sacer and the Insistence of Law." *Theory and Event* 5, no. 2 (2001).

Forsyth, Murray. "Thomas Hobbes and the External Relations of States." *British Journal of International Studies* 5 (1979): 196–209.

Foucault, Michel. *The Archaeology of Knowledge.* Trans. A.M. Sheridan Smith. New York: Pantheon Books, 1972.

———. *The History of Sexuality: Vol. I; An Introduction.* Trans. Robert Hurley. New York: Vintage, 1978.

———. "The Order of Discourse." In *Language and Politics*, ed. Michael J. Shapiro. New York: New York University Press, 1985.

Francis, Diane. "Canadian Refugee Policy for the Dogs." *National Post*, August 14, 1999.

———. "Cities Fight for Fair Refugee Policy." *National Post*, May 15, 2001.

Frost, Mervyn. *Ethics in International Relations: A Constitutive Theory.* Cambridge: Cambridge University Press, 1996.

Galeano, Eduardo. "Salgado: Light Is a Secret of Garbage." In *We Say No*, Eduardo Galeano, trans. Asa Zatz. New York: Norton, 1992.

———. *Upside Down: A Primer for the Looking-Glass World.* New York: Metropolitan Books, 2000.

George, Jim. "Realist 'Ethics,' International Relations, and Post-modernism: Thinking beyond the Egoism–Anarchy Thematic." *Millennium: Journal of International Studies* 24, no. 2 (1995): 195–223.

Gordenker, Leon. *Refugees in International Politics.* London: Croom Helm, 1987.

Green, Linda. "Fear as a Way of Life." *Cultural Anthropology* 9, no. 2 (1994): 227–56.

Grosz, Elizabeth. *Volatile Bodies: Toward a Corporeal Feminism.* Bloomington: Indiana University Press, 1994.

Hammar, Thomas. *Democracy and the Nation State: Aliens, Denizens, and Citizens in a World of International Migration.* Brookfield, VT: Gower, 1990.

Haraway, Donna. "A Manifesto for Cyborgs: Science, Technology, and Socialist Feminism in the 1980s." In *Feminism/Postmodernism*, ed. Linda J. Nicholson. New York: Routledge, 1990.

———. *Primate Visions.* London: Verso, 1992.

Hardt, Michael. "The Withering of Civil Society." *Social Text* 14, no. 4 (1995): 28–44.

Hardt, Michael, and Antonio Negri. *Empire.* Cambridge, MA: Harvard University Press, 2000.

Harrell-Bond, Barbara E. *Imposing Aid: Emergency Assistance to Refugees.* Oxford: Oxford University Press, 1986.

Harvey, David. *The Condition of Postmodernity.* Oxford: Blackwell, 1990.

Hassner, Pierre. "Refugees: A Special Case for Cosmopolitan Citizenship?" In *Re-imagining Political Community: Studies in Cosmopolitan Democracy*, ed. Daniele Archibugi, David Held, and Martin Köhler. Stanford, CA: Stanford University Press, 1998.

Hathaway, James C. "The Evolution of Refugee Status in International Law, 1920–1950." *International and Comparative Law Quarterly* 33, no. 2 (1984): 348–80.

———. *The Law of Refugee Status*. Toronto: Butterworths, 1991.

———., ed. *Reconceiving International Refugee Law*. The Hague: M. Nijhoff, 1997.

———. "Reconceiving Refugee Law as Human Rights Protection." *Journal of Refugee Studies* 4, no. 2 (1991): 113–31.

Hathaway, James C., and R. Alexander Neve. "Making International Refugee Law Relevant Again: A Proposal for Collectivized and Solution-Oriented Protection." *Harvard Human Rights Review* 10 (1997): 115–211.

Hayek, Friedrich. The *Road to Serfdom*. Chicago: University of Chicago Press, 1944.

Hegel, G.W.F. *Philosophy of Right*. Trans. T.M. Knox. Oxford: Oxford University Press, 1967.

Heidegger, Martin. *Being and Time*. Trans. John Macquarrie and Edward Robinson. New York: Harper and Row, 1962.

Held, David, and Anthony McGrew, "Globalization and the Liberal Democratic State." In *Global Transformation: Challenges to the States System*, ed. Yoshikazu Sakamoto. Tokyo: United Nations University Press, 1994.

Hellman, Judith Adler. *Mexican Lives*. New York: New Press, 1994.

Hobbes, Thomas. *Body, Man, Citizen*. Ed. Richard S. Peters. New York: Collier Books, 1962.

———. *Leviathan*. Ed. C.B. Macpherson. New York: Penguin, 1968.

Hoffman, Stanley. *Duties beyond Borders: On the Limits and Possibilities of Ethical International Politics*. Syracuse, NY: Syracuse University Press, 1981.

Holborn, Louise W. *Refugees: A Problem of Our Time: The Work of the United Nations High Commissioner for Refugees, 1951–1972*. Metuchen, NJ: Scarecrow Press, 1975.

Honig, Bonnie. *Democracy and the Foreigner*. Princeton, NJ: Princeton University Press, 2001.

Huntington, Samuel. "The Clash of Civilizations." *Foreign Affairs* 72, no. 3 (1993): 22–49.

Husson, Bernard, André Marty, and Claire Pirotte. "Observations on Crises." In *Responding to Emergencies and Fostering Development: The Dilemmas of Humanitarian Aid*, ed. Claire Pirotte, Bernard Husson, and François Grunewald. London: Zed Books, 1999.

Huysmans, Jef. "The Question of the Limit: Desecuritisation and the Aesthetics of Horror in Political Realism." *Millennium: Journal of International Studies* 27, no. 3 (1998): 569–89.

Hyndman, Jennifer. *Managing Displacement: Refugees and the Politics of Humanitarianism*. Minneapolis: University of Minnesota Press, 1999.

Indra, Doreen Marie, ed. *Engendering Forced Migration: Theory and Practice*. New York: Berghahn Books, 1999.

Isin, Engin F. *Being Political: Genealogies of Citizenship*. Minneapolis: University of Minnesota Press, 2002.

Jackson, Robert. "Armed Humanitarianism." *International Journal* 48 (1993): 579–606.

Jacobsen, Karen. "A Framework for Exploring the Political and Security Context of Refugee Populated Areas." *Refugee Survey Quarterly* 19, no. 1 (2000): 3–22.

———. "Refugees as Security Threats in Sub-Saharan Africa." In *International Migration and Security*, ed. Myron Weiner. Boulder, CO: Westview, 1993.

Jennings, R. Yewdall. "Some International Law Aspects of the Refugee Question." *British Yearbook of International Law* 20 (1939): 98–114.

Jessen-Petersen, Soren. "Statement to the Security Council by Soren Jessen-Petersen, UNHCR." *Refugee Survey Quarterly* 17, no. 1 (1998).

Johnson, Barbara, ed. *Freedom and Interpretation: The Oxford Amnesty Lectures 1992.* New York: Basic Books, 1993.

Johnston, David. *The Rhetoric of "Leviathan": Thomas Hobbes and the Politics of Cultural Transformation.* Princeton, NJ: Princeton University Press, 1986.

Kant, Immanuel. *Political Writings.* Ed. Hans Reiss. Cambridge: Cambridge University Press, 1991.

Keen, David. *Refugees: Rationing the Right to Life; The Crisis in Emergency Relief.* London: Zed Books, 1992.

Keenan, Thomas. "Humanism without Borders." In *Social Insecurity: Alphabet City* No. 7, ed. Len Guenther and Cornelius Heesters. Toronto: Anansi, 2000.

Korn, David A. *Exodus within Borders: An Introduction to the Crisis of Internal Displacement.* Washington: Brookings Institution Press, 1999.

Kumin, Judith. "Revitalizing International Protection: The UNHCR's Global Consultations." *Refuge: Canada's Periodical on Refugees* 19, no. 4 (February 2001): 5–7.

Leader, Nicholas. "Proliferating Principles; Or How to Sup with the Devil without Getting Eaten." *Disasters* 22, no. 4 (1998): 288–308.

Levinas, Emmanuel. "The Name of a Dog, or Natural Rights." In *Difficult Freedom: Essays on Judaism, Emmanuel Levinas*, trans. Seán Hand. Baltimore: Johns Hopkins University Press, 1990.

Levi Strauss, David. "Epiphany of the Other." *Artforum* 29 (February 1991): 96–99.

Lingis, Alphonso. *Foreign Bodies.* New York: Routledge, 1994.

Linklater, Andrew. *Men and Citizens in the Theory of International Relations.* 2nd ed. London: Macmillan, 1990.

———. *The Transformation of Political Community: Ethical Foundations of the Post-Westphalian Era.* Columbia: University of South Carolina Press, 1998.

Lippert, Randy. "Governing Refugees: The Relevance of Governmentality to Understanding the International Refugee Regime." *Alternatives* 24, no. 3 (1999): 295–328.

Lippit, Akira Mizuta. *Electric Animal: Toward a Rhetoric of Wildlife.* Minneapolis: University of Minnesota Press, 2000.

Locke, John. *Two Treatises of Government.* Ed. Peter Laslett. Cambridge: Cambridge University Press, 1988.

Loescher, Gil. *Beyond Charity: International Cooperation and the Global Refugee Crisis.* New York: Oxford University Press, 1993.

———. *Refugee Movements and International Security.* Oxford: Adelphi Papers No. 262, 1992.

Loescher, Gil, and Laila Monahan, eds. *Refugees and International Relations*. Oxford: Clarendon, 1989.

Lubbers, Ruud. "UN High Commissioner for Refugees" (presentation made to the Informal Meeting of the European Union Ministers for Justice and Ministers for Home Affairs. Stockholm, February 8, 2001).

Luciw, Roma, Gray Miles, Peter Wall, and Brian Lin. "The Media versus the Migrants." *Thunderbird: UBC Journalism Review* 2, no. 1 (November 1999).

Lyotard, Jean-François. "The Other's Rights." In *The Politics of Human Rights*, ed. The Belgrade Circle. London: Verso, 1999.

Machiavelli. The Prince. In *The Portable Machiavelli*, ed. Peter Bondanella and Mark Musa. New York: Penguin, 1979.

Macrae, Joanna. "The Death of Humanitarianism? An Anatomy of the Attack." *Refugee Survey Quarterly* 17, no. 1 (1998): 24–32.

Magnusson, Warren. "The Reification of Political Community." In *Contending Sovereignties*, ed. R.B.J. Walker and Saul Mendlovitz. Boulder, CO: Lynne Rienner, 1990.

––––. *The Search for Political Space*. Toronto: University of Toronto Press, 1996.

Maison Européenne de la Photographie. "Sebastião Salgado: Exodes." *Mots Ecrans Photos* 8 (April 2000, Paris).

Maley, William. "Refugees and Forced Migration as a Security Problem." In *Asia's Emerging Regional Order: Reconciling Traditional and Human Security*, ed. William T. Tow, Ramesh Thakur, and In-Taek Hyun. Tokyo: United Nations University Press, 2000.

––––. "Security, People-Smuggling, and Australia's New Afghan Refugees." *Australian Journal of International Affairs* 55, no. 3 (2001): 351–70.

Malkki, Liisa H. "Citizens and Humanity: Internationalism and the Imagined Community of Nations." *Diaspora* 3, no. 1 (1994): 41–68.

––––. "National Geographic: The Rooting of Peoples and the Territorialization of National Identity among Scholars and Refugees." *Cultural Anthropology* 7, no. 1 (1992): 24–44.

––––. *Purity and Exile: Violence, Memory, and National Cosmology among Hutu Refugees in Tanzania*. Chicago: University of Chicago Press, 1995.

––––. "Refugees and Exile: From 'Refugee Studies' to the National Order of Things." *Annual Review of Anthropology* 24 (1995): 495–523.

––––. "Speechless Emissaries: Refugees, Humanitarianism, and Dehistoricization." *Cultural Anthropology* 11, no. 3 (1996): 377–404.

Marrus, Michael. *The Unwanted: European Refugees in the Twentieth Century*. New York: Oxford University Press, 1985.

Martin, Randolph. "Regional Dynamics and the Security of Afghan Refugees in Pakistan." *Refugee Survey Quarterly* 19, no. 1 (2000): 71–78.

Massey, Doreen. *Space, Place, and Gender*. Minneapolis: University of Minnesota Press, 1994.

Massumi, Brian. *Parables for the Virtual: Movement, Affect, Sensation*. Durham: Duke University Press, 2002.

––––. ed. *The Politics of Everyday Fear*. Minneapolis: University of Minnesota Press, 1993.

Mda, Zakes. *When People Play People: Development Communication through Theatre.* London: Zed Books, 1993.

Médecins Sans Frontières. *Populations in Danger.* London: John Libby, 1992.

———. *World in Crisis: The Politics of Survival at the End of the Twentieth Century.* New York: Routledge, 1997.

Mercer, Kobena. *Welcome to the Jungle: New Positions in Black Cultural Studies.* New York: Routledge, 1994.

Mickleburgh, Rod. "27 Boat People See Refugee Claims Rejected." *Globe and Mail,* November 10, 1999.

Milliken, Jennifer. "The Study of Discourse in International Relations: A Critique of Research and Methods." *European Journal of International Relations* 5, no. 2 (1999): 225–54.

Minear, Larry, and Thomas G. Weiss. *Humanitarian Action in Times of War: A Handbook for Practitioners.* Boulder, CO: Lynne Rienner, 1994.

Mitchell, Katharyne. "Different Diasporas and the Hype of Hybridity." *Environment and Planning D: Society and Space* 15 (1997): 533–53.

Montgomery, Charlotte. *Blood Relations: Animals, Humans, and Politics.* Toronto: Between the Lines, 2000.

Mortland, Carol A. "Transforming Refugees in Refugee Camps." *Urban Anthropology* 16, nos. 3–4 (1987): 375–404.

Mouffe, Chantale. *The Return of the Political.* New York: Verso, 1993.

Mousavi, Sayed Askar. *The Hazaras of Afghanistan: An Historical, Cultural, Economic, and Political Study.* New York: St. Martin's, 1998.

Mtango, Elly-Elikunda. "Military and Armed Attacks on Refugee Camps." In *Refugees and International Relations,* ed. Gil Loescher and Laila Monahan. Oxford: Clarendon, 1990.

Neocleous, Mark. "Against Security." *Radical Philosophy* 100 (2000): 7–15.

Nietzsche, Friedrich. *The Gay Science.* Trans. Walter Kaufmann. New York: Vintage Books, 1974.

———. *On the Genealogy of Morals.* New York: Vintage Books, 1969.

Nyers, Peter. "Abject Cosmopolitanism: The Politics of Protection in the Anti-deportation Movement." *Third World Quarterly* 24, no. 6 (2003): 1069–93.

Ogata, Sadako. "Humanitarian Action in Conflict." *Refugee Survey Quarterly* 17, no. 1 (1998): 60–64.

Ong, Aihwa. *Buddha Is Hiding: Refugees, Citizenship, the New America.* Berkeley: University of California Press, 2003.

Parkin, David. "Mementoes as Transitional Objects in Human Displacement." *Journal of Material Culture* 4, no. 3 (1999): 303–20.

Patton, Paul. *Deleuze and the Political.* New York: Routledge, 2000.

Physicians for Human Rights. *The Taliban's War on Women: A Health and Human Rights Crisis in Afghanistan.* Boston: Physicians for Human Rights, 1998.

Pilch, Frances T. "Security Issues and Refugees: Dilemmas, Crises, and Debates." *Refuge: Canada's Periodical on Refugees* 19, no. 1 (July 2000): 25–34.

Pugh, Michael, and Alex Cunliffe. "The Lead Agency Concept in Humanitarian Assistance: The Case of the UNHCR." *Security Dialogue* 28, no. 1 (1997): 17–30.

Roberts, Adam. *Humanitarian Action in War: Aid, Protection and Impartiality in a Policy Vacuum.* Adelphi Paper No. 305. Oxford: International Institute for Strategic Studies, 1996.

Robin, Corey. "Fear: A Genealogy of Morals." *Social Research* 67, no. 4 (Winter 2000): 1085–115.

Robinson, Courtland. "Refugee Warriors at the Thai–Cambodian Border." *Refugee Survey Quarterly* 19, no. 1 (2000): 23–37.

Robinson, Fiona. "Globalizing Care: Ethics, Feminist Theory, and International Relations." *Alternatives* 22, no. 1 (1997): 113–33.

Rosello, Mireille. *Postcolonial Hospitality: The Immigrant as Guest.* Stanford, CA: Stanford University Press, 2001.

Rousseau, Jean-Jacques. "Discourse on the Origin of Inequality." *The Basic Political Writings.* Trans. and ed. Donald A. Cress. Indianapolis: Hackett, 1987.

Ruiz, Lester Edwin J. "In Pursuit of the 'Body Politic': Ethics, Spirituality, and Diaspora." *Transnational Law and Contemporary Problems* 9, no. 2 (1999): 633–52.

Salgado, Sebastião. *The Children: Refugees and Migrants.* New York: Aperture, 2000.

———. *Migrations: Humanity in Transition.* New York: Aperture, 2000.

———. *Workers: An Archaeology of the Industrial Age.* New York: Aperture, 1990.

Sallot, Jeff. "Migrants Not Owed Free Ride, Poll Says." *Globe and Mail,* August 31, 1999, 1.

Santner, Eric L. "Some Reflections on States of Exception." In *Social Insecurity: Alphabet City* No. 7, ed. Len Guenther and Cornelius Heesters. Toronto: Anansi, 2000.

Schmitt, Carl. *The Concept of the Political.* Trans. George Schwab. Chicago: University of Chicago Press, 1996.

———. *Political Theology: Four Chapters on the Concept of Sovereignty.* Trans. George Schwab. Cambridge, MA: MIT Press, 1985.

Schrijvers, Joke. "Fighters, Victims and Survivors: Constructions of Ethnicity, Gender and Refugeeness among Tamils in Sri Lanka." *Journal of Refugee Studies* 12, no. 3 (1999): 307–33.

Scott-Danter, Helen. "Theatre for Development: A Dynamic Tool for Change." *Forced Migration Review* 6 (December 1999): 22–24.

Shahrani, M. Nazif. "Afghanistan's Muhajirin (Muslim "Refugee-Warriors"): Politics of Mistrust and Distrust of Politics." In *Mistrusting Refugees,* ed. E. Valentine Daniel and John Chr. Knudsen. Berkeley: University of California Press, 1995.

Shapiro, Michael J. "Literary Geography and Sovereign Violence: Resisting Tocqueville's Family Romance." *Alternatives* 25, no. 1 (2000): 27–50.

———. *Violent Cartographies: Mapping Cultures of War.* Minneapolis: University of Minnesota Press, 1997.

Shapiro, Michael J., and Hayward Alker, eds. *Challenging Boundaries: Global Flows, Territorial Boundaries.* Minneapolis: University of Minnesota Press, 1996.

Shaw, Karena. "Feminist Futures: Contesting the Political." *Transnational Law and Contemporary Problems* 9, no. 2 (Fall 1999): 569–98.

Sheehan, James J., and Morton Sosna, eds. *The Boundaries of Humanity: Humans, Animals, Machines.* Berkeley: University of California Press, 1991.

Shklar, Judith N. "The Liberalism of Fear." In *Liberalism and the Moral Life*, ed. Nancy L. Rosenblum. Cambridge, MA: Harvard University Press, 1989.

Silove, Derrick, Zachary Steel, and Charles Watters. "Policies of Deterrence and the Mental Health of Asylum Seekers." *Journal of the American Medical Association* 284, no. 5 (August 2000): 604–11.

Simon, Jonathan. "Refugees in a Carceral Age: The Rebirth of Immigration Prisons in the United States." *Public Culture* 10, no. 3 (1998): 577–607.

Skran, Claudena M. *Refugees in Inter-war Europe: The Emergence of a Regime*. Oxford: Clarendon, 1995.

Slater, David. "Spatialities of Power and Postmodern Ethics—Rethinking Geopolitical Encounters." *Environment and Planning D: Society and Space* 15 (1997): 55–72.

Smart, Alan, and Josephine Smart. "Monster Homes: Hong Kong Immigration to Canada, Urban Conflicts, and Contested Representations of Space." In *City Lives and City Forms: Critical Research and Canadian Urbanism,* ed. Jon Caulfield and Linda Peake. Toronto: University of Toronto Press, 1996.

Smith, Michael J. "Humanitarian Intervention: An Overview of the Ethical Issues." *Ethics and International Affairs* 12 (1998): 63–80.

Smith, Michael Peter. "Can You Imagine? Transnational Migration and the Globalization of Grassroots Politics." *Social Text* 39 (1994): 15–33.

Soguk, Nevzat. *States and Strangers: Refugees and Displacements of Statecraft.* Minneapolis: University of Minnesota Press, 1999.

Sokoloff, William W. "Politics and Anxiety in Thomas Hobbes's Leviathan." *Theory and Event* 5, no. 1 (2001).

Sommaruga, Cornelio. "Address to the UN General Assembly, 20 November 1992." *International Review of the Red Cross* 292 (1993).

Spener, David. "This Coyote's Life." *NACLA: Report on the Americas* 33, no. 3 (1999): 22–23.

Spillers, Hortense. "Where the Human Stops." In *Social Insecurity: Alphabet City* No. 7, ed. Len Guenther and Cornelius Heesters. Toronto: Anansi, 2000.

Spivak, Gayatri Chakravorty. "Imperatives to Re-imagine the Planet." In *Social Insecurity: Alphabet City* No. 7, ed. Len Guenther and Cornelius Heesters. Toronto: Anansi, 2000.

Steans, Jill. *Gender and International Relations.* Oxford: Polity, 1998.

Stetz, Margaret D. "Woman as Mother in a Headscarf: The Woman War Refugee and the North American Media." *Canadian Woman Studies* 19, no. 4 (December 1999–February 2000): 66–70.

Stockton, Nicholas. "In Defence of Humanitarianism." *Disasters* 22, no. 4 (1998): 352–60.

Stoessinger, John George. *The Refugee and the World Community.* Minneapolis: University of Minnesota Press, 1956.

Subramaniam, Banu. "The Aliens Have Landed! Reflections on the Rhetoric of Biological Invasions." *Meridians: Feminism, Race, Transnationalism* 2, no. 1 (2001): 26–40.

Sugino, Kyoichi. "The 'Non-political and Humanitarian' Clause in UNHCR's Statute." *Refugee Survey Quarterly* 17, no. 1 (1998): 33–59.

Suhrke, Astri. "Burden-Sharing during Refugee Emergencies: The Logic of Collective versus National Action." *Journal of Refugee Studies* 11, no. 4 (1998): 398–415.

———. "A Crisis Diminished: Refugees in the Developing World." *International Journal* 48 (1995): 215–39.

Taussig, Michael. *The Nervous System*. New York: Routledge, 1992.

Terry, Fiona. *Condemned to Repeat?: The Paradox of Humanitarian Action*. Ithaca, NY: Cornell University Press, 2002.

Thucydides. *The Peloponnesian War*. Trans. Richard Crawley. New York: Modern Library, 1982.

Tickner, J. Ann. *Gender in International Relations: Feminist Perspectives on Achieving Global Security*. New York: Columbia University Press, 1992.

Tilly, Charles. *Coercion, Capital, and European States, AD 990–1992*. Cambridge: Blackwell, 1992.

Tomlinson, John. *Globalization and Culture*. Chicago: University of Chicago Press, 1999.

Torpey, John. *The Invention of the Passport: Surveillance, Citizenship and the State*. Cambridge: Cambridge University Press, 2000.

Tronti, Mario. "The Strategy of Refusal." In *Autonomia: Post-political Politics*. New York: Semiotexte[e], 1980.

Tugendhat, Ernst. "The Moral Dilemma in the Rescue of Refugees." *Social Research* 62, no. 1 (1995): 129–42.

Turack, Daniel C. *The Passport in International Law*. Lexington, MA: Lexington Books, 1972.

Turner, James. *Reckoning with the Beast: Animals, Pain, and Humanity in the Victorian Mind*. Baltimore: Johns Hopkins University Press, 1980.

United Nations. Executive Committee of the High Commissioner's Programme. *Military or Armed Attacks on Refugee Camps and Settlements*, Conclusion No. 48 (1987) (UN Doc. No. A/AC.96/702).

———. Executive Committee of the High Commissioner's Programme. *Safety and Security of Staff*, June 20, 2000 (UN Doc. No. EC/50/SC/INF.3).

———. Executive Committee of the High Commissioner's Programme. *The Security and Civilian and Humanitarian Character of Refugee Camps and Settlements*, January 14, 1999 (Doc. No. EC/49/SC/INF.2).

———. Executive Committee of the High Commissioner's Programme. *The Security and Civilian and Humanitarian Character of Refugee Camps and Settlements: Operationalizing the "Ladder of Options,"* June 27, 2000 (UN Doc. No. EC/50/SC/INF.4).

———. Executive Committee of the High Commissioner's Programme. *Strengthening Partnership to Ensure Protection also in Relation to Security*, September 14, 1999.

———. Executive Committee of the High Commissioner's Programme. *A Study of UNHCR Emergency Preparedness and Response: Preliminary Conclusions from the Persian Gulf*, December 11, 1991, Forty-second session (A/AC.96/788).

———. General Assembly. *Report by Ambassador Felix Schnyder on Military Attacks on Refugee Camps and Settlements in Southern Africa and Elsewhere*, March 15, 1983 (UN Doc. No. EC/SCP/26).

United Nations High Commissioner for Refugees (UNHCR). "Focus: Ethnic Conflict." *Refugees* 93 (1993): 48.

———. "Global Consultations Update." *Prima Facie: The Newsletter of UNHCR's Department of International Protection*, May 2001, 1–4.

————. *Handbook for Emergencies*. Geneva: UNHCR, 1992.

————. *Handbook on Procedures and Criteria for Determining Refugee Status under the 1951 Convention and the 1967 Protocol Relating to the Status of Refugees*. Geneva: Office of the United Nations High Commissioner for Refugees, 1988.

————. *Sexual Violence against Refugees: Guidelines on Prevention and Response*. Geneva: UNHCR, 1995.

————. *The State of the World's Refugees: The Challenge of Protection*. New York: Penguin Books, 1993.

————. *The State of the World's Refugees: A Humanitarian Agenda*. New York: Oxford University Press, 1998.

————. *The State of the World's Refugees: In Search of Solutions*. New York: Oxford University Press, 1995.

————. *Statute of the Office of the United Nations High Commissioner for Refugees*, December 14, 1950 (UNHCR/INF/I/Rev.3).

————. Office of the Chief Mission for Bosnia and Herzegovina. *The Interface between Migration and Asylum in Bosnia and Herzegovina*. New Issues in Refugee Research, Working Paper 44.

Vincent, Andrew. *Theories of the State*. Oxford: Blackwell, 1987.

Virilio, Paul. "Is the Author Dead? An Interview with Paul Virilio." In *The Virilio Reader*, ed. James Der Derian. Oxford: Blackwell, 1998.

Virilio, Paul, and Sylvère Lotringer. *Pure War*. Rev. ed. New York: Semiotext[e], 1997.

Virno, Paolo, and Michael Hardt, eds. *Radical Thought in Italy: A Potential Politics*. Minneapolis: University of Minnesota Press, 1996.

Vries, Hent de, and Samuel Weber, eds. *Violence, Identity, and Self-Determination*. Stanford, CA: Stanford University Press, 1997.

Walker, R.B.J. "After the Future: Enclosures, Connections, Politics." In *Reframing the International: Law, Culture, Politics*, ed. Richard Falk, Lester Ruiz, and R.B.J. Walker. New York: Routledge, 2002.

————. "Gender and Critique in the Theory of International Relations." In *Gendered States: Feminist (Re)Visions of International Relations Theory*, ed. V. Spike Peterson. Boulder, CO: Lynne Rienner, 1992.

————. "The Hierarchicalization of Political Community." *Review of International Studies* 25, no. 1 (1999): 151–56.

————. *Inside/Outside: International Relations as Political Theory*. Cambridge: Cambridge University Press, 1993.

————. "International Relations and the Concept of the Political." In *International Relations Theory Today*, ed. Ken Booth and Steve Smith. University Park: Pennsylvania State University Press, 1995.

————."Norms in a Teacup: Surveying the 'New Normative Approaches.' " *Mershon International Studies Review* 38 (1994).

————. "Security, Sovereignty, and the Challenge of World Politics." *Alternatives* 15:1 (1990).

Warner, Daniel. "The Community of the Refugee." *International Journal of Refugee Law* 3, no. 4 (1992): 731–34.

————. *An Ethic of Responsibility in International Relations*. Boulder, CO: Lynne Rienner, 1991.

———. "Forty Years of the Executive Committee: From the Old to the New."
International Journal of Refugee Law 2, no. 2 (1990): 238–51.

———. "The Politics of the Political/Humanitarian Divide." *International Review of the Red Cross* 833 (1999): 109–18.

———. "Refugees, UNHCR and Human Rights: Current Dilemmas of Conflicting Mandates." *Refuge* 17, no. 6 (1998): 12–15.

———. "Review of Constructing a Productive Other." *International Journal of Refugee Law* 7, no. 2 (1995).

———. "Voluntary Repatriation and the Meaning of Return to Home: A Critique of Liberal Mathematics." *Journal of Refugee Studies* 7, nos. 2–3 (1994): 160–74.

———. "We Are All Refugees." *International Journal of Refugee Law* 4, no. 3 (1992): 365–72.

Weber, Cynthia. "Performative States." *Millennium: Journal of International Studies* 27, no. 1 (1998): 77–95.

———. *Simulating Sovereignty: Intervention, the State and Symbolic Exchange.* Cambridge: Cambridge University Press, 1995.

Weiss, Thomas G., and Jarat Chopra. "Sovereignty under Siege: From Humanitarian Intervention to Humanitarian Space." In B*eyond Westphalia?: National Sovereignty and International Intervention*, ed. Gene Lyons and Michael Mastanduno. Berkeley: University of California Press, 1993.

Weiss, Thomas G., and Larry Minear. "Do International Ethics Matter? Humanitarian Politics in the Sudan." *Ethics and International Affairs* 5 (1991): 197–214.

———. eds. *Humanitarianism across Borders: Sustaining Civilians in Times of War.* Boulder, CO: Lynne Rienner, 1993.

Weldes, Jutta, Mark Laffey, Hugh Gusterson, Raymond Duvall, eds. *Cultures of Insecurity: States, Communities, and the Production of Danger.* Minneapolis: University of Minnesota Press, 1999.

Wendt, Alexander. "Bridging the Theory/Meta-theory Gap in International Relations." *Review of International Studies* 17 (1991): 383–92.

Wheeler, Nicholas J. "Pluralist of Solidarist Conceptions of International Society: Bull and Vincent on *Humanitarian Intervention*." *Millennium: Journal of International Studies* 21, no. 3 (1992): 463–87.

———. *Saving Strangers: Humanitarian Intervention in International Society.* Oxford: Oxford University Press, 2000.

"When Is a Refugee Not a Refugee?" *The Economist*, March 3, 2001.

Whitworth, Sandra. "Where Is the Politics in Peacekeeping?" *International Journal* 50, no. 2 (1995): 427–35.

Wilkinson, Ray. "We Are Very Close to the Limit." *Refugees* 4, no. 121 (2000): 7.

Williams, Michael C. "Rousseau, Realism, and Realpolitik." *Millennium: Journal of International Studies* 18, no. 2 (1989): 185–203.

Xenos, Nicholas. "Refugees: The Modern Political Condition." *Alternatives* 18, no. 4 (1993): 419–30.

Zolberg, Aristide R., Astri Suhrke, and Sergio Aguayo. *Escape from Violence: Conflict and the Refugee Crisis in the Developing World.* New York: Oxford University Press, 1989.

Index